HANGMEN
OF ENGLAND

HANGMEN
OF ENGLAND

A History of Execution
from Jack Ketch to Albert Pierrepoint

Brian Bailey

W H ALLEN · LONDON
1989

Set in Baskerville by Phoenix Photosetting
Printed and bound in Great Britain by
Mackays of Chatham PLC, Chatham, Kent
for the Publishers, W.H. Allen & Co. Plc
175/9 St John Street, London EC1V 4LL

ISBN 0 491 03129 7

Criminals do not die by the hands of the Law.
They die by the hands of other men.

Bernard Shaw

Contents

Acknowledgments

I GRATEFULLY acknowledge the cooperation of the Departmental Record Officer, Home Office, for granting me permission to examine closed Prison Commission files in the Public Record Office.

I am grateful for helpful advice on physical aspects of the death penalty to Professor A. Keith Mant, MD, FRCP, FRCPath, DMJPath, formerly Head of the Department of Forensic Medicine at Guy's Hospital; and Professor Bernard Knight, MD(Wales), MRCP, FRCPath, DMJ, Barrister-at-Law, Professor of Forensic Pathology, University of Wales Medical College, Cardiff.

I wish to express special thanks, also, to Undine Concannon, Archivist at Madame Tussaud's, who not only gave me access to relics of James Berry, but was also most helpful with the illustrations.

I warmly appreciate the help I received from the following: Elizabeth Melrose of the North Yorks. County Library, York; Miss. E. M. Willmott of the Central Library, Bradford; S. J. Eccles, District Librarian, Lancaster; Brian Hughes, Dept. of Education and Arts, Bolton.

Most of my research on John Ellis (Chapter VIII) was done many years ago, and at that time the Howard League for Penal Reform kindly put at my disposal the files of the former National Council for the Abolition of the Death Penalty, for which I remain most grateful.

Several former friends and relatives of Ellis provided me with information, but did not wish to be named, and I am grateful to all of them. Charles Duff gave me permission to quote from *A New Handbook on Hanging* as well as answering particular questions I put to him, chiefly about Ellis, many years ago.

I am also indebted to Albert Pierrepoint and Messrs Harrap for permission to quote from *Executioner: Pierrepoint*.

Introduction

'Dancing in Bailey's Ballroom'

THERE IS IN existence somewhere, although I cannot remember where I came across it many years ago, a tale describing the adventures of some Christian seafarers whose ship was wrecked on a remote and unknown island, and who set out to explore it in some trepidation lest it be inhabited by hostile savages or, worse still, cannibals. The first thing they set eyes on as they moved inland was the rotting corpse of a man hanging on a gibbet. Nothing could have given them greater relief or comfort, for it proved that Christians had been there before.

If the identity of the man who first thought of killing another by putting a rope round his neck and hanging him from a tree were not lost in the mists of primeval barbarism, his name would be honoured nowhere more than in England where, until quite recently, the noose remained a symbol second only to the cross in denoting a tradition and a way of death upon which our society was founded. There ought by rights to be a statue of him on that empty pedestal in Trafalgar Square, and perhaps a bust in the House of Lords.

The English became the chief exponents of hanging as a method of execution much to be preferred, we liked to assure ourselves, to such barbarities as the garotte, the guillotine and the gas chamber, not to mention the electric chair, the firing squad and the cup of hemlock. And so, in course of time, the English became such acknowledged experts in hanging that English executioners were sent abroad to

[1]

train backward foreigners unfamiliar with the techniques, just as English missionaries had taught heathen natives everywhere to worship that other instrument of torture, the cross.

Yet the English themselves, though always supporting the death penalty in the mistaken (or at least unproven and unprovable) belief that it was a deterrent, were also in a curious way ashamed of it. You only have to consider all the familiar euphemisms to see that the English attitude to the death penalty was similar to its attitude to love-making: the less said about it the better. If you *have* to mention love-making, call it anything but sexual intercourse. If you *have* to mention capital punishment, call it anything but killing.

Hence executing someone used to be called 'turning him off', or 'launching him into eternity', or 'topping' or 'despatching' him. Mr Hangman Ellis, even in the present century, liked to call it 'putting him away'. What the jargon of officialdom referred to as 'paying the supreme penalty' was known in underworld lingo as 'taking a leap in the dark', or 'the morning drop', or being 'nubbed' or 'choked by a hempen quinsy'. The rope was the 'hempen necktie'. The gallows was 'Tyburn tree' or the 'wooden-legged mare'. Later on the scaffold became 'Beilby's ballroom', this probably being a corruption of (Old) Bailey, so hanging on the end of a rope there was transformed from 'dancing the Tyburn jig' to 'dancing in Beilby's ballroom'. As for the executioner himself, he was variously known as the 'topsman', the 'sheriff's journeyman', the 'nubbing cove' or – a particularly graphic phrase – the 'crap merchant'.

The collective story of the hangmen of England right up to the abolition of the death penalty for murder in 1965 has never been told. This is a serious omission from our island history which I hope to make good in the following pages, so that those who believe such a venerable English tradition ought not to be allowed to pass away may know the breed of men who have had such a civilising influence, not only at home, but on large parts of the world.

This book, you might say, is my ballroom, and I have called upon a troupe of nimble ghosts to demonstrate the figures they used to cut as, leading processions from condemned cells to execution chambers, they performed the Dance of Death to the applause of the crowd.

I

By Appointment, Butchers of the Nobility

What, think you we are Turks or infidels?
Or that we would, against the form of law,
Proceed thus rashly in the villain's death,
But that the extreme peril of the case,
The peace of England and our persons' safety,
Enforc'd us to this execution?

William Shakespeare
Richard III, 1593

HANGING BY the neck until dead as a legal punishment was apparently introduced into Britain by the Anglo-Saxon invaders, and is thus an English tradition as venerable as Christianity itself. Decapitation preceded it, having been used by the Romans (Alban, the first English martyr, was beheaded by a Roman executioner around 303 AD).

William the Conqueror was extremely sparing in his use of the death penalty, inflicting it only on conspirators against his rule, but Henry I reintroduced it for murder and other crimes, including theft, and there are several mentions of hanging sentences by local manorial lords during the early Norman period, most notably the instance in 1124 recorded in the *Anglo-Saxon Chronicle*, when Ralph Basset 'held a court of the king's thanes at Hundehoh in Leicestershire, and hanged there more thieves than ever before: forty-four of them in all were dispatched in no time, and six had their eyes put out and were castrated.'

We know hardly anything of the men who carried out the law's decrees, however, before relatively recent times, and it is not until the Tudor period that we can begin to gather even tiny bits of information about the men who, by that time, served the State as 'common hangmen'.

Men were hired or commandeered to do the jobs by lords of manors or their bailiffs, or in some cases by those who brought the criminals

[3]

to justice. There was a law in force in Kent, in the reign of Henry VII, to the effect that if a prosecutor could not find a hangman to execute a felon he had brought to justice, he must do the job himself or go to prison.

A fellow named Cratwell is mentioned during Henry VIII's time, but he was clearly not regarded as an expert, and was probably only adept at stringing up common criminals, which any half-wit could do (and often did), for when Ann Boleyn was to be executed in 1536, the headsman of Calais was brought over to do the job. Cratwell was hanged himself two years later, for robbing a booth at Bartholomew Fair.

There were so many executions during the Tudor period that an army of professionals would have been needed to carry them out. It has been estimated that 2000 a year were being put to death in Henry VIII's time, and not many less by Elizabeth's. Many were victims of religious persecution, and the executioners were required to be butchers as well as hangmen – hanging, drawing and quartering was the sentence passed frequently on the Catholic martyrs who died at Tyburn. The answer to the great demand for executioners was to make criminals assist at executions. Shakespeare has the following exchange in *Measure for Measure*:

Provost: Here is in our prison a common executioner, who in his office lacks a helper: if you will take it on you to assist him, it shall redeem you from your gyves; if not you shall have your full time of imprisonment, and your deliverance with an unpitied whipping, for you have been a notorious bawd.

Pompey: Sir, I have been an unlawful bawd time out of mind; but yet I will be content to be a lawful hangman. I would be glad to receive some instruction from my fellow partner.

(Shakespeare gives the executioner the splendid name of Abhorsen!) At York, as we shall see, the principle of using criminals as executioners became so firmly established that they were still doing it in the nineteenth century.

A fellow named Bull was active during the late years of Queen Elizabeth I. It was he who executed Mary Queen of Scots at Fotheringay in 1587, being hired by Secretary of State Walsingham for the purpose in great secrecy, lest Elizabeth should hear of it, at a fee of ten pounds. He was conducted to Fotheringay disguised as a servant, with his axe hidden in a box. He took two strokes to sever Mary's head, but he was still in service in 1593, so he must have been regarded as an efficient enough workman.

This, however, is a relative term. All those hanged in those days died from strangulation, as there was no drop, and a man might take as long as a quarter of an hour to expire. There are many records of victims of the scaffold, assumed dead, being still alive, and it has to be admitted as a distinct possibility that many victims of the common hangman were buried alive in those days. One case recorded by John Stow in his *Survey of London*, occurred in 1587, and it is quite possible that Bull was the executioner:

> The 20 of Februarie, a strange thing happened a man hanged for felonie at Saint Thomas Wateringes, being begged by the Chirurgions of London, to have made of him an Anatomie after hee was dead to all mens thinking, cut down, stripped of his apparell, laide naked in a chest, throwne into a carre, and so brought from the place of execution through the Borough of Southwarke over the bridge, and through the Citie of London to the Chirurgions Hall nere unto Cripelgate: The chest being there opened, and the weather extreeme cold hee was found to be alive, and lived till the three and twentie of Februarie, and then died.

After Bull came one Derrick, who executed, among others, the Earl of Essex at the Tower of London in 1601. The irony is that Essex had apparently saved Derrick from death some years earlier, when Derrick was condemned for rape in France. In accordance with the custom of the time, the earl did so on condition that Derrick served as an executioner. Scott mentions Derrick in *The Fortunes of Nigel*, and the hangman gave his name to the type of crane called a derrick because of its resemblance to the gallows he used. (The gallows itself was known sometimes as a 'derrick' in the reign of James I.) Derrick was active from around 1598 to 1610, and it may well have been he who tortured and executed Guy Fawkes in 1606, Fawkes being hanged last of the five conspirators, and helped on the scaffold because stretching on the rack had made him incapable of mounting it unaided.

Derrick had as his assistant on some occasions Gregory Brandon, who became the public hangman himself in due course. He lived with his wife Alice in Rosemary Lane, Whitechapel, and was frequently in trouble with the law himself. He was convicted of manslaughter in 1611, but pleaded benefit of clergy and got away with being branded on his thumb (laymen who claimed benefit of clergy were branded so that they could not claim it a second time). Brandon may have served as an executioner for nearly thirty years. It seems that the Garter King of Arms, Sir William Segar, was duped by a practical joke into granting Brandon a coat of arms in December 1616, being ignorant of his profession – in consequence of which Brandon and some of his successors were often ironically termed 'Esquire'. Gregory Brandon died about 1640 leaving his son Richard to succeed him.

The executioner had to be a versatile exponent of his inhuman craft, serving not only as headsman and hangman, adept with the axe as with the rope, but being required also to carry out mutilations and public floggings, branding and burning and all the other appurtenances of an ignorantly cruel society's conception of 'justice'. A common nickname for the public executioner at one time was 'William Boilman', because of a savage law in force for seventeen years (1530-47) when poisoners were sentenced to be boiled to death. The executioner also carried out the punishment of *peine forte et dure*, or pressing to death, in which heavy weights were loaded on to the chest of the victim, stretched out on the floor, until he either confessed to the crime he was accused of, or died. If he confessed, he was likely to be hanged after this ordeal, which was so common at one time that a part of Newgate prison was called the Press Yard.

Richard Brandon, Gregory's son, became so well known that he merits an entry in the *Dictionary of National Biography*, for it fell to his lot to deal with the most illustrious victim of all the English executioners – King Charles I. Richard Brandon was popularly known as 'Young Gregory', and for a time the gallows at Tyburn was referred to as the 'Gregorian tree'. It is said that Dick prepared himself from childhood to succeed his father by decapitating cats and dogs. Hardly had he done so, however, before he was clapped into Newgate on a bigamy charge, from which he somehow extricated himself. He, too, lived in Rosemary Lane, with his wife Mary, though whether she was his original wife or the allegedly bigamous one is not at all clear.

The series of performances which made Richard Brandon famous and led to his *magnum opus* began in 1641, when he was required by his masters to execute for treason Sir Thomas Wentworth, Earl of Strafford – really a victim of Charles I's defects in the build-up to the Civil

War. 'My lord of Strafford's condition is happier than mine', the king said tearfully as he signed the death warrant. Brandon beheaded Strafford on Tower Hill on 12 May, and three years later he did the same for the Archbishop of Canterbury, William Laud, who had been languishing in the Tower since Strafford's impeachment, but was not tried until 1644.

Then came the execution of the king, sentenced to death by a revolutionary tribunal as a tyrant, a traitor, a murderer and a public enemy. Rumours abounded regarding this unprecedented public spectacle. It was said that Brandon had refused to execute the king. It was said that two troopers, named Hulet and Walker, had volunteered to do it in disguise. When the executioner and his assistant appeared on the scaffold erected in front of the Banqueting House in Whitehall, on 30 January 1645, they were both masked and disguised. The executioner was said to have grey hair and both he and his assistant were apparently wearing false beards.

When the king was brought out, and had made his speech, the executioner did not appear to ask, as was customary, for the victim's forgiveness. Rumour said that the king had *refused* to forgive him. The king took off his cloak and doublet, his jewels and his insignia, and the executioner was given an 'orange stuck full of cloves' and a handkerchief from the king's pocket. His Majesty asked if the block could be higher, and the executioner told him, 'It can be no higher, Sir.' The king lay down with his head on the block, and Brandon bent down to make sure that his hair was not in the way.

'Stay for the sign', said the king.

'I will, an' it please Your Majesty', Brandon replied.

The king gave the sign, and the executioner beheaded him with one crashing blow of the axe. A huge groan broke from the crowd. Soon other rumours were circulating about the identity of the masked executioner. It was the Earl of Stair, a Scottish judge; it was Captain Joyce, a soldier; it was even Hugh Peter, an army chaplain. One French report went so far as to say that Cromwell and Fairfax had themselves done the job!

In fact, there is little real doubt that the two men were Richard Brandon and Ralph Jones, a ragman who had often assisted Brandon. According to one account, Brandon was 'fetched out of bed by a troop of horse' on the morning of the execution, and afterwards sold the orange he had been given for ten shillings. He was paid thirty pounds for his services and received it all in half-crowns within an hour of the execution. (Many years later, after the Restoration, William Hulet was condemned for executing the king, in an attempt by Charles II to avenge his father's death, but three witnesses swore that it was Brandon, who had long been dead himself by that time.)

Brandon executed other royalists – the Duke of Hamilton, the Earl of Holland and Lord Capel – using the same axe that he had used to kill the king, but it was said that he suffered from remorse, and on 20 June, 1649, he died. If he had, in his stage fright on such a dramatic occasion, forgotten to ask the king's forgiveness; or if the king had indeed refused to forgive him, on the grounds that no one but God could forgive the killing of a king, who ruled by divine right, then that would certainly have preyed on Brandon's mind. It was a universally accepted ritual that the executioner should be forgiven by his victim in order that the executioner should not have any victim's death on his own conscience – a psychological device that was subsequently replaced by the convention that a condemned criminal died by the 'hands of the law.'

Someone named William Lowen carried out a multiple execution a few days after Brandon's death. Twenty-three men and a woman, variously condemned for burglary and robbery, were drawn in eight carts 'unto Tiburne the Fatall place of execution, where William Lowen the new Hangman fastened eight of them unto each Triangle.' But we know nothing of Lowen except that he was a refuse collector, nor how long he served before being replaced by Edward Dun, who was in service after the Restoration and lived at Cripplegate, near Golden Lane.

It was almost certainly Dun, who, when the corpses of Cromwell, Ireton and Bradshaw were disinterred from Henry VII's Chapel in Westminster Abbey, was required to sever the heads, after exposing the remains at Tyburn, and set them on poles on the roof of Westminster Hall. Cromwell's head was not removed whilst Charles II remained on the throne. His trunk was flung into a pit near Tyburn. It was probably Dun who solemnly burnt in public, in Old Bailey in 1660, the poet John Milton's defence of the execution of Charles I, entitled *The Tenure of Kings and Magistrates*.

Edward Dun died in September 1663, and was succeeded by perhaps the most notorious of all the hangmen of England, John Catch or Ketch, usually known as 'Jack Ketch', the name which

[8]

became a common synonym for every succeeding hangman, on account of the universal execration in which he was held by the populace. We know nothing of his origins, but he was confined in the Marshalsea Prison for debt around 1649, before he took office. He was undoubtedly a brutal man, for he carried out his ghastly work in unskilful fashion for twenty-three years without any apparent ill-effect, and died in his bed in November 1686. A woodcut on a broadsheet of 1678 shows a condemned man being drawn to Tyburn and saying, 'I am sick of a traytorous disease.' Ketch is shown, with an axe in one hand and a rope in the other, replying, 'Here's your cure, sir.'

Ketch's individual deeds have not come down to us in any detail until late in his career when, in 1682, he is said to have gone on strike for higher wages, and to have won his case. But the obscurity of Ketch's first twenty years is more than compensated for by the infamy of his last three. The story begins with the execution of Lord William Russell, a son of the first Duke of Bedford. He was accused of high treason in connection with the Rye House Plot to assassinate Charles II, and condemned to death on slender evidence. Sentenced to be beheaded at Lincoln's Inn Fields, on 21 July 1683, he was brought to the scaffold, where Ketch awaited him. The executioner asked his lordship's forgiveness, and Lord Russell gave Ketch ten guineas to despatch him efficiently. But the first blow of the axe merely wounded Lord Russell, who looked up at Ketch and said, 'You dog, did I give you ten guineas to use me so inhumanly?' Ketch struck again. Still the head was not severed from the body, and two more blows of the axe were necessary before the bloody mess was over.

It was alleged afterwards that Ketch had been bribed with twenty guineas not to kill his victim with the first blow, but Ketch denied this and said that the bungling was due to Lord Russell having moved his head at the last moment. Ketch executed Algernon Sidney at the same time, and two years later, the Duke of Monmouth came to his scaffold on Tower Hill. 'Here are six guineas for you,' the Duke said to Ketch. 'Pray do your business well: don't serve me as you did my Lord Russell. I have heard you struck him three or four times.' Then Monmouth gave some more gold coins to his servant, instructing him to give them to the executioner if he did the job properly.

'If you strike me twice,' he said to Ketch, 'I cannot promise you not to stir.' He lay down, then got up again and said, 'Prithee, let me feel the axe.' He put his fingers along the edge and said, 'I fear it is not sharp enough.' But he lay down again, and gave the signal.

Ketch's arms swung over and the axe blade flashed down, but missed the target and wounded the Duke, who half rose and looked at the executioner, then resumed his position. The axe fell twice more, and still the head was not off. Blood gushed and the body still moved. Shouts of horror rose from the crowd. Ketch flung down the axe. 'God damn me, I cannot do it,' he cried. 'My heart fails me.' 'Take up the axe, man,' the Sheriff ordered. Ketch did so, and struck two more blows before the bloody corpse ceased to quiver. But even then, the head was still joined to the trunk, and Ketch finally had to separate it with a knife. The crowd was so enraged by this spectacle that Ketch was in serious danger of being lynched, and had to be escorted from the scene by a military guard.

In the same year as Monmouth's execution, Ketch was involved in the punishment of Titus Oates, the contemptible author of the Popish Plot, who was sentenced to be pilloried, and whipped at the cart's tail from Aldgate to Newgate, and after an interval of two days, again from Newgate to Tyburn. If he was still alive after this, he was to be imprisoned for life and publicly pilloried five times a year, which meant being thrown to the savagery of the mob. He was in danger of his life in the pillory on the first day of his sentence, and next day he was flogged so severely in the presence of a multitude of spectators in the streets of London that he bellowed and swooned as blood poured down his body. Two days later, unable to walk, partly through weakness and partly through deliberate intoxication, he was dragged to Tyburn on a sledge and the flogging was repeated. A witness said that he received seventeen hundred strokes. He somehow survived this barbarity, and the treatment he received, despite the enormity of his crimes, only added to the notoriety of the executioner, Jack Ketch.

Ketch had already had a busy time as a butcher at Tyburn with those convicted of complicity in the Popish Plot. On 20 June 1679, for instance, he had been involved in the hanging, drawing and quartering of a considerable number of Catholics, including the Jesuit priests Thomas Whitbread, William Harcourt, John Fenwick, John Gavan and Antony Turner.

Although there is no evidence that Ketch travelled to the West Country later that year, his name became associated in popular myth with the loathsome Judge Jeffreys and the Bloody Assizes, when seventy-four were hanged in Dorset, and two hundred and thirty-three hanged, drawn and quartered in Somerset. 'At every spot where two roads met,' as Macaulay put it in his *History of England*, 'on every marketplace, on the green of every large village which had furnished Monmouth with soldiers, ironed corpses clattering in the wind, or heads and quarters stuck on poles, poisoned the air, and made the traveller sick with horror.'

'While Jeffreys on the bench, Ketch on the gibbet sits,' the common saying was, and (who knows?) perhaps Ketch was called to assist and possibly instruct the local gang of bloody executioners who were mustered to exact this savage retribution. If Ketch was not the servant of Judge Jeffreys on this occasion, he was certainly the servant of King James II, and carried out many equally barbaric executions in London.

But he did not sit on the gibbet in the first months of 1686, for it appears that he insulted a Sheriff and was dismissed, and sat in the Bridewell instead. A butcher named Pascha Rose was appointed executioner in his place. As butchery constituted a considerable part of the executioner's responsibilities then, he was doubtless even better qualified than Ketch, and may have assisted him on occasions, but alas, on 28 May of that year Rose was himself hanged at Tyburn for housebreaking and theft, and Ketch was reinstated. Not for long, however, since Death soon overtook him, who had meted out death to so many in nearly a quarter of a century of office. We do not know the exact circumstances of Ketch's demise, but he was buried at Clerkenwell and it is recorded that one Johnson was whipped in London in the first days of December, 1686, 'but civilly used by the new hangman, Jack Ketch being buried two days before.'

The nickname 'Jack Ketch' was commonly used of every hangman who followed him for well over a hundred years, so great was the hatred with which he was remembered, and children were terrorised into good behaviour by the threat that 'Jack Ketch will get you.' He was introduced into the traditional Punch and Judy puppet play, although, so far from hanging Mr Punch, who murders his wife and child, Jack Ketch gets hanged himself – a reflection of the popular contempt for the hangman. Ketch more than anyone else was responsible for establishing the public executioner in modern times as a rogue character to be shunned by respectable society. The hangman was henceforth a subject of taboo, a manslayer who was isolated from normal human beings.

[11]

The stories of the public hangmen up to this point have been much concerned with butchery rather than hanging, because the victims who made national news in those times were so often the noblemen who were condemned for treason in London. But we should not forget that thousands of ordinary people whose names and crimes we do not know were also victims of the hangmen of England, and all the executioners we have encountered hanged more people than they beheaded. A large number of these victims were women, convicted of witchcraft. Witches were burnt in Scotland, but in England they were always hanged. The last execution for witchcraft in England occurred in Ketch's time, when Alice Molland was hanged at Exeter in 1685. There was never any danger of the early hangmen of England being made redundant.

II

The Long March to Tyburn

The English are people that laugh at the delicacy of other
nations who make it such a mighty matter to be hanged; their
extraordinary courage looks upon it as a trifle, and they also
make a jest of the pretended dishonour that, in the opinion of
others, falls upon their kindred.

Henri Misson
Memoirs, 1719

THE FIRST man we know of who followed Ketch as the State's chief
agent of death was named Richard Pearse, but hardly anything is
known about him, and we have to skip a few years to the appointment
of John Price. He is said to have been born in London in 1677, the son
of a soldier who was killed in Tangiers when the boy was only seven.
At this age, he was apprenticed to a rag-dealer in order to scrape a
living for himself and his poverty-stricken mother. Later he worked as
a wagon-loader and eventually ended up in the Royal Navy, perhaps
as a result of being press-ganged.

In 1713 Price was discharged from the Navy, and he applied for the
vacant position of hangman for the City of London and the County of
Middlesex. We do not know what he, or indeed the authorities,
considered to be his qualifications for the job, unless it was his sailor's
familiarity with ropes and knots, but he was appointed, and commen-
ced his work in 1714.

The one or more men who filled the twenty-eight years between
Ketch's demise and Price's inauguration are not known to us by
name except for Pearse. Criminals themselves were sometimes
ordered to carry out executions, and in parts of Scotland chimney-
sweeps were occasionally compelled to assist at hangings. In York, in
1731, one Matthew Blackbourn, convicted of a capital offence, is
known to have 'had his Pardon, being made Hangman'.

There were certainly one or more bungling amateurs at work

during the period before Price took up his post. When Captain John Kidd was hanged for piracy at Execution Dock, in May 1701, the rope broke, and the naval veteran had to be hanged again, his corpse afterwards being left to be washed by the Thames tides. Fortunately for Kidd, perhaps, he was practically senseless with drink at the time. Execution Dock was used for the capital punishment of all those who committed crimes at sea. The place was on the Thames shore at Wapping, by the Pool of London, and bodies were customarily left hanging there until three tides had washed them.

Then there was the case of 'half-hanged Smith' at Tyburn in 1705, when the wretched man was reprieved after hanging for fifteen minutes and found to be still alive when taken down. He was bled and treated till he recovered and gave an account of what it felt like to be hanged, saying that when he was 'turned off, he, for some time, was sensible of very great pain, occasioned by the weight of his body, and felt his spirits in a strange commotion, violently pressing upwards: that having forced their way to his head, he, as it were, saw a great blaze or glaring light, which seemed to go out at his eyes with a flash, and then he lost all sense of pain. That after he was cut down, and began to come to himself, the blood and spirits forcing themselves into their former channels, put him, by a sort of pricking or shooting, to such intolerable pain, that he could have wished those hanged who had cut him down.' Smith's offence was housebreaking, and it is possible that Pearse was the executioner in this case.

To return to John Price, however, we do not have a sufficient record of his work to know whether he was, on the whole, a good or bad practitioner. (Efficiency in executioners was, in any case, only relative, since no hanging resulted in 'instantaneous' death.) But we know that there were enough 'hanging days' at Tyburn to give him plenty of experience, in the short time he officiated, of the last agonies as men were literally hanged by the neck until dead, and that these experiences did nothing to deter him from committing the murder which brought Price himself to the gallows.

It seems that Price fell into the habit of living beyond his means, and was first arrested for debt one day at Holborn, when he was on his way home from Tyburn. The debt on this occasion was a trifling sum, and Price was able to discharge it with the change in his pocket and three suits of clothes, formerly the property of the men he had just hanged, and now rightfully his. But soon afterwards two more creditors took out writs against him and Price, now penniless, was installed in the Marshalsea Prison at Southwark, a terrible place holding at that time as many as seven or eight hundred prisoners, all of them poor folk imprisoned for small debts. Two or three prisoners a day died here, and it was reported in 1719 that three hundred had died in less than three months. By this time, Price had of course been made redundant, a fellow named William Marvell being appointed executioner in his place. So having no source of income, Price had no means of paying his debts, and he languished in the Marshalsea for two years until, early in 1718, he and another prisoner escaped by breaking a hole in the wall.

A month or two later, Price was going home drunk in Moorfields one dark night when, passing close to the Bunhill Fields burial ground, he saw an elderly woman standing by the stall where she had been selling apples and gingerbread. There was no one else in sight, and Price threw the woman to the ground and tried to rape her, but she struggled violently, and in a drunken rage, he began to batter her savagely until her screams brought others to the spot and Price was taken into custody.

The woman's name was Elizabeth, and she was the wife of William White, a local watchman. Her injuries were found to be appalling. Apart from a broken arm, they were chiefly to her head, which was bleeding from the mouth and eyes, one of which had been forced out of its socket. A surgeon and a nurse were fetched to attend to her, and she was somehow able to describe to them what had happened, but she died four days later.

Price was brought to trial for murder, and as he had been caught red-handed, the best defence he could offer was that he had struck an object with his foot as he was walking along in the dark, and finding it to be the old woman, was trying to help her up when he was arrested. This story not being swallowed by anyone, he was found guilty and sentenced to death and to be hung in chains, and was clapped into Newgate to await the day of his execution, which was fixed for 31 May 1718.

It was a common practice to hang particularly vile murderers at the places where they had committed their crimes, so a gallows was erected for Price's death at Bunhill Fields, and jubilant crowds lined the route as the villain was transported there in a cart from Newgate, where Price had spent his time getting stupefied with the spirits which could then be obtained by prisoners without difficulty. One report alleged that a 'little girl who used to carry victuals to John Price the hangman in Newgate, has declared that a few days before his execution, he had carnal knowledge of her body. . . .' We need not take this too seriously, however. Executioners were fair game for slander by both press and public, and the paper that carried this report was the gutter press of the day.

The Ordinary of Newgate (the prison chaplain), Rev. Paul Lorrain, reported that, having obstinately refused to confess his guilt in prison, Price finally did so on the scaffold, and moreover cautioned the mob to take warning from his end. The former executioner met his death at the hands of one Banks, who afterwards had the job of fitting the corpse of his predecessor into an iron suit and suspending it from a gibbet at Holloway.

William Marvell, who took Price's place as hangman when the latter was in prison, did not last much longer than the man he replaced, but he did have the distinction of executing at least two of the Jacobite rebels just before the Hanoverian succession finally ended Stuart pretensions to the throne.

Marvell had been a blacksmith by trade when he was appointed by the Sheriffs of London and Middlesex to succeed Price, but he was already a convicted felon himself. No doubt his muscular arms, well practised at striking the iron on his anvil with a heavy hammer, appeared eminently suited to the task of chopping off heads with an axe; whilst putting a rope round a man's neck and shifting the support from under his feet was no task at all, except perhaps to the nerves.

The Jacobite rebellion of 1715 was led by the eleventh Earl of Mar, who bitterly resented George I's deprivation of all his government offices. He raised his standard at Braemar in September, and was soon in command of an army of 12,000 in Scotland and the north of England. Meanwhile, three men, Whitty, Sullivan and O'Hara, who had been sent to London to recruit the Pretender's sympathisers there, were brought to trial for treason and hanged at Tyburn. It is uncertain whether Price or Marvell was their executioner, but one or the other launched them into eternity, as the common euphemism had it.

By the end of the year, the king's troops had thoroughly routed the Pretender's forces, the Earl of Mar and several others, not to mention

James Edward Stuart himself, escaping to the Continent. But 1500 of their followers were taken prisoner at Preston, including seven noblemen who were brought to the Tower of London to await trial for high treason.

Six of them pleaded guilty, and the sentence passed on them was that they 'return to the prison of the Tower from whence you came; from thence you must be drawn to the place of execution; when you come there, you must be hanged by the neck, but not till you be dead; for you must be cut down alive, then your bowels must be taken out, and burnt before your faces; then your heads must be severed from your bodies, and your bodies divided each into four quarters; and these must be at the king's disposal. And God Almighty be merciful to your souls.'

It does not seem to have crossed the minds of judges much, in those days, that God Almighty might not be merciful to those who pronounced such dreadful sentences. They happily persuaded themselves that the 'Law', and not them, was responsible for such barbarity. In the event, only two of the nobles were executed – James, Earl of Derwentwater and William, Viscount Kenmure – and their sentence was commuted to simple beheading.

The London blacksmith, William Marvell, was instructed to do the job on 24 February 1716, on Tower Hill. He severed Lord Derwentwater's head first with one blow from the axe as the rebel earl pronounced the name of 'sweet Jesus'; but the first blow to Lord Kenmure's neck failed to kill him, and a second was necessary to separate the head from the body. The authorities paid Marvell three pounds for each beheading. Lord Kenmure gave him eight guineas, and he probably had a similar tip from his other victim. It was a profitable day's work, and three months later Marvell hanged two more Jacobites at Tyburn, who were wealthy men and probably tipped him handsomely to make short work of it and not leave them thrashing about in the agonies of slow strangulation. When the executioner, or perhaps the victim's friends or relatives, felt inclined to ease his death, they would do so by gripping the hanging victim's legs and pulling down on them so that he quickly lost consciousness.

It is worth nothing that, about this time, John Hamilton was executed for murder in Scotland by the machine known as the 'Scottish Maiden', the British version of Dr Guillotin's device which was to become the grim symbol of the Revolution in France towards the end of the century. The Scottish Maiden was itself a copy of the Halifax Gibbet, a decapitating machine which had been in use in that town until about 1650, and which was copied from more ancient and primitive devices used fairly widely in Europe in earlier times. Hamilton was the last person to die in Britain by means of such a gadget, on 30 June 1716.

In that year Marvell's death was falsely reported, along with the allegation that he had three sons, two of whom had been hanged and the other transported. This report appeared in the same paper which claimed that Price had taken advantage of the little girl in Newgate. It was not known, the report said, who would succeed Marvell as hangman, 'but there are already 14 candidates for it'. Notwithstanding his supposed demise, however, Marvell was arrested for debt in November of the following year, whilst he was actually on his way from Newgate to hang three men at Tyburn, and in the chaos that ensued from this unprecedented interruption of the course of justice, the hangman was thrown into a horse-pond by the mob and had to be taken away for treatment by a physician. The three condemned were returned to Newgate in the absence of an executioner, and were in due course reprieved. A few days after the incident, Marvell was dismissed from office. He gradually descended into poverty and resorted to theft, but he was soon arrested and brought to trial for stealing ten silk handkerchiefs valued at twelve shillings, a capital offence. The jury brought in a verdict of guilty, but only to the value of four shillings and tenpence, which saved the ex-hangman from the gallows. The Shoplifting Act of 1699 had made it a capital crime to steal from a shop any goods valued at five shillings or more. Marvell was transported instead to the American plantations, where so many criminals were sent until Australia became the new dumping ground; and that is the last we know of Marvell.

The man chosen to succeed him was named Banks, formerly a bailiff, who was appointed on 12 November 1717 and, as we have seen, saw to the arrangements regarding his fellow-hangman, Price. Banks also hanged the Marquis de Paleotti, the Italian brother of the Duchess of Shrewsbury. The Marquis had killed a servant, who refused to borrow money for him, by running him through with his sword, and he was hanged at Tyburn in March 1718.

We know very little about the career of Banks – not even how long he remained in office – but there is evidence that Richard Arnet was

London's hangman by 1719, and it was probably he who executed the notorious Jack Sheppard at Tyburn in November 1724. Sheppard was a Cockney thief and highwayman who escaped from prison four times before being finally 'turned off' at the age of twenty-two.

Seven months later the even more notorious Jonathan Wild was hanged at Tyburn, and again we have no certain knowledge of the identity of his executioner, but the mob was so impatient to see the double-dealing Wild hanged that some spectators threatened to knock the hangman on the head if he did not get on with it. It *might* have been Richard Arnet. We do not know for certain that Arnet was Banks's immediate successor. There could have been someone else at work between these two. None of them can have occupied the office for long, but between them they hanged – among others – a couple of young highwaymen named William Spiggot and Thomas Phillips; and the 'Waltham Blacks', seven men who had been poaching the king's deer on Waltham Chase in Hampshire, with their faces blacked to avoid recognition. This case resulted from the recently enacted 'Black Act', which eventually led to something in the region of 250 offences being made capital. One of the seven, Edward Elliott, was only seventeen, and had been arrested whilst trying to catch a live fawn as a present for his girl-friend. The seven were hanged at Tyburn on 4 December 1723, having been brought from Winchester in irons and chained together. Jonathan Wild's pickpockets were active among the crowd at the execution. Two years later, Thomas Barton, who had given evidence against some of those who were hanged, was himself executed for robbing a woman of twelve shillings.

The Black Act, rushed through Parliament in May 1723, was a savage response to increasing poaching and damage in royal forests, particularly in Berkshire and Hampshire. 'Blacks' was the name given to gangs of poachers going armed and in disguise to hunt or kill deer. The government saw this activity as a Jacobite conspiracy, just as a century later it was to see the Luddite Rebellion as an emulation of the French Revolution. In fact, it was just a crime wave in which poor country folk, who believed that deer were wild beasts and not anyone's private property, pursued an illicit but profitable trade in venison. But in a period of legal terrorism, the Act was continually extended and multiplied by interpretation and new Acts to cover a multitude of other crimes against property. For instance, the original

Act referred specifically to men going armed *and* in disguise, but was soon taken by the courts to mean armed *or* in disguise. The Black Act, which remained in force for a hundred years, gave rise to what is commonly called the 'Bloody Code', and we shall have occasion to consider it again.

It may have been Arnet who had the job of burning Barbara Spencer at Tyburn in July 1721. She was a coiner, when making counterfeit coin of the realm was regarded as high treason, and the punishment for this, in the case of a woman, was that she be tied to a stake and strangled, then burnt.

Arnet was certainly the executioner of Catharine Hayes, who was dealt with in like manner in May 1726. At least, it was *intended* that she should be strangled and then burnt, but the executioner bungled the job. No doubt drunk, he failed to strangle her before the fire forced him away, and the spectators were appalled to see the woman shrieking with terror as the flames licked round her and burnt her alive. Mrs Hayes and her two lodgers had killed her husband and then dismembered his body and dumped it in various parts of London; it was one of the earliest recorded cases in England of disposal of a body by dismemberment. The method was no doubt popularised by the Law, which frequently distributed the quarters of traitors to be exhibited in various parts of the country.

In April 1725 an Irishman named Smith was hanged at Tyburn under the Black Act for trying to extort money by means of a threatening letter. He went to his execution dressed in a shroud, as some Catholics were wont to do, but he tried to escape, and the shroud turned out to be his undoing, not only hampering his getaway but making him obvious for recapture.

Richard Arnet died at Deptford in August 1728. Before we consider the career of his successor, John Hooper, the 'Laughing Hangman', it might be instructive to review the proceedings surrounding the death penalty as they existed around this period in the metropolis.

The majority – though by no means all – of the executions ordered in London in the first three quarters of the eighteenth century took place at Tyburn. This was close to where Marble Arch now stands, at the junction of Edgware Road and Bayswater Road, and near the present 'Speakers' Corner' of Hyde Park. There is still a short road called Tyburn Way there. It had already been London's chief place of execution for six hundred years, and possibly much longer. In the

[20]

time of Elizabeth I, the temporary gallows which had replaced the original Tyburn tree, from which malefactors had been unceremoniously strung up for centuries, was itself replaced by a permanent gallows, still commonly called Tyburn Tree or the Triple Tree. It consisted of cross beams on three wooden posts forming a triangle, so that a number of people could be hanged from it at once. It was about two and a half miles from Newgate Gaol, near St Paul's Cathedral.

For a long period there were eight 'hanging days' a year at Tyburn, and they were public holidays, commonly known as 'Paddington Fair'. One late-eighteenth-century resident who recalled the hanging days wrote: 'It was common through the whole metropolis for master-coach-makers, frame-makers, tailors, shoe-makers, and others who had engaged to complete orders within a given time, to bear in mind to observe to their customers "that will be a hanging-day and my men will not be at work".'

Noisy crowds lined the streets as criminals to be hanged, or beheaded, or burnt, were conveyed from Newgate or the Tower to Tyburn in open horse-drawn carts or hurdles. The condemned had their arms pinioned to prevent escape; they faced backwards, and already had the ropes loosely round their necks. They were accompanied in the carts by the prison chaplain, constantly exhorting them to confess their sins and make their peace with God. The carts were preceded by mounted law-officers with the Under-Sheriff and the city Marshal at their head.

At St Sepulchre's Church, as the solemn procession left Newgate, the bell was tolled. Sometimes, if the criminals were held in particular odium by the mob, they would be pelted with stones or vegetables as they passed. Mandeville, in his *An Enquiry into the cause of the frequent executions at Tyburn* described how they:

> took care to swallow what they could, to be drunk, and stifle their Fear; yet the Courage that strong Liquors can give, wears off, and the Way they have to go being considerable, they are in Danger of recovering, and, without repeating the Dose, Sobriety would overtake them: For this Reason they must drink as they go; and the Cart stops for that Purpose three or four, and sometimes half a dozen Times, or more, before they come to their Journey's End. These Halts always encrease the Numbers about the Criminals; and more prodigiously, when they are very notorious Rogues. The whole March, with every Incident in it, seems to be contrived on Purpose,

to take off and divert the Thoughts of the Condemned from the only Thing that should employ them. . . . It is incredible what a Scene of Confusion all this often makes, which yet grows worse near the Gallows; and the violent Efforts of the most sturdy and resolute of the Mob on one Side, and the potent Endeavours of rugged Gaolers, and others, to beat them off, on the other; the terrible blows that are struck, the Heads that are broke, the Pieces of swingeing Sticks, and Blood, that fly about, the Men that are knock'd down and trampled upon, are beyond Imagination. . . .

There was a house at Tyburn with iron galleries at the windows of the upper floors, from which the Under-Sheriff and other official observers watched the executions, and open galleries were erected for those members of the public who were prepared to pay for seats. These grandstands were called 'Mother Proctor's Pews', being owned by a widow Proctor who obviously had an eye for the main chance.

The cart carrying the condemned was halted beneath the gallows, and the executioner tightened the noose round the standing prisoner's neck, then the horse was moved on, drawing the cart away and leaving the prisoner hanging, to die by strangulation. If the rope was tight enough, unconsciousness was sometimes caused quickly by pressure on the carotid arteries, but more often than not the condemned died slowly of asphyxia, which would take several minutes, and might be accompanied by evacuation of the bowel and bladder – hence the nickname for the hangman, the crap merchant, and the old euphemism for being hanged – pissing when you can't whistle.

The mob was generally excited by the criminal's convulsions as he instinctively struggled against throttling, but if there was some sympathy for him he was put out of his misery by the executioner or someone else pulling his legs to produce unconsciousness through strangulation. When the victim was dead, his body was taken down by the executioner, usually to be either hung in chains on a gibbet, or to be dissected by a teacher of anatomy. A law originating in the time of Henry VIII allowed the surgeons of London to have the corpses of a certain number of executed murderers each year in order to train their apprentices in surgery, and it was the job of the executioner to assist the beadles of the Worshipful Company of Barber-Surgeons in conveying such corpses as they were entitled to from Tyburn to Chirurgeons' Hall. This could be a dangerous business. The public

[22]

abhorred the idea of dissection, and criminals themselves often dreaded this sentence more than hanging in chains, because the whole point of the sentence was as an additional punishment for specially heinous crimes – it prevented, according to the religious doctrine of the time, material resurrection of the body on Judgment Day.

Friends and relatives of a man or woman condemned to be delivered to the surgeons sometimes fought physically with the officials over the corpse when it was taken down from the gallows, and in consideration of the danger they were in, in performing their duty in this way, executioners were customarily given Christmas boxes by the Barber-Surgeons' Company for their year's trouble on the surgeons' behalf. In December, 1730, for instance, the Company's accounts included seven shillings and sixpence paid to the hangman, receipted with the signature of 'John Hooper Executioner'.

We first hear of Hooper when he was a turnkey at Newgate. He was appointed to attend a Major Oneby, who was awaiting execution for murder, and it is recorded that he (Hooper) was so ugly that when the Major saw him, he said, 'What the devil do you bring this fellow here for? Whenever I look at him I shall think of being hanged!' But soon Hooper made himself welcome to the prisoner by his gift of mimicry and his fund of jokes. In earlier times he might have earned his keep as a court jester. Major Oneby left him five shillings in his will.

When Richard Arnet died, Hooper applied for the position of hangman, and was appointed on 15 August 1728. We know of few of Hooper's clients by name, but he was kept busy enough, though few of them perhaps found him as diverting as Major Oneby had done. Japhet Crook, for instance, was hardly amused by this wise-cracking agent of the devil. Crook was convicted of forging deeds of conveyance in 1731 to defraud a couple at Clacton-on-Sea of two hundred acres of land, and was condemned to be put in the pillory for an hour, then to have his ears cut off and his nose slit and seared with an iron, before being imprisoned for life. It fell to John Hooper to carry out this sentence. When Crook had stood his hour in the pillory at Charing Cross, he was placed in a chair on the platform ready for the torture. Hooper stood behind the chair and sliced off his ears with a sharp knife, holding them up for the mob to see. The wounds were staunched by a surgeon, then Hooper slit the victim's nostrils with a pair of scissors and applied a red-hot iron to the bleeding nose, whereupon Crook shot out of the chair and was allowed to forego completion of the operation.

Sarah Malcolm was one of Hooper's victims on the scaffold. She was a twenty-five-year-old killer of some notoriety, having murdered her mistress and two fellow-servants, and she was hanged in the middle of Fleet Street, close to the scene of her crimes in The Temple, on a specially erected gibbet.

Shortly before his retirement, John Hooper was called before the Court of Aldermen to be severely reprimanded for selling the bodies of some of his victims to private surgeons, instead of delivering them to the Barber-Surgeons' Company for whom they were properly intended. The shortage of corpses for teaching anatomy and surgery was becoming acute, and competition for the available bodies was fierce. No doubt jolly Jack made a tidy profit out of this amusing little sideline.

His gallows humour lasted less than seven years, however. Perhaps he got into worse trouble and was dismissed, or perhaps he died. We do not know. But by the beginning of March 1735 he had been replaced by John Thrift, who managed, in spite of all the odds, to hold down the job for nearly eighteen years.

It was not Thrift, but some unnamed provincial hangman, who in 1738 was reported to have been so drunk when he prepared two men for the gallows at Hereford, for housebreaking, that he was convinced there were three for execution, and was only prevented by the gaoler from whipping a noose round the parson's neck as well.

Nor was it Thrift who hanged Dick Turpin, executed for horse-stealing in 1739 at York. They employed their own hangmen in that county, and it may have been the afore-mentioned Matthew Blackbourn who hanged him, but whoever it was received an ivory whistle from the highwayman. Witnesses saw Turpin's right leg tremble as he mounted the scaffold, but he stamped to control it, and when the noose was fixed, he did not wait for the cart to be drawn away, but, taking the law into his own hands, as it were, jumped off it and died instantly from the drop instead of being strangled to death slowly. His body was stolen from its grave by a surgeon next day, but a group of local people recovered it from his garden and reburied it in quick-lime so that it would no longer be of use to the anatomists.

Several of Turpin's former cronies had been hanged in London by Thrift, however, almost as soon as he was appointed. They were

[24]

members of the notorious Gregory gang who terrorised the Epping Forest area of Essex. Executed at Tyburn in March 1735, they were all hung in chains at Edgware, and it was not long before their gang-leader, Samuel Gregory, joined them. It is recorded that he was hanged in June of the same year, and that he 'behaved himself in such a scandalous Fashion during Prayers the mob threw dirt at him. He was afterwards hanged in Chains at Edgware.'

Thrift was evidently a man of nervous temperament, and illiterate. He either possessed criminal tendencies himself, or he was very unlucky. He was always getting himself into trouble. He was accused by a woman of robbing her, but was acquitted, she being imprisoned instead. Perhaps she was a friend or relative of a Tyburn victim, and bore a grudge against the hangman. Then Thrift was attacked by the mob at Tyburn when he hanged a fellow named Thomas Reynolds, a Herefordshire collier who had been condemned under the Black Act for being armed with a pick-axe and being disguised in 'a woman's gown and a woman's straw hat', in the course of destroying turnpikes at Ledbury. The man being cut down and put in a coffin, he suddenly threw back the lid and sat up! Thrift got him back on the scaffold and was about to hang him again when the mob took exception and beat Thrift badly. They carried the victim away to a house, where he 'vomited three pints of blood' and soon died.

Failure to kill the condemned was a not uncommon occurrence in those days, and it occurred again a few years later in Thrift's career. The victim this time was William Duell, convicted of rape and murder, and sentenced to be hanged and then to be handed over to the surgeons for dissection. But when he was already lying naked on the surgeon's table, he was found to be still alive, and in a few days he had fully recovered. Instead of being hanged again, he was transported.

It was Thrift, no doubt, who hanged James Hall in 1741. Hall had murdered his master, John Penny, in his bedroom, by beating him on the head with a stick, then cutting his throat and holding the body so that the blood ran into the chamber-pot. The motive was theft. Hall was hanged in the Strand, and his corpse hung in chains at Shepherd's Bush.

In January 1743 Thrift was the hangman when Thomas Rounce was taken from Newgate to Execution Dock to be hanged for treason on the high seas. 'Jack Ketch rode upon the Hurdle,' a newspaper reported, 'dress'd in a White Frock, with a Knife and Steel by his Side, and a drawn Scymetar in his Hand.' Rounce was first hanged, and after he had 'hung about 15 Minutes, the Executioner cut him down, ript up his Belly, and threw his Heart and Bowels into a Fire prepar'd for that Purpose. He was then quartered, and his Quarters put into a Coffin, and deliver'd to his Friends.' The report added that the crowd was 'so great that several People had their Legs and Arms broke, and were otherwise terribly bruised.' This was the year in which Handel's *Messiah* brought tears to the eyes of the more sensitive in London society, all of whom, no doubt, approved of the death penalty.

The Vagrancy Act of 1744 made 'rogues and vagabonds' liable to whipping and increased the income of the executioner, particularly in London. But it was the '45 Rebellion that provided Thrift with his high point, or perhaps his low point, as an executioner. He was required in July 1746 to hang, draw and quarter nine Jacobites on Kennington Common. One by one Thrift had to take the hanged men down from the gallows, cut off their heads, disembowel them and throw their hearts and entrails into a fire. Less than three weeks later, he was called upon to behead Lords Kilmarnock and Balmerino on Tower Hill. The story is told of Balmerino that, whilst under sentence of death in the Tower, he begged for his wife Peggy to be brought to him, and the instant she arrived, he stripped her and made love to her.

Thrift had to get himself drunk to tackle the job. He seems to have been intimidated by the thought of executing his betters, and it is debatable whether he or their lordships were more nervous of the event. Thrift wept as he begged Lord Kilmarnock's forgiveness, but he received a purse of guineas as an incentive to do the job properly, and somehow managed to dispatch Lord Kilmarnock with one blow. Lord Balmerino was less fortunate. The scaffold was strewn with fresh sawdust and 'that no appearance of a former execution might remain, the executioner changed such of his clothes as appeared bloody'. Lord Balmerino was brought out and took his place on the block, but this time Thrift took three blows to sever the head from the body.

Three blows were necessary again in December, when Thrift executed Charles Radcliffe, the brother of Lord Derwentwater, whom Marvell had beheaded somewhat more efficiently thirty-one years

earlier. But when Lord Lovat came to Thrift's scaffold in the following April, the executioner seems to have recovered his confidence.
Perhaps he was helped by the fact that there was no public sympathy
for Lovat, a Scottish despot and reprobate who had raped the widow
of the tenth Lord Lovat and forced her to marry him in order to secure
his own succession to the title.

The eighty year-old Simon Fraser, Lord Lovat, was fat, and a story
circulated in London that he had petitioned the king to be hanged
instead of beheaded, as his neck 'is very short and his shoulders
almost as high as his head, so that unless he stretched it out, his
shoulders must receive most part of the blow. . . .' If this request was
made, it was turned down, and in fact Thrift struck off Lovat's head
with one blow so accurate and forceful that the axe was lodged nearly
two inches deep into the block. Lord Lovat was the last person to be
beheaded in England.

In addition to these various lords who were executed in the
time-honoured manner, more than a hundred of Bonnie Prince
Charlie's followers were hanged, many of them by Thrift. He was
now an object of hatred to all those who had any sympathy for the
Jacobite cause, and one night in 1750, when he was returning to his
home just off Drury Lane, he was followed by some youths shouting
'Jack Ketch' and other various insults at him. The noise drew a larger
and rather menacing crowd as he reached his door, and Thrift ran
into the house and emerged again with a sword, threatening the mob
if they did not clear off. It appears that he gave chase to some of them,
and in Short's Gardens, a few yards away, there was a scuffle in which
a fellow named David Farris was killed. Several of those present
swore that the hangman was the killer. Thrift was imprisoned to
await trial for murder.

The trial came in April 1750, and Thrift pleaded innocence, saying
that a friend who had come to his assistance had struck the fatal blow
entirely in self-defence. The 'friend', however, was a little circum-
spect in agreeing to this version of events, and in due course the Lord
Chief Justice, Sir William Lee, pronounced Thrift guilty as charged
and sentenced the hangman to death. He was reprieved, however,
and ordered instead to be transported to the American colonies, but
after spending many weeks in prison he was granted a free pardon
and released, and was soon busy with the ropes on the City's behalf
again. Perhaps a man who had killed so many enemies of the people

legally was thought too useful to sacrifice merely for the illegal killing of one person – and a Jacobite sympathiser at that!

I am not sure if it was Thrift who hanged Mary Blandy at Oxford in April 1752. If it was, this act cannot have increased his popularity, for there was a great wave of public sympathy for this rather stupid young woman who had poisoned her father so that she could marry a scoundrel named Cranstoun, who was already married. She claimed that the powders she administered to her father were sent to her by Cranstoun to appease her father's opposition to him, and that she did not know they were harmful. When she came to the scaffold, she asked the hangman not to 'hang me high, for the sake of decency.' Her ghost, riding a white horse, was long said to haunt a lonely road near Henley-on-Thames, where the family lived, and where Mary became known as the 'murdered maid'.

Thrift hanged one William Parsons in February 1752, but three months afterwards he fell ill, and died at his home on 5 May. There was a riot at his funeral six days later. He was buried in the churchyard of St Paul's, Covent Garden, though he was not a native of that parish, and at a time when the overcrowding of city churchyards was on the verge of becoming a national scandal, there was local resentment by parishioners of *any* intruder, let alone the public hangman! But eventually the mob was dispersed, and the burial took place. Among the mourners was one 'Tullis'.

The newspapers sometimes spelt his name 'Tollis' as well, but his name was Thomas Turlis, as his own careful signature shows beyond doubt. We know hardly anything about his private life, but it appears that he had already been employed on occasions while Thrift was still active, and it could have been Turlis who hanged Mary Blandy, though it is equally possible that the Sheriff of Oxfordshire employed some local jobbing hangman entirely unknown to us. A fellow named Elliot had testified at Thrift's trial for murder that he had acted for him whilst the hangman was in prison, and one Joseph Barnet seems to have served as assistant to Turlis for a short time until he (Barnet) was transported for theft.

Turlis served as hangman for nearly twenty years – two years more than his predecessor – but his greatest claim to fame came nearly half-way through his term of office, when he was called upon to execute Laurence Shirley, Earl Ferrers, the only peer of the realm to be hanged for murder. This execution was a landmark in the sad history of the death penalty for another reason, too.

Towards the end of 1759, the so-called 'Triple Tree' at Tyburn – the permanent triangular gallows which had stood for nearly two hundred years – was removed as an obstruction to the increasing amount of traffic in and out of London. It was replaced by a new movable scaffold, which was brought out for each hanging day and then stored away again until the next. This contraption had a raised staging reached by a set of wooden steps, and eighteen inches above the staging was a platform which could be collapsed so that the victim fell suddenly, before the rope reached its full extent and jerked the head to a halt, causing unconsciousness, if not necessarily death, more rapidly than by the old system of stringing a man up and removing the support for his feet. (The old method was still employed for some years, particularly when there was more than one victim to be hanged.) Lord Ferrers was not the first victim to be hanged by means of a drop, but he was certainly among the earliest subjected to what was intended as a more humane technique. A drop of a mere eighteen inches was not nearly enough, however, and victims of the gallows continued to be strangled to death for a long time yet.

Laurence Shirley was the descendant of an ancient and distinguished Leicestershire family, whose seat was Staunton Harold Hall, near Ashby-de-la-Zouch. Laurence was the fourth Earl Ferrers. He was a hard drinker with a violent temper, and his long-suffering wife divorced him for cruelty when he kicked her unconscious in front of the servants. One day he called into his presence an old family retainer named Johnson, for whom he had developed a passionate hatred, ordered him down on his knees and shot him dead. After his arrest he was taken first to Ashby, then to Leicester Gaol and finally to the Tower of London, to await trial by the House of Lords in Westminster Hall. He conducted his own defence, using all his eloquence to convince their lordships that he was insane, which was undoubtedly true, but they did not believe him, and he was sentenced to be hanged at Tyburn on 5 May 1760.

Huge crowds gathered to see the execution. Lord Ferrers was dressed in his white satin wedding suit and travelled in his own landau, attended by his liveried servants and accompanied by an escort of cavalry and infantry. The march to Tyburn from the Tower took nearly three hours because of the mass of people lining the route. As the Earl himself observed: 'I suppose they never saw a lord hanged, and perhaps they will never see another.' He understood the Englishman's weakness for a free show.

Popular myth has it that Lord Ferrers was hanged with a silk rope, but there is no truth in this – he had to make do with hemp, like a common criminal. On the scaffold, Ferrers gave his five guineas to the executioner's assistant, by mistake, and a scuffle then broke out between the agents of death until the hangman himself, Thomas Turlis, had recovered the money. In due course, these grotesque proceedings continued, but when the Earl was actually hanged, his feet were touching the ground, so Turlis and his henchman had to grab his legs and pull hard. 'He suffered a little by delay,' Horace Walpole observed rather nonchalantly, 'but was dead in four minutes.'

Another notorious murderer of this period was Eugene Aram, but Turlis was not his executioner, this honour going to the hangman customarily employed by the Sheriff of Yorkshire, partly to save the expense of bringing a man all the way from London and partly, no doubt, because whatever Londoners could do, Yorkshiremen always reckoned they could do better themselves. Aram was a scholar who became a schoolmaster. But he and a crony named Houseman killed a shoemaker, Daniel Clark, in order to rob him of £200 worth of silver plate and jewellery. They dumped the body in a cave by the River Nidd at Knaresborough in 1744, the skeleton being found fourteen years later. Houseman then turned King's Evidence, and Aram was convicted and sentenced to death, in spite of a long and ingenious speech in which he suggested that the skeleton was not that of Clark but possibly that of a hermit or anchoress who had lived in the cave centuries ago. Forensic science was hardly thought of then, but no one believed this theory. Aram failed in a suicide attempt whilst in prison, and he was hanged at York by the local exponent of the gallows art, and hung in chains in Knaresborough Forest after his skull had been presented to the College of Physicians.

York's place of execution was also called Tyburn at this period. The gallows had been erected in 1708 at a spot called 'the Mount', outside the city walls beyond Micklegate Bar, where executions had been carried out since the fourteenth century. The site is now part of York's racecourse. Tyburn was last used in 1801, after which York Castle became the scene of executions for the county, and the gaol of those for the city.

[30]

Meanwhile, in London, Turlis had been practising his various arts by disembowelling a Jacobite rebel, Doctor Cameron, hanging an assortment of forgers and murderers, and carrying out the whippings and floggings he was required to administer. In 1761 he hanged Theodore Gardelle, a Swiss painter of miniatures, who killed his London landlady, Mrs Anne King, in the course of attempting to rape her. He dismembered the body and made clumsy attempts to dispose of it, and he was hanged in the Haymarket and his corpse hung in chains on Hounslow Heath.

In 1763, another and less common duty of the hangman was imposed on Turlis when he was ordered to burn publicly a journal containing a seditious libel, issue No. 45 of the *North Briton*, whose author and publisher was John Wilkes, Member of Parliament for Aylesbury. Wilkes had made an unprecedented attack on the King's Speech, alleging that it contained a lie. The symbolic execution was to take place on 5 December in front of the Royal Exchange.

On the appointed day, at noon, a small bonfire was lit in the presence of the Sheriff and a large crowd. Turlis received the offending literature from one of the officials. But between the sentence and the execution, the government which had condemned the publication had fallen, and the mob was mainly on the side of Wilkes. As Turlis stepped towards the fire to drop the *North Briton* into the flames, the incensed mob suddenly surged forward, pelting the law officers and the hangman with mud and stones, manhandling the constables, and wrecking the Sheriff's coach. Turlis, though covered and bruised by a barrage of missiles, stood his ground long enough to do his duty, casting the publication into the fire; but no sooner had he done so than someone in the crowd snatched it out again, and the scene becoming ever uglier, Turlis ran for cover.

Turlis had narrowly escaped execution himself earlier in the year, when he had been charged with stealing coal from the cellar of one of his neighbours. He knew better than anyone that he was liable to be hanged if caught, but the deterrent value of the death penalty was as much a myth then as it is now. He pleaded poverty and was not only let off, but was appointed hangman for Surrey, as well as for London and Middlesex, so as to increase his income. The Sheriffs must have valued Turlis highly.

One of the most despised murderers who came Turlis's way was Elizabeth Brownrigg, a midwife who so cruelly treated a sixteen-

[31]

year-old bound apprentice, Mary Clifford, that the girl died. She was not the first victim of Mrs Brownrigg's savagery, but she was the most extreme case. She was tied up naked and beaten mercilessly, sometimes with a cane, sometimes a horsewhip, and sometimes a broom-handle. She was made to sleep in a coal-hole and fed on bread and water. On other occasions, the girl's arms were tied up to a hook in the kitchen ceiling while her naked body was beaten until blood was running down it. Once, Mrs Brownrigg seized the girl's cheeks with her fingers and forced the skin down so violently that blood ran from Mary Clifford's eyes, and on another occasion, her tongue was cut with scissors.

Eventually, it came to the notice of Mary Clifford's mother-in-law that the neighbours had frequently heard shrieks and moans from the Brownriggs' house, and at length the house was entered by law officers who found Mary Clifford in a cupboard, in a critical condition. She was taken to St Bartholomew's Hospital, but died a few days later. Mr and Mrs Brownrigg and their eldest son John, who had also whipped and otherwise ill-treated Mary, were indicted for murder. The charge was reduced to misdemeanour for the two men, who were imprisoned for six months. Mrs Brownrigg was found guilty of murder and sentenced to death. She made her last journey to Tyburn on 14 September 1767, through a crowd that, for once, was more hostile to the criminal than to the executioner, and Thomas Turlis, after hanging the madwoman, assisted her corpse on the way to Surgeons' Hall, where it was dissected, the skeleton being preserved for many years.

As to the deterrent value of the death penalty, Sarah Metyard, a milliner, was hanged, along with her daughter, for a very similar crime less than a year later. Crime is a reflection of the social climate, regardless of the state of the Law, and Georgian society was violent and brutal. While all these acts were being committed illegally, Thomas Turlis was doing the same thing legally, and being paid for it. He was paid a pound for whipping four women in May and June of that year, and ten shillings for whipping Mary Dolley from Cavendish Square to Duke Street, as well as earning several similar fees for whipping men in the same period. The medieval whipping post had given way to the 'cart's tail' in many such instances of corporal punishment, and the sentences of the courts were usually specific, ordering that, for instance, a woman should be stripped to the waist and whipped until the blood ran down her back.

Hardly surprising that the common hangman was held in such contempt by the majority of the populace, and especially by the poor, whose social circumstances made them most likely to become his victims. When Turlis hanged three men at Kingston-on-Thames in April 1768, the mob stoned him, and he was cut and bruised. And in March of the following year, he was again cut and bruised about the head and face when he put a man in the pillory at Southwark.

Punishment, as Freud pointed out in *Totem and Taboo*, 'will not infrequently give those who carry it out an opportunity of committing the same outrage under colour of an act of expiation. This is indeed one of the foundations of the human penal system and it is based, no doubt correctly, on the assumption that the prohibited impulses are present alike in the criminal and in the avenging community.'

As for Thomas Turlis, he died suddenly whilst returning home from an execution at Kingston, in April 1771. He was the last hangman to use Tyburn as the chief scene of his work throughout his career.

III

Slaughter of the Innocents

'Jesu!' said the Squire, 'would you commit two persons to Bridewell for a twig?'
'Yes,' said the Lawyer, 'and with great lenity too; for if we had called it a young tree they would have been both hanged.'

Henry Fielding
Joseph Andrews, 1742

IN 1783, twelve years after Turlis's death, the last execution took place at Tyburn. The site where, over a period of six centuries, English men, women and children had been variously flogged, mutilated, hanged, burnt, beheaded and disembowelled in the name of the law of a Christian country, had become an inconvenience to the rapidly expanding capital. It has been estimated that as many as 50,000 people may have been done to death there. Henceforth, the chief place of execution for the metropolis was to be in front of the rebuilt Newgate Prison, in Old Bailey.

The executioner for London and Middlesex at this time was Edward Dennis, who had probably succeeded Turlis in 1771. In that year John Wilkes was elected Sheriff of London, and made an appeal to the citizens to instruct their MPs to 'move for a revision of those laws which inflict capital punishment for many inferior crimes'. It was not to be. The savagery of the Georgian laws to protect property gave Dennis one of his first jobs, when he hanged eighteen-year-old Mary Jones at Tyburn for the theft of four pieces of muslin valued at five pounds ten shillings. The girl's husband had been press-ganged, and she had been turned into the streets with her two children to beg. She was hanged because she was poor, and her infants were left without a mother. It was said that one of them was at her breast when she was carted to Tyburn.

There was nothing especially unusual about this case. During the course of the eighteenth century, the Industrial Revolution produced a vast increase in urban population, with the inevitable consequences of overcrowding, slums, disease, inequality and rising crime rates. The government was made up largely of land-owning country squires, and law and order were in the hands of parish constables. The latter were as unequal to their task as the squires were to bringing about urgently needed social reforms. The government's answer to the growing problems was to extend the death penalty to even the pettiest of crimes. The wealthy and powerful believed that there was a 'criminal class' which must be eliminated for the sake of society as a whole. By the end of the century, there were well over two hundred capital crimes on the statute book, the majority of them crimes against property – the obsession of Georgian criminal law. The various enactments originating from the Black Act of 1723 were framed so broadly that the death penalty could be imposed for innumerable unspecified variations of the same offence, and it is impossible to compute precisely how many crimes there were which could be punished by death. Some say more than three hundred.

Popularly known as the Bloody Code, this legislation made it an offence punishable by death for a man, woman or child to steal turnips, shoot a rabbit, pick a pocket, damage a fish-pond, cut down an ornamental tree, set fire to a haystack, consort with gypsies, write a threatening letter, impersonate a pensioner of Greenwich Hospital, or appear on a public highway with a sooty face. Such crimes were punished with a barbarism unparalleled in the history not only of England but of the whole civilised world. The records of children hanged during this period are numerous. It was probably Dennis who hanged a boy named Peter McCloud in May 1772 for attempted house-breaking. Five years later a fourteen-year-old girl was in Newgate waiting to be burned alive for 'petit treason'. At the instigation of her master she had secreted some whitewashed farthings in her clothing. 'Good God, sirs,' Sir William Meredith exclaimed in the House of Commons, 'we are taught to execrate the fires of Smithfield and we are lighting them now to burn a poor harmless child for hiding a whitewashed farthing.'

No time was allowed to pass between sentence and execution. Unless the day after the trial was a Sunday, the condemned was hanged next morning. No person in England was less likely to be unemployed at that time than the public hangman, particularly the hangman for London and Middlesex. London was the nation's crime capital, and one estimate reckoned that more than a hundred thousand people were making a living from crime in the city towards the end of the eighteenth century.

I am indebted to E. P. Thompson's *Whigs and Hunters* for the splendid story told by Henry Fielding about the judge Sir Francis Page, who, when a horse-thief was brought before him under the Black Act and claimed to have found the animal, said: 'Thou art a lucky fellow: I have travelled the circuit these forty years, and never found a horse in my life: but I'll tell thee what, friend, thou was more lucky than thou didst know of; for thou didst not only find a horse, but a halter too, I promise thee.'

Edward Dennis hanged the Perreau brothers in January 1776. They were dissimilar twins, Robert being a respectable tradesman, Daniel a wastrel, who induced his brother to join him in financial speculations which brought them close to bankruptcy. They then took to forging bonds to the value of several thousand pounds. When they were brought to book, they accused Daniel's mistress, Mrs Margaret Rudd, of being the forger. She, however, was acquitted and the brothers sentenced to death. Many believed that Robert should be reprieved as the innocent dupe of Daniel, and a petition in his favour was signed by seventy-eight bankers and merchants. But there was little inclination to be merciful at that time, and the law took its course.

The brothers were not the only ones to be hanged that day at Tyburn. There were also two Jews, convicted of housebreaking; a young highwayman; and two men condemned for coining. Two long cross-beams were erected on the scaffold for this event. The two Jews were hanged side by side on one, and the five Christians in a row on the other. 30,000 people are said to have turned out to see the event on a cold January day when there was snow on the ground. Dennis obviously needed an assistant for this complicated multiple execution, and the man who helped him was named William Brunskill, an illiterate, humble and obsequious fellow, whom we shall meet again.

Another famous forger met his maker at the hands of Dennis in the following year, when it was said that the crowds lining the route to Tyburn were the greatest ever known, exceeding even the gatherings at the executions of such as Jonathan Wild and Lord Ferrers. The victim on this occasion was Rev. William Dodd, Doctor of Divinity and Chaplain to the King. He had forged a single bond when he had fallen into debt to several tradesmen. He was a respected preacher and the author of many charitable works, and no one believed he would be executed, even when he was declared guilty and the dread sentence was pronounced.

Dr Samuel Johnson was prominent among those who tried to save him, and wrote Dr Dodd's speech in his own defence, as well as a petition to the king and a letter to the newspapers on Dodd's behalf. It was all to no avail. Rumour was rife among the sympathetic populace when Dodd was driven to Tyburn in a mourning coach. It was said that Dennis had been bribed to fix the noose so that it would not strangle the reverend gentleman, and that as soon as he was cut down he would be rushed to the house of a surgeon who would be ready to resuscitate him.

There was another criminal to be hanged that day, named Harris, and when the two men were on the scaffold, Dr Dodd did all he could to comfort his fellow victim. Just before the cart was driven away, Dr Dodd was seen to whisper something to Dennis, and when the two men were left hanging, the executioner immediately steadied the clergyman's legs, but if this action had anything to do with a conspiracy to defraud the gallows of a victim, the plan did not work. Dr Dodd was soon dead. One of the jurymen who had found him guilty was himself hanged for forgery soon afterwards.

Dennis numbered another unfortunate clergyman among his clients, in a great *cause célèbre* of 1779, when Rev. James Hackman was condemned to death for the murder of Martha Ray, mistress of the Earl of Sandwich, First Lord of the Admiralty. Miss Ray had been the earl's mistress since she was eighteen, and bore him several children, but in 1774 she had an affair with an army officer, James Hackman, whom she had met at Lord Sandwich's country home. Hackman tried to persuade her to leave the earl and marry him, but she refused. Early in 1779 Hackman left the army and was ordained a deacon in the Church of England, but he was still so infatuated with Martha Ray that, when he still failed to win her, his jealousy overcame him. One night in April, as Miss Ray was leaving the Covent Garden Theatre, Rev. Hackman shot her in the head. Knowing she was in the theatre, he had waited for her with two pistols. He claimed that he had intended to commit suicide in front of her, and that the second pistol was a precaution in case the first misfired. Dr Johnson took some interest in this case, too, though not to the extent of wanting to save the passionate clergyman from the gallows. He believed that the possession of two pistols proved an intention to murder, as indeed did the jury, and the judge, who sentenced Hackman to be hanged by the neck until he was dead.

In the summer of the following year, hangman Dennis became marginally involved in the Gordon Riots. Dickens, in *Barnaby Rudge*, involves him deeply, and represents him as being hanged as one of the ringleaders in the attack on the recently rebuilt Newgate Prison. Dickens has Dennis begging for his life in abject terror, saying, 'The King and Government can't know it's me; I'm sure they can't know it's me; or they never would bring me to this dreadful slaughterhouse. They know my name, but they don't know it's the same man. Stop my execution – for charity's sake stop my execution, gentlemen – till they can be told that I've been hangman here, nigh thirty year. . . .' But this is a case of artist's licence, and not one of Dickens's most sensible imaginings. Why would the hangman attack the chief source of his income?

Dennis's real participation in the Gordon Riots was very minor. He was arrested for aiding a mob in High Holborn in the looting of a Catholic shopkeeper's premises, and brought to trial at the Old Bailey early in July 1780. Dennis claimed that someone in the mob had recognised him as he approached (he lived in Newtoners Street close by), and cried out, 'Here's bloody Jack Ketch!' whereupon he and others had threatened to burn Dennis unless he helped them. The judge bent over backwards in his summing-up to give Dennis the benefit of the doubt, but the jury, less inclined to look kindly on the common hangman, found him guilty, and he was sentenced to death. Dennis dropped to his knees and begged for mercy, but he was taken with the other convicted rioters to Tothill Fields Prison to await execution. For some reason, however, he escaped being hanged and eventually got a free pardon. Perhaps once again the authorities felt that they could not do without this experienced public servant when there were so many others to be launched into eternity. It seems even more likely when we learn that, whoever was doing the hanging during Dennis's enforced absence, he was a bungler. 'The present "Jack Ketch" is a disgrace to his office', a correspondent wrote to the *Public Advertiser*. 'He handles the unhappy convicts with as little concern as a butcher would a sheep or a bullock.' Could this have been William Brunskill, who had been assisting Dennis for several years?

Dennis himself executed William Ryland, a popular engraver who turned his talent to forging an East India Company bill of exchange, and was hanged for it in August 1783. On 7 November that year the last execution occurred at Tyburn, when John Austin was hanged there. The fatal tree was felled at last. Executions in future were to take place in front of Newgate, once more rebuilt after extensive damage in the Gordon Riots.

The decision to end executions at Tyburn was made for good practical reasons. Not only was the expansion of London leading to increased traffic which was obstructed on execution days, but the West End of the capital was becoming a fashionable residential and business area for which the scaffold and the noisy and unruly mobs lining the route were hardly a good advertisement. But the change provoked a famous outburst from Dr Johnson, who fumed with characteristic bombast against the complaint that Tyburn drew a multitude of spectators: 'Sir, executions are intended to draw spectators. If they do not draw spectators, they do not answer their purpose.' He need not have worried. The Old Bailey drew spectators as well.

Johnson's opinion would unquestionably have been supported in a referendum on the subject, but wiser heads were being shaken over the public taste for retribution even before Sir Samuel Romilly took up the cause. Even Edmund Burke noted with some discomfort that the House of Commons would pass *any* Bill for the imposition of the death penalty, and Sir William Meredith argued in the Commons in May 1777 that the death penalty was not a deterrent.

Nevertheless, Dennis and William Brunskill hanged ten people in front of Newgate Prison on 9 December 1783. The new scaffold was a timber structure on wheels, which was kept inside the prison yard and pulled out into the street by horses for hanging days. It had a platform which was released by a pin or bolt to produce a drop of two or three feet. (The *Gentleman's Magazine* said two or three *inches*, but this cannot have been correct – the rope would have stretched by that much and the victims' feet would always have touched the ground, so far from bringing 'immediate death' as the magazine reported.)

It would appear that Dennis was still working two years later, for there is a record that he was presented in 1785 with a robe by the

Sheriffs, apparently intended as a kind of uniform, but he found it restricted his movements and duly sold it. But in 1786 Edward Dennis died in his bed and was buried in the churchyard of St Giles-in-the-Fields on 26 November. 'In his office of Finisher of the Law, Surveyor of the New-drop, and Apparator of the Necklace,' said one facetious obituary, 'alias Yeoman of the Halter, &c, he acquitted himself with the approbation of all – but the parties concerned.'

Dennis had on more than one occasion petitioned the Sheriffs to appoint his son to succeed him, but there is no evidence that they did so. After Richard Brandon, the position of public hangman was not again to be regarded as in any sense hereditary – in London at least – until the end of the nineteenth century. But there was a family of hereditary hangmen named Otway at work in Somerset at this time, it would seem, although at Bridgwater in 1785 another local executioner was hanged for theft. His name was Thomas Woodham, and he had served the Sheriff of Gloucestershire, and possibly helped out in Somerset on occasions. He is said to have been seventy years old at the time of his offence, so he must have been desperate to assault a man and rob him of one shilling and sixpence.

The man who succeeded Dennis was his former assistant Brunskill, who carried out a multiple execution the day after Dennis's death, hanging seven criminals at once before a critical audience in Old Bailey, to which he bowed humbly at the conclusion of his maiden performance.

In March 1789 Brunskill carried out the last execution in Britain in which a woman was burnt. The victim's name was Murphy, and she was convicted of coining, a crime for which, like the murder of a husband, a woman was sentenced to be 'burnt with fire until she was dead', although in practice the victim was invariably strangled before the bonfire was lit. Murphy's male accomplices were hanged on the same day. In 1790, this punishment for women was abolished.

That year was also notable for a clear demonstration of the sheer idiocy of imposing the death penalty for crimes against property. A man named Williams was arrested for stabbing a girl named Anne Porter. His knife wounded but did not kill her. He was charged with wounding and with the capital offence of 'unlawfully wilfully and maliciously spoiling, tearing, cutting and defacing the cloak, gown, petticoat and shift' of his victim, and pronounced guilty by the jury. An appeal to the Court of Errors got the verdict overturned on the grounds that Williams's intention was to damage the girl, not her clothes, and therefore he was not guilty of 'wilfully and maliciously' doing so. Williams was saved from the gallows. He got two years for wounding the girl.

Business was not too good for the new executioner in his early years. In January 1794 he petitioned the Court of Aldermen for higher pay, saying that his income was not sufficient to provide for himself and his family, and he could not obtain other employment because of his calling. The obvious solution to this problem, from his point of view, would have been to hang more people, but what was actually happening was precisely the opposite. From 1788, two years after Brunskill's appointment, transportation to Australia had begun to take place on a large scale for many of the crimes for which the death penalty was prescribed in the Black Act. In the ten years from that date, only 191 executions were carried out in London and Middlesex, compared with 531 in the previous decade, when the scaffold had rivalled smallpox and fever in reducing the population of London. In the ten years from 1799 to 1808, the figure fell even further, to 126. If the threat of the death penalty would not reform the criminal class, the reasoning went, better to rid the country of these people in another way. Besides, as a reaction to the savagery of the Bloody Code, juries were regularly refusing to convict on capital charges, by undervaluing stolen or damaged property, and the legalised terrorism with which the governments of the first four Georges had sought to suppress the 'criminal class' eventually back-fired. The prosecutor of two men in Leicestershire, Joseph Bland and John Edgson, who were arrested in 1793 for destroying trees, refused to proceed against them when the judge pointed out that it was a capital offence under the Black Act.

In 1797, Brunskill bungled an execution when hanging two men for murder. Martin Clench and James Mackley were being made ready on the Newgate gallows by Brunskill and his assistant John Langley, whilst the Ordinary of Newgate, Rev. John Villette, and a Catholic priest were administering the last rites. Suddenly the platform collapsed, and the six men fell, the four officials tumbling in a heap at the feet of the two condemned, who died by one means or another in any case. The two clergymen were badly bruised and shaken, and Brunskill had to try to explain away the failure of the bolt holding the platform.

[42]

In 1803 Brunskill was called on to hang the Irish Colonel Edward Despard and his six associates on the roof of Horsemonger Lane Gaol, the new Surrey county prison in what is now Union Street in Southwark, a borough notable for its prisons in those days – there were seven at one period, including the notorious Marshalsea. Horsemonger Lane, where the new prison had been completed five years earlier, was at the centre of an area much favoured by the criminals, prostitutes and body-snatchers of London because it was outside the City's jurisdiction.

Despard was the chief conspirator in a foiled plot to assassinate George III, and he and his companions were sentenced to be hanged, drawn and quartered, but this was subsequently changed to beheading after hanging. The men were brought out two at a time, Despard coming out last on his own, and the seven men were hanged. Then a masked man severed the head of each one, and as he did so Brunskill held each one up to the crowd, declaring, 'This is the head of a traitor', in the time-honoured manner.

Ugly scenes of a different sort occurred at Newgate four years later, when John Holloway and Owen Haggerty were hanged for murder by Brunskill. Many believed them innocent, and a dense and agitated crowd, said to number forty thousand, gathered to see them hanged, resulting in the crushing of many spectators in the tumult. The pressure of the crowd was so great that women were screaming for help, and when a pie-man's basket was knocked to the ground, people started to fall over it and one another. Meanwhile, the two men were hanged, Holloway crying out, 'I am innocent, innocent by God! Innocent, innocent, innocent!' When the execution was over, and the mob started to disperse, more than thirty were found to have been trampled to death, some of them women and children, and a large number had to be treated for their injuries.

Two years after this event, Brunskill hanged Captain Sutherland of the merchant navy, who had murdered his young negro servant in a drunken temper. The law took its course at Execution Dock, although there were many who were affronted by the execution of a British officer for the killing of a mere negro, and huge crowds again gathered to witness the spectacle, not only along the route from Newgate and on the shore-line, but also from boats and barges on the river. The captain was observed to give Brunskill his prayer-book before the hangman 'turned him off.'

[43]

Perhaps the most famous criminal to come Brunskill's way was John Bellingham, the man who assassinated Spencer Perceval. Bellingham was a merchant who had gone bankrupt, and blaming government measures for his failure, went to the lobby of the House of Commons and shot the Prime Minister on 11 May 1812. The man was a lunatic and insanity was pleaded in his defence, but he was sentenced to death for all that, and Brunskill hanged him at Newgate within a week of his crime. A large crowd gathered, and most people, it seemed, were on the side of the criminal, for some called out 'God bless you!' as he appeared on the scaffold, and Brunskill had to perform his duty to considerable barracking. Bellingham's last words were, 'I thank God for having enabled me to meet my fate with so much fortitude and resignation.' The people's healthy disrespect for government ought not to have gone so far as applause for an assassin, no doubt, but it was combined with a long-lasting show of defiance of the authority represented by the gallows, and perhaps exhibited some sympathy for a man who was clearly out of his mind and ought not to have been executed.

Meanwhile, Sir Samuel Romilly was leading the campaign to abolish the death penalty for the multitude of trivial offences that were still on the statute book. 'There is no country on the face of the earth,' he said, 'in which there have been so many different offences according to law to be punished with death as in England.' But against his proposal to abolish the death penalty for shoplifting to the value of five shillings or more, the Lord Chief Justice, Lord Ellenborough, made his notorious objection that repeal of this law would lead to no man being able to 'trust himself for an hour out of doors without the most alarming apprehensions, that, on his return, every vestige of his property will be swept off by the hardened robber.'

Brunskill had been ill of late, and in 1814 he had a stroke. The man who had long assisted him, John Langley, was called upon to take charge of executions meanwhile, but in May of the following year, Brunskill submitted his humble resignation to the Court of Aldermen, having been rendered incapable of carrying on by the partial paralysis of his seizure. By that time, Langley had felt confident enough of his succession to have taken on an assistant of his own, one James Botting by name. Brunskill was awarded a pension of fifteen shillings a week. He had been the chief hangman for twenty-eight years, easily the longest-serving London executioner we know of up to that time, although his contemporary in Lancashire, a fellow named Edward Barlow, is said to have served for thirty-one years, hanging all those condemned to death at Lancaster Assizes during that period. (The *Lancaster Gazette* of 22 March 1806, said that Barlow had been the county hangman for twenty years; but when the same paper reported his death in 1812, it said he had been hangman for thirty-one years!)

Barlow was a Welshman, commonly known as 'Old Ned' and, according to later reports, was as great a villain as any of those he hanged. One account says that he was guilty of 'nearly every vile act, was many times convicted, and twice sentenced to transportation for life.' He is usually credited with about 130 executions at Lancaster between 1782 and 1812, though some fanciful accounts credit him with hangings up to 1835, twenty-three years after his death, including the hanging of nine men at once in 1817! Even the former figure is almost certainly an exaggeration. As Barlow was in prison from 1806, his true number of executions was probably nearer 100, and his true length of service probably twenty-five years.

Up to the turn of the century, Lancashire's hangings were carried out on a gallows known as the 'Tyburn shape' on Lancaster Moor, overlooking Morecambe Bay. Barlow was clearly loathed by the local population, and was sometimes physically assaulted and pelted with 'missiles of the foulest description'.

In March 1806, Old Ned was convicted of stealing a gelding from a Mr Wright of North Meols, near Hoylake, and was sentenced to death, but the sentence was commuted to ten years imprisonment, and Barlow died in Lancaster Castle in December 1812. He was probably in his late sixties, though his age is as uncertain as his length of service and the number of his victims. After his death the London executioner was invited to Lancashire on occasions as a sort of guest artist, although Lancashire's Sheriff probably swallowed his pride and engaged the man from Yorkshire on occasions, to save expenses. It is known that the Sheriffs of England's northern counties sometimes employed Scottish executioners, too, rather than bring a man all the way from London.

Brunskill's successor in London served for one of the shortest terms on record. John Langley was only two-and-a-half years at the job before death removed him from office. We know little about Langley except that he had assisted Brunskill for many years, ably enough to be appointed in his place without competition, after his master's attack of apoplexy. He was a married man of forty-eight then, and he and his wife Elizabeth had three children.

It may have been Langley who hanged one of the last victims to be executed under the Black Act. William Potter, an Essex man, was hanged in 1814 for cutting down his neighbour's orchard. Few ordinary people were conversant with the ninety year-old law by this time. Potter was not aware that he had committed a capital offence, and even the committing magistrate was surprised. He and the prosecutor signed a petition against the sentence, but it was an abortive gesture.

Langley's most famous client was undoubtedly Elizabeth Fenning, a twenty-one-year-old servant in the house of a couple named Robert and Charlotte Turner in Chancery Lane. The premises were owned by Robert's father, Orlebar Turner, who lived at Lambeth and was a well-to-do law stationer. The house in Chancery Lane was also his sales office. Besides his son and daughter-in-law and Elizabeth Fenning, a housemaid and two apprentices lived there. Old Mr Turner habitually joined Robert and Charlotte for dinner on weekdays. Elizabeth had been employed there as cook for only a few weeks. She was intelligent, conscientious and good-looking.

On 21 March 1815, Elizabeth served the family steak and dumplings for dinner and, naturally enough, sampled her own cooking before doing so. Within minutes, all three of the Turners were suffering from stomach pains and vomiting. So was Eliza Fenning, in the kitchen, and one of the apprentices, Roger Gadsden, who had also sampled a small portion of dumpling. Two physicians were called to treat them all, and in due course they all recovered.

Old Mr Turner, meanwhile, remembered that a packet of arsenic which was kept in a drawer in the office for use on mice which infested it had disappeared, and he had one of the physicians examine the contents of the pan in which the dumplings had been cooked. Arsenic was found in it. Elizabeth Fenning was arrested and brought before a magistrate, who committed her to Newgate to await trial for attempted murder.

The trial was a disgrace to a supposedly civilised country. The evidence was entirely circumstantial, and the Turners – especially Charlotte – were very hostile and damaging to Miss Fenning's cause, implying that Eliza was resentful and bent on vengeance because Mrs Turner had caught her going to the apprentices' room one night

[46]

partly undressed, and threatened to dismiss her. The judge was biased, refusing to admit evidence on Eliza's behalf and virtually instructing the jury to convict her.

After she was declared guilty, she wrote to her fiancé: 'They have, which is the most cruellest thing in this world, brought me in guilty.' And then she told him, 'I may be confined most likely six months at least.' In fact, she was sentenced to death. Appeals for clemency were made to the Prince Regent, the Home Secretary (Lord Sidmouth) and the Lord Chancellor (Lord Eldon), but to no avail. Elizabeth Fenning, hysterical with disbelief, protested her innocence continually until the morning of her execution, when John Langley bound her arms and led her out to the scaffold with two other condemned criminals. A large crowd was waiting. The Ordinary exhorted her to confess her guilt, but she would not do so, and Langley hanged her, after tying a dirty handkerchief round her eyes, which she objected to but had to accept. Her father had to pay fourteen shillings and sixpence before he was allowed to take his daughter's body away for burial. This sum was called 'executioner's fee'.

It turned out that Robert Turner had suffered from some sort of mental derangement and had threatened to destroy himself and his wife. It was he who had bought the arsenic.

Langley's last job was at Snow Hill in March 1817, when he and Botting hanged an Irish sailor, John Cashman, who had plundered a gunsmith's premises during the so-called Spa Fields riots of the previous December. In April, Langley was admitted to the London Hospital, and on the twenty-seventh he died, aged fifty-one, to be succeeded by his former assistant James Botting, the son of a Brighton man who ran a low dive in that town.

Elizabeth Langley petitioned the Court of Aldermen for financial assistance, on the grounds that through the unfortunate occupation of her husband, and the contempt it had brought on her, she was unable to earn her living and provide for her children.

With Langley's death coincided the end of mutilation as an 'additional punishment', the last sentence of hanging and drawing in England occurring at Derby in 1817, when three men convicted of high treason were hanged, but beheading was substituted for disembowelling.

James Botting, or 'Jemmy' as he was known, was an illiterate, surly and repellent character who seemed to revel in the task he had taken on. He is reckoned to have executed 175 people in his few years of office, but his chief claim to fame is the regularity of his complaints to the Aldermen – written by someone else and signed with his mark – about his pay and working conditions, making what was by now the traditional and heart-breaking hangman's protest that, in effect, the number of people he was required to kill was insufficient to support him.

Even whilst he was assistant to Langley he had asked for higher wages, and hardly had he succeeded to the highest rank of his chosen profession before he was asking to be allowed to employ an assistant, which request – oddly enough – was refused. The Court of Aldermen declared that 'an assistant to the public executioner is unnecessary.' We can only put this decision down to ignorance. The Aldermen had never had to hang two or three people at once! It is true that the number of executions was diminishing at this time, partly because of the increasing use of transportation as an alternative way of ridding the country of its criminals, and partly because of juries' refusals to convict on capital charges for offences against property.

In fact, in 1818, the first full year of Botting's reign, the death penalty for shoplifting, in force for 119 years, was finally abolished. Much of the credit for the gradual disappearance of the Bloody Code is due to Sir Samuel Romilly, the hero of British penal reform, who had campaigned for years against the death penalty, but died by his own hand, after the death of his wife, just before his efforts at last produced a change in the law. He had poured scorn on an old law which had resulted in only one person being executed out of the last 1872 convictions for the capital charges of shoplifting and theft from dwelling houses, and held up to the Commons as an example of the law's absurdity the case of Bridget Mackallister, who was charged with stealing a £10 banknote from a house in 1808. Stealing to the value of more than forty shillings carried the death penalty. The jury had brought in a verdict of guilty, but declared that the banknote was worth only thirty-nine shillings!

Nevertheless, there were still many occasions when it was necessary for assistance to be given to the executioner, and the Aldermen soon relented, appointing one James Foxen as assistant to Botting. Soon afterwards, it appears that the hangman for London and Middlesex was granted a weekly wage of one pound, in addition to the usual perks, for as Botting pointed out in one of his submissions,

John Langley 'had always received small fees from the undertakers and friends of the criminals executed, also the privilege of rubbing persons afflicted with wens, for which it was usual to receive 2s. 6d. for each person.' Thus Botting became the first salaried civil servant among the hangmen of England, and for the next half-century the men who succeeded him in London were not left wanting because of the gradual diminution in the number of clients, or 'parties' as Botting always called them.

In Scotland, on the other hand, they were sacking hangmen for incompetence. John Simpson was dismissed in December 1818 following his inefficient handling of an execution at Edinburgh, when Robert Johnston was to be hanged for robbery. When the platform fell, the condemned man's toes were still touching the boards, so that he was only half suspended, and he struggled in this position for five minutes before he was cut down, after cries of horror broke from the crowd and the officials were pelted with stones. Then the mob rushed the scaffold, carried Johnston away to revive him, and attacked Simpson, causing him some injuries. Johnston was carried back to the scaffold when soldiers and police had restored some order, and a second attempt was made to execute the half-conscious prisoner. First his trousers fell down, then when Simpson released the platform Johnston got a hand free and struggled to free his neck from the pressure of the rope, until Simpson forced his hand away, and amid shouts of horror from the crowd, the body twitched for several minutes before life was extinct.

That it was necessary for the hangman to have at least one assistant in these modern times was proved on 1 May 1820, when Botting's instructions were to hang the five leaders of the Cato Street conspiracy, in front of Newgate Gaol. The intent of these radical extremists had been to assassinate the Cabinet and take over the country. They proposed to cut off the heads of the Ministers and carry them through the streets of London on poles. Their chief was Arthur Thistlewood, who had been involved in the Spa Fields affair for which Botting had helped to hang John Cashman three years earlier.

Inspired by Tom Paine and the French Revolution, the fanatical and possibly deranged Thistlewood seems to have believed that an armed insurrection in London, following the recent outrage of the Peterloo Massacre in Manchester, would have the support of the people and end in the establishment of a republic, with himself as

[49]

president. But the government had been watching Thistlewood and his crazy henchmen for three years, and had a spy in their midst. The authorities pounced on the Cato Street hayloft where the conspirators did their plotting, and the five were brought to trial and condemned to death for treason. The sentence of the court was that they should be hanged and beheaded. It was the last occasion in England on which such a reinforcement of the State's punishment for treason was ordered. Naturally, a huge crowd turned out to see it done.

Botting hanged the five men, after one of them, James Ings, had cried out, 'Give me death or give me liberty!' (an inaccurate echo of the American statesman Patrick Henry). Their bodies were left dangling for half an hour. Then a masked figure in a seaman's jersey mounted the scaffold and severed the heads of the five, Botting holding them up in turn. The man who did the decapitations was so speedy and skilful that rumours quickly spread as to his identity. He must be an experienced surgeon. Someone in the crowd put it about that he came from Argyll Street. This could only mean Thomas Wakley, subsequently founder of the medical journal *The Lancet*. A gang of conspiratorial remnants or sympathisers raided his house during the night, set fire to it, and seriously injured the surgeon, who was not in fact responsible for the beheading at all. The masked man was a body-snatcher named Parker, who had been paid twenty pounds by the Under-Sheriff to do the job, his qualifications being that he was, as he so eloquently put it, 'in the habit of cutting of nobs for the purpose of getting the gnashers.' (There was a market for the teeth from corpses at that time – fashionable people wanted real teeth in their dentures.)

By 1824 Jemmy Botting had been replaced and he was in the debtors' prison, but he was released with a small pension, and eventually returned to Brighton where, after suffering a stroke like Brunskill before him, he lingered on, practically bedridden, until 1837. It was said that he was much troubled in his last years by the ghosts of all those he had killed.

Botting's successor, predictably, was James Foxen, his former assistant. He too was illiterate and brutal, though a little more sociable than his predecessor. He called his victims his 'gentlemen' instead of his 'parties'. It seems he had some competition, however. He described himself in a letter to the Court of Aldermen in 1828 as 'one of the Executioners at the Old Bailey'. His fellow hangman was one Thomas Cheshire, who spent most of his long career as an assistant, but carried out executions by himself on some occasions. Why it was thought necessary to appoint two hangmen when executions were becoming less frequent is not entirely clear, but one reason may have been that the London hangman was increasingly in demand in other parts of the country, since it was no longer worth while for most counties to have their own specialists.

It was Cheshire, for instance, who hanged John Thurtell at Hertford in January 1824 for the so-called 'Elstree murder', the Hertfordshire authorities having asked the Keeper of Newgate to 'send down a proper man' for the job.

John Thurtell was the son of a mayor of Norwich. He fell in with a gang of low sporting types and decided to kill William Weare, a solicitor, apparently because the latter had cheated him in a game of billiards. Weare having accepted an invitation to spend a weekend at a cottage owned by Thurtell's crony William Probert at Radlett, he travelled with Thurtell in a gig from London, and on arrival at Radlett, Thurtell suddenly pulled out a pistol and fired point blank at Weare's face, but the bullet glanced off his cheekbone. Thurtell then fell upon his terrified victim and cut his throat with a penknife. He then rammed the barrel of his pistol at Weare's head with such force that it penetrated the skull and filled the barrel with blood and tissue. Meanwhile, Probert and another crony, Joseph Hunt, had turned up, and they dumped Weare's body in a pond in the garden until later, when they took it to another pond at Elstree. But some labourers at Radlett soon found the bloody pistol and penknife which Thurtell had carelessly dropped, and a major murder hunt was in progress in no time. When two Bow Street runners questioned Probert, he immediately offered to turn King's Evidence before Hunt, who was a professional singer, had the chance, though Hunt hastily showed them where the body was.

The trial at Hertford Assizes was before Mr Justice Park, and is notable as the last trial in England conducted under the Tudor procedure whereby an accused had to defend himself during inquisition by his accusers. Thurtell and Hunt were tried together (the latter as an accessory before the fact), and the guilt of Thurtell was so generally taken for granted by the press that the judge was led to remark that if 'these statements of evidence before trial which corrupt the purity of the administration of justice in its source . . . are not checked, I tremble for the fate of our country.'

[51]

Thurtell's speech in his own defence was a long and rambling mixture of emotional blackmail and dubious argument, which impressed some commentators as being exceptionally eloquent, for some unaccountable reason. Perhaps they were carried away by the fact that the defendant was, at any rate, literate. 'My lord,' Thurtell began, 'and you, gentlemen of the jury, under the pressure of greater difficulties than perhaps it has ever before fallen to the lot of man to sustain, I now appear before you to vindicate my character and preserve my life.' But in the face of his obvious guilt, it is debatable whether some of his remarks were best calculated to vindicate his character: 'calumniated and charged as I am,' he said, 'what bosom can refuse a sigh? What eye can deny a tear?' He explained that he had been reared by 'a kind, affectionate and religious mother, who taught my lips to utter their first accents in praise of that Being who guides the conduct of your hearts and of the learned judge upon the bench.' He then proceeded, with touching Christian feeling, to accuse Probert of being the real murderer, and called upon the words of Voltaire, the Apostle Paul and the Newgate Calendar in his defence – a mixed bag of witnesses which did not unduly impress Mr Justice Park, who commented that the Newgate Calendar, 'for anything I know to the contrary, may be mere books of romance.'

Nor was the jury to be diverted from the obvious truth by smooth words, and the twelve good men and true took only twenty minutes to find both Thurtell and Hunt guilty. They were sentenced to death, Thurtell's body being ordered to be handed over to the surgeons for dissection. Cheshire got thoroughly drunk the night before, as was the custom with executioners, telling stories of his experiences in return for free drinks, and getting involved in a brawl, during which some of his tackle was stolen. When he got to the gaol the turnkeys locked him up in a cell to sleep it off.

Hunt's sentence had been commuted to transportation meanwhile, and he lived to old age in Botany Bay. But Cheshire was sober enough by morning to do an efficient job on Thurtell, whose neck broke 'with a sound like a pistol shot' when the drop fell. Probert got his come-uppance in the following year when he was hanged for stealing a horse.

Foxen's first famous victim was Henry Fauntleroy, the banker hanged for forgery in November 1824, after he had defrauded the Bank of England of over a quarter of a million pounds. There was a lot

of public sympathy for this 'gentleman', and a vast crowd of spectators turned up, half expecting him to be reprieved at the last minute,
but it did not happen, and Foxen hanged him without so much as a
by-your-leave. The Ordinary of Newgate, Rev. Horace Cotton, was
reprimanded by the authorities because the sermon he customarily
delivered to the condemned was so powerful on this occasion that it
was felt to be unnecessarily harrowing to the prisoner's feelings.
Another euphemism for suffering the death penalty at Newgate was
born around this time – leaving the world 'with your ears stuffed with
cotton'.

Things did not go so smoothly for the executioner when Foxen
came to hang Charles White in January 1827. White was a young
bookseller who had burnt his house down in order to claim the
insurance. It was a particularly senseless act, as his business was
prospering, and White cannot have thought of the consequences. He
protested his innocence and cursed his judges, and even planned an
escape. He fought frantically on the morning of his execution, and
after Foxen had bound him, managed to struggle free. Foxen had
been provided with two assistants in view of White's behaviour in
gaol, and they secured him again and held him whilst Foxen prepared
him for the drop. But when the trap fell, White jumped suddenly,
catching himself partly on the platform so that he did not fall through
completely, and grasped at the rope round his throat, having again
loosened his hands by the violence of his struggle for life. His tongue
was hanging from his mouth and his face was horribly contorted.
There were shouts of horror from the crowd. Foxen forced White's
feet off the platform so that he was properly suspended on the rope,
then hung to the legs of the convulsive figure until all movement
ceased.

A year after this event Foxen sent in his resignation, stating that he
was now sixty, and in a poor state of health, and unable to perform his
duties. But he changed his mind for some reason, and in August 1828
he went to Bury St Edmunds to hang William Corder, perpetrator of
the famous 'Red Barn murder', which outdid even the 'Elstree murder' in the sensation it created and the long-lasting impression it
made on the public.

William Corder was a young farmer at Polstead when he met
Maria Marten, a mole-catcher's daughter, and made her his mistress. A child was born to them, but soon died. Maria's father pressed

Corder to marry her, and on 18 May 1827, Corder told her that they were to be married that very day at Ipswich. She was to meet him later at the red-tiled outhouse on his farm. Maria complied. Corder later informed her father that she was having a holiday on the Isle of Wight. He then went to London, having borrowed money from his mother, and advertised in the *Sunday Times* for a wife. By this means, he met a young school teacher, married her, and helped her to start a girls' school in Ealing.

Meanwhile, Maria Marten's stepmother, who claimed to be a medium, said that she had seen Corder in a dream, shooting Maria and burying her in the red-roofed barn. When Mr Marten remembered that her son – Maria's stepbrother – had seen Corder going towards the barn on the day of the supposed wedding with a pickaxe and shovel, he went to investigate, and soon dug up his daughter's corpse. Corder was arrested and brought to Bury St Edmunds to be tried for murder, and was quickly found guilty and sentenced to death.

When Foxen prepared to do his duty before a large crowd of Suffolk spectators, someone, the Under-Sheriff or the prison governor perhaps, queried the drop he was giving, and becoming very bad-tempered, the hangman grumbled as he made an adjustment, handling the victim rather roughly, and withdrew the bolt without ceremony, protesting afterwards that he didn't 'like to be meddled with'. He said that no man in England 'has had so much experience as me, or knows how to do his duty better.' This was very debatable. Foxen then went to claim Corder's clothes, as was his right, and made an undisclosed sum from the sale of the rope he had used, which he cut up into short lengths so as to disappoint as few eager customers as possible.

In December, no longer thinking of resignation, apparently, Foxen hanged Joseph Hunter, a Quaker, along with three other men. Hunter's crime was forgery, and again there was much sympathy for him as opposition grew to the death penalty for this crime, but when the traditional cry of 'Hats off!' went up in Old Bailey as the condemned mounted the scaffold, it was in no way a mark of respect for men about to die, but an instruction to those spectators at the front so that those at the back could see.

Two months later, in the winter of 1829, Foxen died suddenly at his home in Booth Street, Hoxton, after catching a chill. He was sixty-

'Half-hanged Smith' being taken down alive after hanging for several minutes, 1705. *(By courtesy of the Trustees of the British Museum)*

Simon Fraser, 12th Baron Lovat – the last man in England to be executed by beheading. The portrait is by Hogart[h] (*National Portrait Gallery*)

The axe and headsman's block in the Tower of London, believed to have been used by John Thrift to execute Lord Lovat in 1747. *(By courtesy of the Board of Trustees of the Royal Armouries)*

'The Idle Apprentice Executed at Tyburn', from Hogarth's series of engravings 'Industry and Idleness', 1747. Note the hangman on the triple tree awaiting his victim. *(By courtesy of the Trustees of the British Museum)*

William Calcraft, the longest-serving hangman known to English history. *(BBC Hulton Picture Library)*

Calcraft's business sign. No doubting which craft he took most pride in! *(BBC Hulton Picture Library)*

Madame Tussaud's models of William Marwood and Charles Peace, exhibited in the Chamber of Horrors, stand on a real gallows acquired from Hertford Gaol in 1878. (*By kind permission of Madame Tussaud's*)

James Berry, the former Bradford policeman who became chief hangman of England in 1884.
(*BBC Hulton Picture Library*)

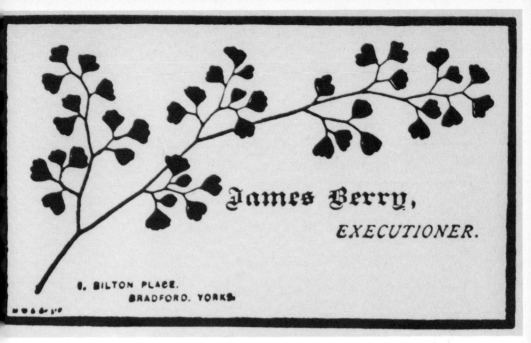

Berry's business card. It was printed in black, green and gold.

A late nineteenth century execution chamber. This artist's impression shows the trap-doors open, and the hatch through which medical officers and executioners descended by steps into the pit. The pulley system evident on the uprights was for raising the corpse after its obligatory hour's hanging. (*By kind permission of Madame Tussaud's*)

One of James Berry's lantern slides, showing a 'victim' pinioned, noosed and hooded, and about to get a drop of what looks like roughly five feet. The model for this photographic reconstruction may well have been Berry himself. Who else would have done it? (*By kind permission of Madam Tussaud's*)

one. The newspapers were not complimentary to him, hinting that he was not the most efficient of his ilk, but compared with his surviving colleague, Cheshire, Foxen was himself a gentleman. When they told Cheshire that Foxen was dead, he snarled, 'How the devil can I help it!'

IV

Money for Old Rope

As it came on very dark, he began to think of all the men he had
known who had died upon the scaffold. . . . He had seen some of
them die, – and had joked, too, because they died with prayers
upon their lips. With what a rattling noise the drop went down;
and how suddenly they changed, from strong and vigorous men
to dangling heaps of clothes!

Charles Dickens
Oliver Twist, 1838

ON 6 JULY 1840, an execution took place outside Newgate Gaol in the
presence of some distinguished witnesses. The condemned man was
Francis Courvoisier, a Swiss butler, who had cut the throat of his
employer, the aged Lord William Russell, uncle of the Duke of
Bedford. Charles Dickens and William Makepeace Thackeray were
among the spectators. 'I can see Mr Ketch at this moment', Thackeray wrote shortly afterwards, 'with an easy air, taking the rope from
his pocket. . . . It seems to me that I have been abetting an act of
frightful wickedness and violence, performed by a set of men against
one of their fellows. . . .'

It was several years before Dickens published *his* impressions of the
occasion, but he eventually wrote about the execution to the editor of
the *Daily News*:

From the moment of my arrival, when there were but a few score boys
in the street, and those all young thieves, and all clustered together
behind the barrier nearest to the drop – down to the time when I saw
the body with its dangling head, being carried on a wooden bier into
the gaol – I did not see one token in all the immense crowd; at the
windows, in the streets, on the house-tops, anywhere; of any one
emotion suitable to the occasion. No sorrow, no salutory terror, no
abhorrence, no seriousness; nothing but ribaldry, debauchery, levity,
drunkenness, and flaunting vice in fifty other shapes. I should have

[57]

deemed it impossible that I could have ever felt any large assemblage of my fellow-creatures to be so odious. . . .

Of the effect upon a perfectly different class, I can speak with no less confidence. There were, with me, some gentlemen of education and distinction in imaginative pursuits, who had, as I had, a particular detestation of that murderer; not only for the cruel deed he had done, but for his slow and subtle treachery, and for his wicked defence. And yet, if any one among us could have saved the man (we said so, afterwards, with one accord), he would have done it. It was so loathsome, pitiful, and vile a sight, that the law appeared to be as bad as he, or worse; being very much the stronger, and shedding around it a far more dismal contagion.'

The executioner of Courvoisier, called 'Jack Ketch' by Thackeray, still using the hangman's common nickname a century and a half after Ketch's death, was in fact one William Calcraft, who had by then been operating for eleven years.

At the demise of James Foxen, his obvious successor would appear to have been Thomas Cheshire, a man of considerable experience if disreputable conduct. But although there is evidence that he offi-ciated at a few executions immediately after Foxen's death, it seems that he did so only as a temporary or 'acting' hangman, for he was quickly passed over by the authorities in favour of this other man, Calcraft, who was appointed executioner for London and Middlesex on 4 April 1829, at a weekly salary of a guinea with a supplement of a guinea for every execution he carried out. He also subsequently got an annual retainer of five guineas from Horsemonger Lane Gaol, with an additional guinea for every execution he carried out there.

The rejection of Cheshire is testimony to the low estimation in which he was held, for the job of assistant had been regarded as ideal preparation for stepping into the boots of the master for at least a century. But Cheshire, familiarly known as 'Old Cheese', was a ghoul. He had been a soldier once, and almost enjoyed a flogging more than a hanging, always provided, of course, he was adminis-tering it, giving being more blessed than receiving. His mother was a Methodist when she was sober, which was not often, and if her son took after her, it was in her devotion to the pub and not the chapel. He habitually wore an ankle-length greatcoat of the colour of snuff, and small boys would follow him in the streets with childish bravado. His wife Ann was charged on one occasion with throwing four children down a cellar when they had followed the drunken woman shouting 'Jack Ketch' after her.

Calcraft was born at Baddow near Chelmsford in 1800, and worked locally as a cobbler at first, then went to London, working first for a brewery in what is now Clerkenwell Road, then as a butler at Greenwich, and then selling meat pies in the streets. 'Trade was bad for me,' he explained later. 'In fact, I could not get anything to do. Being in no way particular what I turned my hand to to earn money, as long as it was honestly come by, I attended the execution of the Quaker Joseph Hunter and sold pies to the people round the scaffold.' During this period, when the crowds at Newgate and Horsemonger Lane were good prospects for his pies, he met both James Foxen and Thomas Cheshire. In due course, Calcraft offered himself as assistant to Foxen for a double execution at Lincoln, and was also employed to flog juvenile offenders at Newgate. With these qualifications, he applied for the vacant position when he heard of Foxen's death. It was the year in which the Home Secretary, Sir Robert Peel, introduced his police force to the metropolis.

Unlike Cheshire, William Calcraft was a quiet and respectable-looking man, married with two young sons, and his hobby was rabbit-breeding. He went to church with his wife on Sunday mornings, and occasionally brought one of his children with him when he called at Newgate to collect his salary.

It was scarcely more than a week after his appointment when Calcraft was called on to do his first job, outside Newgate Gaol. The victim was Esther Hilmer, who had killed a ten-year-old girl apprentice by flogging and starving her. Mrs Hilmer attempted suicide in prison, and struggled so violently against her gaolers when the time of her execution arrived that she had to be confined in a strait-jacket, and was dragged to the gallows wearing only a long black skirt over her nightdress. The execration in which this woman was held by the crowd assembled in Old Bailey was such that when Calcraft mounted the scaffold he was cheered loudly.

The woman had been a tambour-worker, and out of seven parish girls she had charge of, three had died. The broadside circulated at her execution contained the lines:

> Since Mother Brownrigg's ancient doom,
> Now sixty years and more,

> Such treatment to poor infants,
> Was never heard before.

This was scarcely true. Child-killing was alarmingly common. But if the public's memory was short, so was Esther Hilmer's – the well-known fate of 'Mother Brownrigg' had no deterrent effect on her behaviour towards her charges.

Nor was authority to be moved by the tender age of some of society's wrongdoers. In 1831 Calcraft did a job in his native town, Chelmsford, hanging a boy of nine for setting fire to a house.

Among Calcraft's early and infamous victims were the body-snatchers, John Bishop and Thomas Head, alias Williams, who had murdered an Italian boy and a woman in order to sell their bodies to teachers of anatomy. A man named James May was also convicted with them, but was later reprieved on the strength of Bishop's and Williams's confessions. (The murderer William Burke, Hare's partner in crime, had been hanged in Edinburgh three months before Calcraft's appointment. One source says that the executioner was named Williams, although another says that Williams was not made Edinburgh's hangman until 1833.)

Bishop and Williams were brought out to the scaffold in front of Newgate Gaol on 5 December 1831, before a huge crowd which one observer estimated at 30,000. When Calcraft released the trap doors, Bishop died instantly, it appeared, but Williams struggled for some minutes in his death agonies, the vast mob meanwhile shouting and yelling and pressing towards the scaffold to such an extent that many people were injured, including a soldier and several policemen, and some had to be taken to St Bartholomew's Hospital for treatment. Williams's corpse followed them there, in due course, to become a subject of close inspection by students of anatomy, their colleagues at King's College receiving Bishop's body.

Soon afterwards, another alleged body-snatcher came to grief in that grisly period of our social history, though body-snatching was not in itself a crime. A couple named Edward Cook and Elizabeth Ross (sometimes known as Cook, sometimes as Reardon) were charged with murdering at Whitechapel in August 1831 an old woman named Catherine Walsh, who sold laces and cotton in the streets around Aldgate, and selling her body to the surgeons. There was insufficient evidence against Cook, though he was well known as a drink-sodden body-snatcher. Nor was there a body in the case, but the chief witness against the woman was her twelve-year-old son, who said he had heard his mother tell his father that she had sold the body to the London Hospital. Eliza Ross, thirty-eight, was found guilty on this evidence alone and hanged in January 1832. A publican told a newspaper reporter that she had been well known as a body-snatcher twelve years before the execution. She was also a thief and a violent drunkard. It was said that all the cats in the neighbourhood disappeared because she skinned them for profit. Cook was known to sell the skins of hares to furriers. Ross consistently denied having murdered Walsh, claiming to the very end that she had left her 'husband' and her son sitting with the old woman and 'never saw her after'. When her corpse was taken down, it was delivered to the Royal College of Surgeons, where executed murderers were brought for distribution to the anatomy schools.

The slow death of Williams from strangulation was to become almost a trade mark of Calcraft's executions. Despite the invention of the drop to give victims of the gallows a quicker death, Calcraft never mastered the art of using it to the victim's advantage, always adopting a short drop as well as fixing the noose with a clumsy slip-knot. It was a matter of the executioner's judgment how much drop a man should be given to kill him quickly, and Calcraft's judgment was never very good. It was well known for him or his assistant to appear under the scaffold and hang on the victim's legs to speed his death. When he hanged John Tawell at Aylesbury in 1845, *The Times* reported the execution as follows:

> The length of drop allowed him was so little that he struggled most violently. His whole frame was convulsed: he writhed horribly, and his limbs rose and fell again repeatedly, while he wrung his hands, his arms having been previously pinioned, and continued to wring his hands for several minutes, they being still clasped, as though he had not left off praying. It was nearly ten minutes after the rope had been fixed before the contortions which indicated his extreme suffering ceased.

A job as principal came Tom Cheshire's way in 1834, when two men were sentenced to be hanged at Horsemonger Lane Gaol for a murder they had committed at Hyde, near Manchester. Joseph Moseley and William Garside were cotton-spinners, and they had shot their employer's son following a dispute about their wages. But a difference of opinion arose between the authorities of Lancashire and Cheshire about which was responsible for the execution, and the matter being referred to the Court of King's Bench, it was decided that the two culprits should be executed in Surrey! Cheshire was engaged to carry it out, and did so efficiently, no doubt with the usual 'fiendish delight' betrayed by the gleam in his eyes.

'Old Cheese' continued to assist Calcraft on occasions, when needed, but he gradually disappears from the scene after about 1837. *The Times* published an obituary of him in July 1830, but as with Mark Twain, reports of his death appear to have been greatly exaggerated. It was said that a body-snatcher had once sworn to Cheshire that he would have the hangman's corpse, in consequence of which Old Cheese went about in mortal terror of the resurrection men, and wanted to be buried inside Newgate, but we cannot rely on the report that he was buried in St Sepulchre's churchyard instead, and do not know if the body-snatchers got him or not. If he did not die until around 1837, it is unlikely that they did, for the Anatomy Act of 1832 had made the resurrection men more or less redundant.

In 1837, the year of Queen Victoria's accession, Calcraft hanged James Greenacre at Newgate for the murder of Hannah Brown, whom he had cut up and distributed in various parts of London south of the river. Greenacre had been a prominent tradesman and politician at Southwark, and in the condemned cell he was visited by Members of Parliament and even, it is said, noblemen. Calcraft wore a black suit for the occasion with a gold watch chain hanging from his pocket.

His dress was less formal when he was required to whip or flog felons through the streets, a punishment for which he was paid half-a-crown a time, and which was still resorted to frequently in his early days. It was soon abolished in public, though floggings continued to be administered inside prisons.

The number of executions taking place was rapidly diminishing, however. In the year of Calcraft's appointment, Peel was Home Secretary in Wellington's government. 'It is impossible to conceal from ourselves,' Peel said, 'that capital punishments are more frequent and the criminal law more severe on the whole in this country than in any country in the world.' But during the next thirty years, the Bloody Code was to disappear by degrees. A Select Committee in

[62]

1819 had recommended the repeal of twenty-seven of the old statutes, but the judges and the bishops, in particular, had strongly opposed such extreme measures, and Peel himself thought abolition for theft a 'most dangerous experiment'. But by 1835 the death penalty had been abolished for sacrilege and returning from transportation; by the following year, for forgery and coining; by the year after that, for burglary and theft from dwelling houses. The hanging of tarred and chained corpses on gibbets disappeared from the English landscape in that period, too, as well as the law ordering murderer's corpses to be delivered for dissection by anatomists.

These long overdue reforms were to have serious financial consequences for practising and aspiring hangmen throughout the land. Yorkshire had engaged its own executioners from time immemorial, rather than bring men all the way up from London. Since Brunskill's time, the Yorkshire hangman had been John or William Curry, who was still disposing of Yorkshire's criminals some years after Calcraft's appointment in London. Curry, also known as Wilkinson, was a labourer from Thirsk who was in prison for life at York Castle when a vacancy arose for a hangman in 1802. He was offered a reduction of his life sentence in return for accepting it. He had been arrested in August 1800 after stealing five sheep at Heworth, near York. The minutes of meetings of the City of York Association for the Prosecution of Felons, Cheats, &c., show that two guineas were paid to Thomas Dale 'for his journey into Leicestershire with Pardoe to apprehend Curry.' He was originally condemned to death, for the *second time*, having already been convicted of sheep-stealing seven years before. Consequently, he became known as 'Mutton Curry'. He fortified himself with gin for his grim task, and was frequently jeered by the crowds at executions.

In January 1813, Curry hanged fourteen Luddite rioters for their part in the famous raid on Cartwright's mill at Rawfolds – the incident described in Charlotte Brontë's novel, *Shirley*. The trial judge remarked that because of their number, they 'might hang more comfortably on two beams.' Curry hanged seven of them at eleven in the morning, and the other seven at half-past one.

On one notorious occasion, in 1821, when he was required to hang one man at the castle and another at the city gaol, Curry was roughly handled by the mob whilst he was walking from one venue to the other, and drank so much to calm his nerves that he was scarcely able to climb on to the scaffold. When the assembled spectators jeered he shook the rope at them and shouted, 'Some of you come up and I'll try it!' But he was hardly able to get the noose over the proper victim's head without assistance, and the crowd began to shout 'Hang him – hang Jack Ketch – he's drunk!'

Once at a multiple execution he fell through the trap himself, along with his victims, and was badly bruised when he emerged to roars of laughter from the spectators. Curry retired in 1835 after more than thirty years service in his native county, and died in the parish poor-house at Thirsk six years later, no doubt finding a pauper's grave in the churchyard and coming in the end to unmarked dust like his victims. At his retirement, the *Yorkshire Gazette* took it upon itself to recommend a successor, proposing a petition to His Majesty craving the use of Jonathan Martin in this service, 'so that that notorious individual, already execrated by all honest and good men, may become the abhorrence also of all malefactors and dishonest persons, and thus be held in universal detestation and loathing.' Jonathan Martin was the man who had set fire to York Minster in 1828, and the brother of John Martin the painter of apocalyptic landscapes. The authorities did not act on this suggestion.

After Barlow, Lancashire's sheriffs sometimes called on the London executioners to do their dirty work, and one tale concerning Calcraft is related about a double execution he carried out at Lancaster. On the morning afterwards, before leaving for London, he was breakfasting with some men who had got into conversation with him, and asked how the two men had died the day before.

'How did they conduct themselves before appearing on the drop?' said one.

'Oh, very well indeed,' Calcraft replied, 'especially the soldier. By-the-bye, he wore a medal; but it seems he willed it to the priest – that priest was a very nice sort of man – who visited him; and as I like to act fairly – though you know it was my property – why, I took it off, gave it to the governor, who in turn gave it to the priest. I wouldn't do anything wrong on any account, and as it was his last wish – why, there, poor fellow!'

The northern skill and experience in putting their own criminals to death was to stand Yorkshire and Lancashire in good stead in the future, but for the time being the drop in the number of executions made it more expedient to hire the London man when needed rather than go to the expense of training and maintaining local experts, although Yorkshire held out against this move for some time yet.

Scotland came to this conclusion before the stubborn Yorkshiremen. A man named Thomas Young was evidently in practice for twenty-six years in Glasgow, up to 1840, on a wage of a pound a week with free lodgings and fuel, and his term of office was almost matched by Donald Ross of Inverness, who had finally been dismissed in 1834 when the town council worked out that it had cost them £400 for every man hanged in the last twenty years – much more expensive than importing an English executioner when required, which was not often, Scotland having shown England the way in abandoning its devotion to the death penalty for every conceivable misdeed. In 1837, for instance, only one execution took place in Scotland, and in due course, even murderers there were rarely executed. The death penalty fell into disuse in Scotland long before it was officially abolished throughout Britain. (In Ireland, incidentally, a woman commonly referred to as 'Lady Betty' was apparently carrying out executions around the time of Calcraft's appointment in London. A stout, middle-aged woman of swarthy complexion, she seems to have operated chiefly in Roscommon, and to have undertaken public floggings as well as hanging. Her name was used as a threat to naughty children.)

It is recorded that on some occasions Scottish hangmen were employed in the north of England, one John Murdoch in particular being mentioned in this respect. He followed Young, being paid a retainer by the authorities of Glasgow, and continued to work until he was in his eighties.

Crimes against the person were slowly and properly assuming a greater degree of offence to society than crimes against property, and murder was by this time the only crime that, in practice, at any rate, was normally punished by death, although the last execution for *attempted* murder was not to take place until 1861, at Chester. The death penalty for rape was abolished in 1841.

'Justice' could still be savage when it chose. On one occasion Calcraft was engaged to carry out an execution at Bristol. The condemned was a maidservant, Sarah Thomas, who had been provoked into killing her mistress by the cruel treatment she had received. Half-starved and unable to stand the customary beatings any longer, Sarah had gone into her mistress's bedroom one night with a large stone, and hit her on the head with it. Sarah was seventeen. She screamed and struggled when they came to take her to the gallows, crying 'I won't be hanged; take me home!' Calcraft pulled the bolt rapidly as soon as the warders had got her into position. 'I never felt so much compunction,' he was reported to have said afterwards, '. . . in having to bring that young girl to the scaffold. . . . She was, in my opinion, one of the prettiest and most intellectual girls I have met with. . . .'

His mind was taken off this distressing episode next day, however, when he arrived at Norwich Castle, after a long and tiring journey, to hang James Rush there. This man had murdered the Recorder of Norwich, Mr Isaac Jermy, and his son, in a frenzied attack on the family home, in which he also wounded Mr Jermy's daughter-in-law and a maidservant.

It was as well for Calcraft's income that the sheriffs of other counties engaged him during 1849, for there was a curious lull in the London hangings. There were none at all at Newgate in that year. But what London lacked in public entertainment, the provinces made up for. When John Gleeson was hanged at Liverpool in September, the crowd was estimated to number a hundred thousand. 'All the vacant ground in front of the prison, and spreading down to the canal,' it was reported, 'presented much the same appearance with respect to numbers as Aintree or Epsom on the Cup or Derby Day.'

Later that same year, 1849, Calcraft was called upon to execute Frederick George Manning and his wife Marie on the roof of Horsemonger Lane Gaol. They had murdered Patrick O'Connor, Marie's former lover, for financial gain, and buried his body under the kitchen floor of their home at Bermondsey. They tried to blame each other at their trial. The usual enormous crowd gathered outside the prison on the morning of the execution, although it was very cold – the hanging of a husband and wife was a novelty not to be missed. Mrs Manning wore a black satin dress, and the material went out of fashion for decades as a result.

Charles Dickens was again present at this execution, having hired the roof and kitchen of a house for the occasion 'for the extremely moderate sum of Ten Guineas. . . .' He wrote to *The Times* the same day: 'I have seen, habitually, some of the worst sources of general contamination and corruption in this country, and I think there are not many phases of London life that could surprise me. I am solemnly convinced that nothing that ingenuity could devise to be done in this city, in the same compass of time, could work such ruin as one public execution, and I stand astounded and appalled by the wickedness it exhibits. I do not believe that any community can prosper where such a scene of horror and demoralisation as was enacted this morning outside Horsemonger Lane Gaol is presented at the very doors of good citizens, and is passed by unknown or forgotten.'

A lengthy debate in the newspaper's pages followed the execution and Dickens's first letter; much of it concerned with the rights and wrongs of abolishing executions in public, which Dickens was by no means the first to think necessary. Henry Fielding, the author of *Tom Jones* and a London magistrate, had argued for executions to be carried out in some privacy a century before.

Dickens returned to the desirability of executions being conducted in the privacy of the prison in another letter, in which he proposed that a murderer's execution 'should be conducted with every terrible solemnity that careful consideration could devise. Mr Calcraft, the hangman (of whom I have some information in reference to this last occasion), should be restrained in his unseemly briskness, in his jokes, his oaths, and his brandy.'

This suggests that Calcraft, at nearly fifty years old, was no longer the quiet and respectable man he had been at first, but was being coarsened and brutalised by his profession. When Lord Macaulay had suggested in Parliament that abolitionists were victims of 'a kind of effeminate feeling', Dickens had wondered 'what there may be that is specially manly and heroic in the advocacy of the gallows', and sarcastically declined to 'express my admiration of Mr Calcraft, the hangman, as doubtless one of the most manly specimens now in existence. . . .'

Calcraft had, in fact, been summoned around this time for refusing to come to the assistance of his mother, Sarah, who was a pauper incarcerated in the workhouse at Hatfield Peveril, near Chelmsford. She was about seventy-four years old, and had another son and a daughter, but William was judged best qualified to support her – an opinion he vigorously disputed. Asked by the magistrate if he had any children to support, Calcraft said, 'Yes, I have got three of them', and denied that he was still making money from his old trade of cobbler. When an order was made for three shillings a week against him for his mother's support, he said, 'Ah, but you'll never get it from me! I can't pay it, and, if you do, I must run in debt, I suppose.' Calcraft himself lived in Devizes Street, and was shunned by his neighbours now, leaving home for his appointments by darkness, to avoid attracting attention, with the canvas bag in which he carried his 'tackle'.

Since the demise of Tom Cheshire, Calcraft had occasionally used as his assistant, when he required one, a fellow named Smith, formerly a Black Country nail-maker and latterly a farm labourer, described as a tall, wiry man, who sometimes wore a brown velveteen jacket and a bowler hat, although one report describes him as wearing a 'long white smockfrock.' One source says that Smith had been in trouble for failing to maintain his wife.

In June 1856, in order to save the expense of bringing Calcraft all the way from London, the Sheriff of Staffordshire commissioned George Smith to take charge of an execution himself at Stafford. The condemned man was the notorious Dr William Palmer of Rugeley, convicted of poisoning John Parsons Cook and suspected of poisoning his wife and a number of other people as well, for financial gain.

A large crowd gathered to witness the execution outside Stafford Gaol, some people paying a guinea for one of the front seats on the raised platforms which had been erected all round the front of the prison; others paying local householders for a position in one of their windows or even for being allowed to stand in their gardens. It was estimated that there were twenty thousand visitors to Stafford that day, in addition to the natives, and three hundred police were stationed round the gaol. A huge roar broke out when Dr Palmer mounted the scaffold, asking, according to one report, 'Are you sure it's safe?' He said 'God bless you' as he shook hands with Smith, and his death came quickly, much to the disappointment of the mob, who never felt they had had their money's worth unless there was a convulsion or two, and they shouted 'Cheat!' and 'Twister!' before they began to disperse.

Mr Hangman Smith, who came from Dudley, sold the rope to souvenir hunters at a shilling an inch. It was not the only execution he carried out himself, but it was certainly the most famous, and even upstaged Calcraft – not that the latter was bothered about such things: it seems he could scarcely remember *whom* he had executed.

Smith, the Midlander, may well have been the one who hanged a murderer in front of the new County Gaol in Welford Road, Leicester, in 1847, before a crowd of twenty thousand, who included

[68]

patients of the nearby Infirmary. (No records survive to tell us what effect this shock therapy had on their recovery rate.) Smith seems to have been employed whenever executions were to be carried out in Cheshire and Staffordshire, and sometimes in other Midland counties, as, for instance, in 1860, when he was engaged to execute one Francis Price at Warwick, and was roughed up by a gang afterwards whilst he was waiting for his train. Their anger was motivated by Smith's alleged action in dropping Price before the victim had finished saying his prayers. One man jumped on Smith and the two fell on to the line, where twenty or thirty other men joined the fight, some threatening to push him under the engine when the train came in. Smith was rescued by the station master and locked in a waiting-room for his own safety until his train arrived.

Neither Smith nor Calcraft got any jobs in Yorkshire, for the authorities there persisted in employing their own hangmen to succeed Curry. Nathaniel Howard, a coal-porter, hanged sixteen condemned at York between 1840 and 1853, and some time after him came Thomas Askern of Maltby, who carried on in Yorkshire until after Calcraft's retirement, though there is good reason to believe that he was not more skilful than the London hangman, for his rope broke when he attempted to hang one Johnson at Leeds, and this was not the first bungled execution attributed to him. Askern died a year before Calcraft.

1854 was a quiet year for the hangmen of England – there were only five executions in the whole country in that year. But Calcraft was kept busy enough in the early 1860s. There was a wave of what we now call 'mugging' in the streets of towns, especially in the impoverished north of England, and the reaction against it resulted in more executions during 1863 than in any year since the 1830s, when the Bloody Code had more or less disappeared. By 1861, the number of capital offences, well over two hundred half a century before, had been reduced to four.

Calcraft executed James Mullins in 1860, a former policeman who murdered his employer, Mrs Emsley; and Franz Müller, a German tailor, who murdered Thomas Briggs in a railway carriage in London and threw the body out on to the line. Müller is said to have confessed his guilt only seconds before Calcraft hanged him, in 1864. It was one of the eight executions at Newgate in that year, in a total of only nineteen in the whole country. The vast and disgraceful crowd present at Müller's execution did much to convert responsible opinion to the idea of abolishing public hangings. *The Times* reported the scene as follows:

> Before the slight slow vibrations of the body had ended, robbery and violence, loud laughing, oaths, fighting, obscene conduct and still more filthy language reigned round the gallows far and near. Such too the scene remained with little change or respite till the old hangman (Calcraft) slunk again along the drop amid hisses and sneering inquiries of what he had had to drink that morning. After failing once to cut the rope he made a second attempt more success-fully, and the body of Mueller disappeared from view.

Calcraft entertained an even larger audience when he travelled to Scotland in the following year to hang Dr Edward Pritchard for the murder of his wife Mary and his mother-in-law. It is said that a hundred thousand people had gathered in and around Glasgow's Jail Square on the morning of the execution, 28 July.

The Scots were customarily hostile to the criminal; the Irish to the executioner. When Calcraft was asked to execute three Fenians at Manchester for the murder of a policeman, he received threatening letters and became extremely nervous. He was far from being alone in this respect. There was widespread agitation over Fenian activity at this time, and the Queen herself was thought to be in danger. She said in one of her letters that 'We shall have to hang some of them,' but found it in her to pray for O'Brien, Allen and Larkin on the night before their fatal drop.

Calcraft did the job, hanging the three outside Salford Gaol in November 1867. After all, when he was working away from London and Middlesex, where he was employed on a salary basis, he charged county sheriffs £10 for each execution, so there was £30 for him in this job. The three men became known as the 'Manchester Martyrs'.

But Calcraft was not finished with the Irish yet. Hostility towards him continued when another young Fenian, Michael Barrett, was condemned to death in London in the following year for his part in an explosion at Clerkenwell, when part of a wall of the local House of Detention had been blown up in an attempt to free Irish prisoners, and several innocent people, including children, had been killed. Calcraft hanged Barrett at Newgate in 1868. Barrett had claimed that he had been in Glasgow at the time of the explosion, and there were many who believed him. He mounted the scaffold calmly, ignoring the noisy crowd and paying attention only to the priest pronouncing the litany for the dying. Unusually for one of Calcraft's victims, he died without a struggle, and when Calcraft returned to cut the body down after an hour, the hangman was bombarded with verbal abuse, one person in the crowd shouting out, 'Come on, body-snatcher!'

The authorities, meanwhile, had finally been persuaded, slowly and painfully, that the death penalty carried out in public was a demoralising spectacle which did much more harm than good. So far from acting as a deterrent, it probably had exactly the opposite effect to that intended, reinforcing the common conception of life as a cheap and worthless thing. It was in the year of Dr Palmer's execution that a Select Committee had been set up to enquire into the matter, and had recommended the abolition of public executions, notwithstanding the testimony of men such as the former Detective Inspector Haynes who, when asked if it was his opinion that capital punishment had very little effect in deterring, answered: 'Quite the reverse. I believe capital punishment deters very materially from the commission of crime; and I have not the slightest doubt that if capital punishment were done away with, scarcely any man's life would be safe in this country.'

The Committee saw that the evidence was against him, however. Its members knew of many cases such as that of Thomas Wicks, whom Calcraft had hanged for murder in 1846, and who had witnessed most of the hangings in London for some years. And they were familiar with the many eye-witness reports of earlier times which showed that no gathering provided a better opportunity for pickpockets to practice their skills than a public execution, even though the culprit being hanged might himself be a pickpocket.

Nevertheless, it was not for another twelve years after the Committee sat that executions in public finally vanished as an English tradition of more than a thousand years. They were abolished by the Capital Punishment Amendment Act. The execution of Michael Barrett, on 26 May 1868, was the last public execution in Britain, and no one can have been more relieved than Calcraft. Mrs Frances Kidder, whom Calcraft had hanged for murder at Maidstone on 2 April, turned out to be the last woman executed in public.

When Calcraft was called to Maidstone again, a few months later, to hang Thomas Wells, the deed was done inside the prison. There were plenty of witnesses, for justice had to be seen to be done. Newspaper reporters were now to be allowed in to prisons to see executions, and sheriffs continued to treat executions as 'occasions', and brought invited guests along to see the show. Thomas Wells was a railway porter, who had killed his boss Mr Walsh, the station master at Dover. The railways were providing a scene of crime new to the nineteenth century. Calcraft gave Wells the customary short drop, so that he lurched and struggled against strangulation, and took three or four minutes to die. Smith of Dudley was the executioner's assistant.

Smith was Calcraft's assistant again at Newgate when Alexander Mackay was hanged for murder, and one reporter wrote that 'signs of life were visible for a longer time after the bolt was drawn than we remember to have seen on a similar occasion.'

Calcraft was summoned for debt in 1869, having apparently owed thirteen shillings and nine pence for two years to the County Inn at Taunton, where he had stayed when called to the town for an execution. Calcraft had written to the landlord, Mr Sulley, complaining that the sum was exorbitant, and that he should not have sent a bill in an open envelope to expose him: 'i suppose you thought of fritening me but i was born too near a wood to be fritened by an Owl,' he wrote, and repeatedly accused Sulley of meanness. All the same, the magistrate ordered him to pay up within a month.

In August 1870 Calcraft hanged Walter Millar at Newgate for the murder of Elias Huelin, a vicar, and Anne Boss, and seven days later he was at Aylesbury to dispose of John Owen, who had killed a family of seven at Denham. The family was that of Owen's employer, Emmanuel Marshall, the village blacksmith. Owen had an insane grudge against him and, breaking into his house one night armed with a sledgehammer, he killed Marshall, his wife, his sister, his mother-in-law and three children. He told journalists at his execution that he was innocent.

Calcraft was by now an old man. At seventy, he was surly and sinister-looking, with his long hair and beard and his scruffy black attire and fob-chain. He wore a tall hat and had a slouching gait, but this forbidding appearance was sometimes relieved by a rose in his button-hole – he was fond of flowers. His wife had died and he had become even more of an outcast than before, moving house, no longer going to his 'local' or meeting his rabbit-fancier friends, and conducting his 'business' with a glassy-eyed indifference to everyone around him. At Sheffield once, a reporter at the prison said to one of his colleagues, 'I wonder if that bloodthirsty scoundrel Calcraft has arrived.' An old man in black shambled out from the shadows and said, in a low voice that chilled the marrow, 'The bloodthirsty scoundrel is here.'

I think it was Askern, rather than Calcraft, who was engaged to execute Mary Cotton at Durham in March 1873. She was a forty-year-old mass-murderer whose victims, all poisoned, numbered possibly as many as twenty.

By this time, it was a Welshman who most often assisted Calcraft. Robert Evans of Carmarthen was a dilettante of the scaffold, though he claimed to be moved by 'humane motives'. He was a lawyer's son and was trained as a doctor, but never practised. He occasionally acted as chief executioner himself when required, and was wont to urge the Home Secretary to have executions carried out by prison officers rather than by the 'ignorant, brutish persons' who were too often employed as hangmen.

At length, the authorities of London and Middlesex decided to pension off Calcraft as he was clearly getting past it. He protested that he was still able to do the job as well as any man, but he had to accept their decision. He carried out his last execution in Newgate Prison on 25 May 1874. The victim was James Godwin, who had killed his wife. George Smith of Dudley had died early the previous month, and despite the presence of the 'Medical Executioner' (Evans the Rope? Evans the Drop?) as Calcraft's assistant, Godwin 'died hard' as the pressmen reported, struggling helplessly against strangulation, and taking a few minutes to lose all sensation. No wonder it was known to many as 'dancing at Bailey's ballroom'.

Calcraft had been a bungling and incompetent executioner for forty-five years. It was a record of service to the public that was not to be broken by any other hangman. He had made a modest living for nearly half a century by putting his fellow men and women to death and administering the occasional whipping and flogging (for which he was paid an allowance for supplying his own birches and cat-o-nine-tails); adding a bit on the side by selling his ropes to souvenir hunters, making what he could out of the hangman's perquisites, the clothes and personal effects of the victims, and so on. And, as far as we

[73]

can tell, he managed somehow to take his mind off his job as soon as he went home, keeping off the subject in conversation and behaving as if he were a man who had just come home after a day's work in a factory. Calcraft seems to have been unique; as indifferent to the cumulative effects of his trade as to the repetitive strangling of his victims.

He was awarded a pension of a guinea a week, equal to his former salary, and he lived on for another five-and-a-half years before dying on 13 December 1879, at his home in Poole Street, Hoxton. He was seventy-nine years old.

V

The Long Drop

Now he's only twelve stone so he should have eight foot eight,
but he's got a thick neck on him so I'd better give him another
couple of inches. Yes, eight foot ten.

Brendan Behan
The Quare Fellow, 1956

AT THE TIME William Calcraft was superannuated by the shrievalty of
London and Middlesex, there was a certain man living at Horncastle
in Lincolnshire, a cobbler by trade, who had shown such a serious
and responsible interest in the method of hanging criminals that he
had been employed on one or two occasions by the High Sheriff of
Lincolnshire to carry out executions at the county gaol, and reports of
his proficiency were such that the authorities in London chose him to
succeed Calcraft as their executioner. They had clearly known of this
man by reputation when they had made the decision that Calcraft's
time had come. The new man's name was William Marwood. He was
fifty-four years old.

Marwood was born at Horncastle in 1820, and he and his wife lived
in one of the tiniest houses in the town, a little two-storey cottage in
Church Lane, close to Holy Trinity church. He was poor, but worked
hard at his last. As he was not a very literate fellow, and never
committed his thoughts and experiences to paper, we do not know
what first led him to take such a keen interest in the matter of capital
punishment, but he was a man with a scientific turn of mind, who
evidently came to the conclusion that he could do the job more
efficiently than Calcraft, with whose reputation he was obviously
familiar though he had never, it seems, seen a public execution.

Marwood realised that what was needed to produce 'instant' death
instead of slow strangulation at the end of a rope was a longer drop,

[75]

which would result in dislocation of the cervical vertebrae. He began to explain his theories to the authorities until, at length, he was asked to put them into practice at Lincoln. It soon became clear that this man was no fool, and the Sheriffs of London and Middlesex appointed him on a retainer of twenty pounds a year, with a fee of £10 for each execution.

Marwood was a meek sort of fellow, or he might have pressed for a better deal than this. Calcraft was the last hangman of England to receive a salary, and no hangman after him was able to earn his living as an executioner. But no doubt Marwood saw the possibility of a substantial increase in his income from this appointment, and was quite content to continue working as a cobbler in between jobs. Marwood got £10 plus his expenses for every execution he carried out, and in his time the clothing and personal effects of the condemned were still regarded as the property of the executioner, so that the sale of these sensational souvenirs, as well as the ropes he used, could bring him in a tidy sum.

Nor was he in any way ashamed of his alternative employment. He soon put a sign by his front door reading 'Crown Office', and he told Major Arthur Griffiths, a former army officer and prison governor who became an Inspector of Prisons, that he had taken up the appointment in the belief that he could be useful to his generation. His advertisement and new-found local fame proved useful to himself. People living in and around Hornchurch who had never been near his little workshop before now brought him their shoes for mending, especially after he had hanged Henry Wainwright in 1875.

Wainwright was a popular and respected man in the East End of London when he was suddenly arrested for murder in September of that year. He had been married for thirteen years, and carried on his father's trade as a brushmaker in Whitechapel Road. He was a keen churchgoer, and gave lectures and readings from popular authors and poets. But unknown to his admirers, Wainwright was leading a double life. He had fallen in love with a twenty-year-old milliner's apprentice, Harriet Lane, whom he had set up in a house where she eventually bore him two daughters. He paid her £5 a week and bought her nice clothes, until he ran into debt and was forced to cut her allowance.

Harriet gradually took to drink and became difficult, and Wainwright decided she must be disposed of. He shot her twice in the head and cut her throat, and dismembered the body, burying the parts in a

[76]

workshop adjoining his premises. Above this room Wainwright's assistant and his wife lived as tenants, and they soon started to complain about an unpleasant smell, whilst Harriet's father and a friend pestered Wainwright as to her whereabouts. He, meanwhile, was declared a bankrupt, and thought it prudent to remove the remains of Harriet Lane from premises which would shortly belong to someone else. So he parcelled them up and asked an unsuspecting youth named Stokes to keep an eye on the parcels while he fetched a cab. In his absence, Stokes took a look at the parcels and found a severed hand. In due course, two policemen acquainted with this fact accosted Wainwright during his cab journey and found all the remains of Miss Lane.

Marwood executed Wainwright four days before Christmas, 1875, at Newgate. Nearly a hundred people had gathered to witness the hanging, and when Wainwright saw them he shouted: 'You curs! So you have come to see a man die!' They had, and they were not disappointed.

Wainwright was the first of several of the most notorious Victorian murderers to come to Marwood's fatal threshold within less than a decade, so the hangman came to be famous in spite of the fact that all executions now took place behind closed doors, and it was not long before he was such a household name that children in the streets made a riddle of it: 'If Pa killed Ma, who'd kill Pa?' Answer: 'Marwood'. His name cropped up in musical hall songs, too:

> I'd sooner be by a Serpent stung,
> Or hugg'd by a grizzly Bear,
> Or crush'd by one of Pickford's Vans,
> Or blown into the Air;
> I'd sooner be by Marwood hung –
> Or slowly fade away,
> Than have the least connection
> With deceitful Emma Hay.

Marwood later described the method he had almost perfected in a letter dated 7 June 1879, reproduced in facsimile in *St Stephen's Review* in 1883. It was written in an unpractised hand beneath an oval cartouche bearing the words 'Wm. Marwood, Executioner, Church Lane, Horncastle, Lincolnshire, England', and read:

Sir,

in Replie to your Letter of this Day i will give you a Compleat Stait-
ment for <u>Executing</u> a Prisoner – 1-Place Pinnion the Prisoner Round the
Boady and Arms tight – 2 Place Bair the Neck – 3 Place Take the Pris-
oner to the Drop 4-Place – Place the Prisoner Beneath the Beam to stand
Direct under the Rope from the Top of the Beam 5-Place strap the
Prisoners Leggs Tight 6 Place Putt on the Cap 7-Place Putt on the Rope
Round the <u>Neck thite.</u> Set the Cap be Free from the Rope to hide the
Face angine Dow in Frunt 8-Place Executioner to go Direct Quick to the
<u>Leaver</u> Let Down the Trap <u>Doors Quick</u>
No – greas to be Putt on the Rope all Rops to be Well <u>Tested</u> before
Execution and all Rops to be kept Dry in good <u>Auder</u>
<u>Sir</u> the arraingements of the Place of Execution you Can git at H.M
Prison Newgate London it wanting 2 Feet Deeper in the Pitt beneath
then it is <u>Perfect</u> say 10 <u>Feet beneath</u>
<u>Sir</u> Pleas i thought it would be the Best Way to give you a Clear
understanding in the araingements of a <u>Execution</u> of a <u>Prisoner</u>
to Prevent aney Mistake in the Araingement in the Matter
in Question
<u>Sir</u> i shall be glad to asist you in all improvements
Sir i Remain your Humble Servant
Wm Marwood
Church: Lane – Horncastle Lincolnshire

This brief outline of his procedure modestly omits some of the
important innovations Marwood had made in the method of execution, which led him to take a pride in his craft to the extent that he
would speak derisively of his predecessor Calcraft, saying 'He *hanged*
them. I *execute* them.' Marwood never referred to himself as a hangman; always as an executioner.

His first major contribution to the science of execution was the
'long drop'. As we have seen, it had been realised for a long time
that a drop as opposed to the simple removal of the support for the
victim's feet would lessen his agony by exerting pressure on the neck
resulting in strangulation within two or three minutes. But the drop
given, Marwood realised, was always too short to achieve the
optimum result – 'instantaneous' death from cervical dislocation –
and the time it took for the condemned to die depended on his or her
weight and other factors, such as the quality of the rope. Marwood,
by dint of experiment and practical experience, developed the technique of hanging which, with some refinements, remained in force

for the next ninety years or so; that is, until abolition of the death penalty.

Marwood is usually given exclusive credit for the invention of the 'long drop', but of course medical men were well aware of the theory behind it, and Marwood was merely the first executioner to put the idea into practice. The aim was to produce fracture of the cervical vertebrae, and in time executioners came to have almost a scientific knowledge of how to produce this effect by the length of drop given, and were latterly able to achieve fairly consistent fracture between the second and third vertebrae, although it could happen in other positions, for instance between the first vertebra and the skull. The fracture might be accompanied by severance of the spinal cord.

Marwood devised the deep pit beneath the scaffold which would allow a condemned man to be given a drop of anything between seven and ten feet, according to the victim's weight and build, and if the job was done properly, the drop would result in 'instantaneous' death, the head being jerked suddenly backwards when the rope reached its full extent. To ensure that this happened, Marwood paid much more attention to the ropes he used than previous executioners had done. Instead of the coarse rope always used before, he ordered Italian silk hemp ropes, three quarters of an inch thick, and stretched them before use by hanging bags of sand on them. This prevented the ropes from stretching when victims were dropped through the traps, which would result in longer drops than had been intended and could have disastrous results.

Instead of the clumsy slip-knot with which all previous hangmen had fixed the rope round the victim's neck, Marwood devised a metal ring, which was prevented from moving, once in place, by a leather washer. This resulted in a tightening of the rope as it jerked, again speeding the process of killing by exerting such pressure as to produce immediate unconsciousness if it did not break the neck as intended. Because of the way ropes are made, it was found by experience that the 'knot' must be placed under the victim's left ear, or under the angle of the left jaw, to jerk the head backwards. Placed on the right side, the rope would jerk the head forward and result in strangulation.

Marwood also devised a simple pinioning arrangement which fastened the victim's arms to a leather belt round his waist. This prevented the victim from raising his pinioned hands to his throat in an attempt to relieve his agony, as often happened when a man was being slowly strangled to death.

Marwood gave such satisfaction to all the authorities who employed him that they soon included those in Yorkshire, who now abandoned their practice of appointing their own executioners, perhaps because a man of such proven competence was living not far away in Lincolnshire. Besides which, the railways were now making travel from outside the county much speedier than the old slow coach journeys by road.

In May 1878, Marwood executed Vincent Knowles Walker, at York Castle, for a murder at Hull. But unfortunately for the hangman's local reputation, this job did not go as well as he hoped. The drop he gave was insufficient, and the man 'died very hard', reports said, 'so much as seven minutes elapsing before life was fully extinct'. Clearly there was still a lot to be learned. The Yorkshire authorities must have thought this man was no better than Calcraft, or their own bungler, Askern.

It was a very different matter when Marwood hanged Joseph Garcia in Wales later that year. Garcia was a Spanish sailor, and he killed a whole family named Watkins – husband, wife and three children – at their home at Llangybi near Usk. Such was the local outrage and strength of feeling against the murderer that Marwood, like Calcraft on a similar occasion, was cheered and clapped as he left the prison at Usk after the execution. A crowd of people escorted him to the railway station, where he was compelled to speak to them, and thanking them for their applause, said he hoped he would have occasion to come that way again soon!

Three months afterward, Marwood was again invited to Yorkshire, where a man was awaiting execution at Armley Gaol, Leeds. He was to be one of Marwood's most infamous clients. His name was Charles Peace.

Born in Sheffield, Peace had become a talented and incorrigible tearaway, living by theft and spending several periods in prison. He was a small, agile man, who had lost at least one of the fingers on his left hand, and he was very ugly. He married a widow named Hannah Ward and in due course set up shop as a picture-framer and retailer of musical instruments and bric-a-brac. But then he took a fancy to a neighbour, Katherine Dyson, whose husband Arthur was a railway engineer. At first she encouraged him, sending him notes when her husband was out, but later, when Dyson started to warn Peace to stay away from his wife, Katherine realised the error of her ways and discouraged her amorous neighbour. Peace began to make such a thorough nuisance of himself – peering through their windows; accosting Mrs Dyson in the street and threatening her and her husband – that a warrant was put out for his arrest, and he fled to Hull with his wife and step-son.

The Dysons decided to move house, but Peace turned up at their new home in due course, trying to get Mrs Dyson to come out to him. One night, she went to the outside lavatory, and when she opened the door to leave, Peace was standing there with a revolver. She screamed and locked herself in the lavatory. Dyson heard her and rushed out of the house to investigate, and chased Peace to the street where Peace fired two shots, one of the bullets entering Dyson's brain. Peace fled, and then went on the run, travelling as far as Oxford and Bristol, committing burglaries and eventually settling briefly in Nottingham with another woman, Susan Thompson.

Peace and Susan then went to London, where his wife and step-son joined them, and they all lived together – along with an assortment of pets – in the same house, where Susan, 'a dreadful woman for the drink and snuff', so Peace said, gave birth to a son. Friends who were invited to the house were treated to recitations by the man they knew as John Ward, and he also played a fiddle which, however, he did not keep in his violin case – that being reserved for the burglar's tools he took out with him at night.

But someone had tipped off the police about the activities of this new resident, and early one morning several constables turned up at the house. Peace made his exit through a window and tried to run away, but was chased by a policeman whom he shot in the arm before being overpowered. He was charged, under the name John Ward, with burglary and wounding with intent to murder the police constable, and sentenced to penal servitude for life.

Meanwhile, police had discovered the true identity of this man 'Ward', and it was arranged to take him by train to Yorkshire to stand trial for the murder of Arthur Dyson. As the train was nearing Sheffield, Peace escaped through the window of the carriage, which had been opened by his guards so that he could urinate out of it, but he injured himself as he fell and was soon recaptured. He was tried for murder at Leeds Assizes, found guilty and sentenced to death. In the condemned cell at Armley Gaol, he confessed that he had also killed a policeman in Manchester, a crime for which a young man named William Habron had been sentenced to death two years before. Peace had been at his trial and kept quiet until now. Fortunately for Habron, the sentence had been commuted to life imprisonment, and he was now in Portland prison. He was released with a full pardon and awarded £1,000 compensation.

On the morning of his execution, Peace complained of his breakfast that 'This is bloody rotten bacon'. When Marwood had him on the scaffold and was putting the white hood on his head, Peace said, 'Stop a minute – I must hear this', and listened to the chaplain reading the service. Then the old reprobate insisted on addressing those present, who included some newspaper reporters, on his religious feelings as he met his death. Marwood obligingly let him finish, then put the rope round his neck.

'Can't I have a drink?' Peace said. 'Oh, it's too tight, it's too tight.' Marwood spoke to him quietly, saying it wouldn't hurt, and pulled the lever. Charlie Peace died without a struggle. The Yorkshiremen could have no doubts about Marwood's efficiency this time. 'I expected difficulties', Marwood said afterwards, 'because he was such a desperate man, but bless you, my dear sir, he passed away like a summer's eve.'

Five months later, Marwood hanged Kate Webster at Wandsworth prison. She was an Irish woman who had killed an elderly widow, Julia Thomas, who employed her as her housekeeper at Richmond. Webster hacked her to death with an axe after a quarrel, then dismembered her on the scullery floor (taking a break for a drink at the 'local'). She disposed of the remains, some of which she boiled in the kitchen copper, by parcelling them up and throwing them into the Thames at various points, the head going in at Hammersmith Bridge. She was caught by being too eager to dispose of her mistress's property, but had to be traced to Ireland and brought back for trial.

Soon after this Marwood was invited to give a lecture at Sheffield. Never one to hide his light under a bushel, the hangman stood before an eager audience of 600 and began to give them commentaries on the Bible, interspersed with reflections on the Irish question and the forthcoming election (in which Disraeli was about to be defeated by Gladstone). This was not what the Sheffield folk had come for, and they began to get restive. When Marwood observed that 'the wheel of Time is constantly casting people into Eternity', someone in the audience shouted 'So's the rope!' Further interruptions followed, and when the chairman tried to restore order, some of the crowd demanded their money back. So this experience was not a success, but visitors to his cottage in Horncastle found Marwood entertaining enough. Often on the pretext of wanting shoes mended, they would call hoping to see his relics, and he would show them the rope he had used to hang Charlie Peace, and explain why he considered himself the most humane of executioners.

He had an uncommon experience at Newgate in 1880 when he was about to execute Charles Shurety for murder. The prison governor received a letter in an OHMS envelope, marked 'Immediate', just as Marwood was about to make his final preparations to hang the condemned man. The letter purported to be from the Home Office, countermanding the order for Shurety's execution. The governor and the sheriff decided, however, that the letter was a forgery, and instructed Marwood to proceed, which he did. Later, it was proved that the letter had been written, for no obvious reason, by a Dr Whitefoord, who was given two months in prison and a fine of £50 for attempting to obstruct the course of justice.

In the following year, the most famous of Marwood's victims was Percy Lefroy, a youth who had killed a man named Frederick Gold by pushing him out of a train when Gold had resisted Lefroy's attempt to rob him. Lefroy was said to be in a state of collapse when he was taken to the execution chamber at Lewes prison, though Marwood denied it. 'When I tap a prisoner on the shoulder,' he said, 'he nearly always comes to me.'

Dr George Lamson came to him five months later at Wandsworth, perhaps second only to Charlie Peace among Marwood's famed victims. He was a young and handsome GP who had become a morphine addict whilst serving as an army doctor in the Balkans. Unable to maintain a medical practice for long, he took to forgery and other crooked schemes for making money. In 1881 he poisoned his invalid brother-in-law for gain, and it was rumoured that he had similarly murdered another brother-in-law who had died a few years earlier, though Lamson vigorously denied this.

After he had been sentenced to death, there were several attempts to have him reprieved, and there were two stays of execution while the arguments were considered by the Home Secretary, but Lamson eventually walked calmly to the gallows with Marwood on 28 April, 1882, and earned the hangman's commendation, for what it was worth. 'The doctor died like a gentleman,' Marwood said afterwards.

Everything did not always go so smoothly, however, even for a conscientious hangman like Marwood. When he executed James Burton at Durham, the slack in the rope caught the condemned man's arm as he dropped, breaking the fall and leaving the man hanging in the opening. He had to be pulled up and prepared all over again, then pushed through the still-open trap. This incident led in due course to the slack in the rope being tied up with a thread, to keep it out of the way until the victim fell, when of course the thread broke and released the full length of the rope.

A month after Marwood had hanged Lamson, the so-called Phoenix Park Murders occurred in Dublin. The victims were Thomas Henry Burke, Permanent Under-Secretary for Ireland, and Lord Frederick Cavendish, Gladstone's newly appointed Chief Secretary of State for Ireland. The two men were ambushed by Irish nationalists, calling themselves Invincibles, as they walked through the park together to the Viceregal Lodge. The real target of the assassins was Mr Burke, an Irish Catholic loyal to the Crown's representative at Dublin Castle, and known to the republicans as a 'castle rat'.

A gang of Invincibles lay in wait for Burke, and as he approached with his companion, four men leapt out, one of them, named Brady, driving a long knife into Burke's back. Lord Cavendish tried to beat the man off with his umbrella, but Brady stabbed him repeatedly while one of his companions, Kelly, cut the fallen Burke's throat. Long and careful police work led in due course to the arrest of twenty-seven men, three of whom turned informers. At the subsequent trial Brady, Kelly and three others, named Curley, Fagan and Caffrey, were sentenced to death, all the others getting long terms of imprisonment. One of the informers, and the chief prosecution witness, was James Carey, who had been the leader of the gang, and after the trial he was shipped for his own safety to South Africa where, however, he was soon shot dead by an Irish nationalist named O'Donnell.

Marwood travelled to Ireland to execute the five condemned men on different dates during May and June 1883. He was accompanied by two detectives acting as bodyguards, for English hangmen were always, naturally enough, in some personal danger in Ireland. It may have been his experiences in Ireland rather than in England that led him to lament his unhappy lot in social terms. 'My position is not a happy one,' he told the man who was to succeed him. Once, when returning from Ireland, Marwood had become acquainted with an Irishman on board the ship and spent most of the night drinking with him. A steward who had served the two men that night recognised Marwood on a later trip and asked him what had happened to his friend. 'Oh,' Marwood said casually, 'I've just hanged him.'

When Marwood fell ill and died, in September 1883, three months after hanging the Phoenix Park murderers, rumour – ever seeking the sensational – had it that the Invincibles were responsible for his death. In fact, he died of pneumonia, at the age of sixty-three. They buried him in Holy Trinity churchyard, close to his lifelong home, and gave him a six-foot drop. In his twelve years as an executioner, he, more than anyone, transformed death by hanging from a brutal and ignorant hit-and-miss affair into a procedure which at least had some semblance of a humane technique about it.

Ever since Marwood's time, the word 'instantaneous' has been used freely of death brought about by efficient execution. But no one knows that such a death was ever literally instantaneous. The authorities liked the public to think so – it took away some of the discomfort that might have been felt by the sensitive when, reading the morning paper over their toast and marmalade, they were informed that a murderer had been executed and 'death was instantaneous'.

We need not take seriously Aubrey's tale about Sir Everard Digby, who – executed for his part in the Gunpowder Plot in 1606 – had his heart plucked out and, when the executioner cried 'Here is the heart of a traitor!' answered him, 'Thou liest'. But there is plenty of apparently impartial evidence that people whose heads were chopped off in France showed unmistakeable signs of awareness for a few seconds after their heads were severed from their bodies. And no less an authority than the pathologist Sir Sydney Smith, Professor of Forensic Medicine at Edinburgh University, went on record as doubting that death by hanging was really instantaneous, as far as the consciousness of the victim was concerned, since the heart would go on pumping blood and the pulse would continue to beat faintly.

It is certainly hypocrisy to pretend that the white hood put over the victim's face was a gesture of humanity towards the victim. It was no such thing. By the time this was done, the victim had walked to the execution shed or chamber, seen the hangman and the noose, and been placed carefully on the division between the trap doors and pinioned. All that remained to be done when the white hood was pulled over the head was adjusting the noose – a matter of a second or two. If we had been that sensitive about the feelings of the victim we would never have hanged him at all. The white bag was a gesture to the feelings of the necessary spectators. Sometimes with a short drop the head remained above the level of the floor or platform, visible to all, and even when it was not, those whose duty it was to look down into the pit – the prison governor, for instance – could be very upset if they saw the distorted features of a man they had come to know quite well.

All we can say with certainty is that, given the fact that men and women were executed, the long drop was an improvement on slow strangulation, and William Marwood's intentions seem to have been genuinely humanitarian, although there is a curious story about a visit he made once to Madame Tussaud's, where he had sat for his effigy to be modelled for the Chamber of Horrors. He was apt to call there when he was at a loose end (so to speak) in London, and wander round with his old terrier, 'that has caught rats in my business bags.' One day someone aware of Marwood's identity heard him remark that his dog was dying, and said, 'Why not hang him, then?' 'No, no,' Marwood retorted. 'Hang a man, but my dear old dog, never!'

Marwood's immediate successor was Bartholomew Binns, who had some experience of actual executions, having been an assistant on a number of occasions. Binns carried out his first execution at Wandsworth two months after Marwood's death, when his victim was one Henry Powell, who had murdered his employer's son. Binns also hanged Patrick O'Donnell, the Irish republican, for the murder of James Carey, the chief witness against the Phoenix Park murderers.

Binn's reign was short-lived, however. His character was hardly what was required of an executioner in these days when any grounds for censure were liable to lead to demands for the abolition of the death penalty. On one occasion Binns and an assistant, Alfred Archer, had been prosecuted and fined for travelling by rail without paying the fare, and in March 1884 Binns was criticised for an inefficient execution at Walton Gaol, Liverpool, when the victim's heart had continued to beat for a quarter of an hour after the drop. The prison governor reported that in his opinion Binns had no idea how to do his work properly. 'He put the rope round the culprit's neck and hanged him, but it was by accident whether the hanging was successful or not.' Clearly this man would not do, and another was soon appointed in his stead.

VI

It Won't Hurt a Bit

The Executioner: As a master in my profession, I have to consider its interests. And, after all, my first duty is to my wife and children.

Bernard Shaw
Saint Joan, 1924

JAMES BERRY, who applied for the job of executioner when William Marwood died, was a shoe salesman in Bradford. But he had been a police constable until 1882, and had known Marwood and discussed with him the business of hanging. Indeed, he was apt to claim that he had actually assisted Marwood in the execution of Charlie Peace at Leeds, but this cannot be so. He also claimed that he had watched Calcraft at work on one occasion in Manchester, and whilst this is possible, he was only a youth at the time, when thousands of other people had seen Calcraft on the job, too. Berry was thirty-one when he applied for the position, and said afterwards, somewhat equivocally, that he 'had a great distaste for the work', but looked upon the vacancy as his 'one chance in life'.

He was born in February 1852 at Heckmondwike, the son of a wool stapler and one of a large family. His most notable achievement at school seems to have been his ability to write fine copperplate script, but he worked as a mechanic and as a joiner for some years before joining the Bradford Borough Police Force when he was twenty-two. Not long afterwards he married Sarah Ann Ackroyd, who in due course gave birth to a son whom they named Luther, and the family settled at 1 Bilton Place, Bradford, a terraced Victorian brick house off City Road, north-west of the town centre. Berry was a thick-set figure of average height with a florid complexion and sandy hair. He had a scar on his right cheek caused by a horse's kick when he was ten, and another on his forehead caused by a criminal resisting violently when PC Berry arrested him.

Berry's application to the Sheriff of London to succeed Marwood was unsuccessful. Out of about 1,400 applicants, some of whom offered to do the job without payment, Berry's name was placed on a short-list of twenty, and he was invited to attend an interview at the Old Bailey at his own expense, which he did. But the job was given to Binns.

Berry soon took another route towards achieving his goal. Early in 1884 he applied to the magistrates at Edinburgh to be appointed executioner of two men awaiting death at Calton Gaol. He gave the names of the Chief Constable of the West Riding Police and the High Sheriff of London as referees. The two condemned were William Innes and Robert Vickers, both miners. They had killed two gamekeepers who had caught them poaching, and their execution was to be the first in Edinburgh for about five years.

Berry was called to Edinburgh three days before the execution was due to take place, the prison governor, Mr J. E. Christie, and the magistrates having decided that Berry was probably the best man available and awarded him the commission. He had to take with him an assistant, and the man he chose was one Richard Chester. That night in the room he had been given in the prison precincts, Berry knelt down and 'asked the Almighty to help me in my most painful task. . . .'

From then until the abolition of the death penalty, over eighty years later, the leading hangman of England was always from Yorkshire or Lancashire; the heir, so to speak, not of Ketch, Brunskill and Calcraft, but of Curry, Barlow and Askern.

Berry recorded in his memoirs that for the double execution at Edinburgh he used Italian hemp ropes, five-eighths of an inch thick after stretching, as Marwood had found best for the job. He tested the ropes, the lever and the trap-doors using bags of cement as substitutes for human beings, and worked out that the drop for Innes would be ten feet and for Vickers, the heavier of the two, eight feet. (There are many careless contradictions in Berry's memoirs. Only a few pages after stating that the drop for Vickers was eight feet, he says that it was eight feet six inches.) He was naturally very nervous at this, his first execution, and on the day before it, he could not eat his 'late dinner' at 4 p.m., though it consisted of rice pudding, blackcurrants, chicken, vegetables, potatoes and bread.

During that night Berry hardly slept, and imagined all sorts of disasters – the rope breaking; himself trembling too much to do the job, and so on. He was up at five o'clock. By seven, groups of people had begun to gather on Calton Hill. Berry went to the execution shed and prepared his equipment. Shortly after eight o'clock, he pinioned the two prisoners and the usual procession walked to the scaffold. Innes and Vickers were stood in their places and quickly prepared, but as the white cap was placed over the head of Vickers, he fainted. He had to be held up for the moment it took Berry to adjust the noose and pull the lever, and then in a flash the two dead men were dangling below. As he travelled home to Bradford, Berry had in his pocket not only his fee for the job, but also testimonials from the prison governor and surgeon to the effect that he had carried out his duties to their complete satisfaction and that the two condemned had died instantaneously. It was noted by witnesses, however, that Innes's head had blood on it, resulting from the trap-doors rebounding and hitting the body as it descended.

The services of Bartholomew Binns having now been dispensed with, especially after his conduct had led to questions in the House of Lords, Berry succeeded to the position of leading hangman and was soon travelling all over the country. A few months after his trip to Edinburgh, he hanged Mary Lefley at Lincoln. She had been condemned to death for the murder of her husband, who had died after eating a rice pudding laced with arsenic. She protested her innocence to the end and, hysterical with terror, went shrieking to the scaffold. Berry himself came to believe years afterwards that she was innocent of the murder, but in any case Berry's first experience of hanging a woman gave him a strong aversion to the task in the future, as it did other executioners. He told a reporter that he hoped he would never have to hang another woman. But it was not long before he had to repeat the experience. When he came to hang Mary Britland at Strangeways, for the murder of her landlady, the prisoner was a complete physical wreck, lying in her cell crying and moaning, and she had to be more or less carried to the gallows. As Berry put the white cap over her face, she uttered a cry which a reporter described as being 'such as one might expect at the actual separation of body and spirit through mortal terror'.

Berry's first full year as an executioner – 1885 – gave him some more experiences he would never forget. In February of that year he was called to Exeter to execute John Lee, convicted of murdering Emma Keyse, his employer, at Babbacombe. The wealthy Miss Keyse employed Lee as a footman, and he apparently killed her when she reduced his wages, battering her to death and then making a clumsy attempt to burn the body.

When Berry inspected the scaffold at Exeter Prison (it had been erected by prisoners in a coach house where the prison's transport was normally kept), he found it old-fashioned but satisfactory. An iron hook was suspended from the cross-beam, and the trap-doors were of thin wood and light in weight. There were no catches to grip the doors in a vertical position when they fell open. Berry pointed out these details to the governor, as faults that ought to be remedied for the future.

On the morning of the execution Berry pinioned Lee, who was very calm, and conducted him to the scaffold with the usual officials in attendance. He stood Lee in position, pinioned his legs, put on the white cap and adjusted the noose, then stepped back quickly and operated the lever. Nothing happened. Berry stamped on the doors with one foot, but they failed to open. Then the warders present joined him in trying to force the trap-doors open, whilst the chaplain continued to read from the Book of Common Prayer. After a minute of this noise and confusion it was clear that the trap-doors were not going to work, and Berry removed the noose, cap and leg-strap from Lee, and had him taken to a room nearby whilst he tested the scaffold again. It seemed all right. Lee was brought back and prepared again. This time Berry pulled the lever with such force that he bent it, but the trap-doors again remained closed, and despite further stamping, they could not be made to open. Lee was again removed, his face ashen, like those of all the officials present. The reporters witnessing these events through a window from outside soon let the crowd which had gathered outside the prison know why the black flag had not been hoisted at the expected time.

Two warders helped Berry in trying to put matters right. They made various adjustments to the edges of the doors, and Berry tested them all over again and was satisfied that nothing was wrong with them. For the third time the solemn procession made its way to the execution shed. Lee was again pinioned, hooded and noosed. Berry pulled the lever. Nothing moved. The chaplain swayed and almost fainted. The prison governor, in a state of extreme distress, agreed with the Under-Sheriff that no further attempt should be made to execute Lee, and he was led back to his cell and given the breakfast reserved for Berry, which the hangman could not face.

When the Home Secretary was informed of the facts, he ordered that Lee's sentence be commuted to one of penal servitude for life. Lee served twenty years, being released in 1905, and he then disappeared into obscurity. It is believed that he died in America in his late sixties. Berry was required to submit a report to the Under-Sheriff, and that official must have been satisfied that there was a technical fault in the construction of the scaffold, for the fiasco seems not to have reflected on Berry's growing reputation as a reliable operator.

Berry came to the conclusion that the fault with the Exeter scaffold was due to iron reinforcing bands on the under-side of the trap-doors, which were slightly bent, and were straightened by the weight of a man standing on them so that they projected past the opening and prevented the doors from falling open. Another theory was that a board in front of the trap-doors caught the edge of the doors when the chaplain was standing on it. Others seem to have thought that rain had warped the trap-doors themselves. At any rate, this unique incident not only led Berry to test scaffolds with a weight on them in future, but it also resulted in the Home Office issuing a design for a standard recommended scaffold. The experience upset Berry a great deal, but if he thought this was disturbing, he had seen nothing yet.

Three months later, he was at Worcester to hang a man named Moses Shrimpton, a hardened criminal who had spent more time in prison than out of it, and had committed a murder in the course of poaching. Berry gave the man a nine-foot drop, but when he looked at the body in the pit, he saw that Shrimpton's head had been pulled almost from his body by the force of the rope's jerk, and blood had splashed the walls of the pit and was running down the dead man's body. Berry attempted to explain away this ghastly miscalculation by blaming the weak tissues of the victim due to his advanced age, but he was soon to get another severe demonstration of the fact that, notwithstanding Marwood's careful calculations and the table of drops which Berry had inherited from him, there was no such thing as a foolproof method of execution by hanging.

In November of the same year, Berry travelled to Norwich to execute a farmer, Robert Goodale, for the murder of his wife Bathsheba. He had hit her with an iron bar and thrown her body down a well, forty feet deep. Weighing fifteen stone, Goodale was nevertheless in bad physical condition, and warders at the prison told Berry they did not think the execution could be carried out safely. But Berry had his duty to do (and his fee to collect). He reduced the drop by two feet as a precaution, to five feet nine inches, when he would normally have reckoned on seven feet eight.

When the appointed time came, Goodale struggled with Berry and the warders, and screamed for mercy. Warders had to drag him from the condemned cell to the scaffold, and he collapsed completely on sight of it, one of the warders also fainting from the ordeal. Other warders held Goodale up while Berry prepared him, and let go as the hangman pulled the lever. As soon as the rope reached its full stretch it rebounded through the opening, with nothing attached to it. The officials looked into the pit and saw the head in the bag, no longer white, lying on the ground near, but not attached to, the bloody trunk. This time Berry himself collapsed. He had to be revived with brandy, and still felt ill when he got back to Bradford.

These ghastly events made Berry resolve briefly to give up the job, but he reflected subsequently that he now had no future except as an executioner. He would be recognised as Berry the hangman wherever he tried to get another job. Besides, he was a Yorkshireman. He was not going to have it said that he was not equal to the task, and he was always capable of reassuring himself that, if anything did go wrong, it was not his fault.

Nevertheless, these incidents led to a committee of enquiry being set up, under the chairmanship of Lord Aberdare, to consider the existing method of execution. The Aberdare Report, published in 1888, stated that death by hanging was caused either by suffocation, if the length of drop was insufficient, or by dislocation or fracture of the cervical vertebrae and rupture of the spinal cord. With the latter, the risk of decapitation was always present, but this was preferable 'in the true interests of humanity' to the intense agony a prisoner would suffer in the course of suffocation or asphyxia, the medical experts considering that a man might remain sensible to pain for between one and three minutes if the drop was insufficient. The committee recommended that a revised table of drops should be adopted, along with other technical measures to ensure efficient execution and instantaneous death.

The bulk of the evidence the Aberdare committee heard was from medical witnesses, one of whom, Dr Marshall, described an execution he had observed Berry carry out on a man named Hewitt at Gloucester in 1886:

> I descended immediately into the pit, where I found the pulse beating at the rate of 80 to the minute, the wretched man struggling desperately to (I presume) get his hands and arms free. I came to this conclusion from the intense muscular action in the arms, fore arms and hands, contractions, not continuous but spasmodic, not repeated with regularity but renewed in different directions and with desperation. From these signs I did not anticipate a placid expression on the countenance, and I regret to say my fears were correct, for on removing the white cap (about 1½ minutes after the fall) I found the eyes starting from the sockets, and the tongue protruded; the face exhibiting unmistakable evidence of intense agony.

The recommended drop was based on producing a blow of 1260 foot pounds. This figure was to be divided by the weight of the prisoner in pounds, and the result would be the length of the drop in feet. Thus, a man of twelve stone should be given a drop of seven and a half feet to ensure 'instant' death. The calculation made no allowance for the build of each individual, which executioners had become accustomed to judging according to their experience, but it approximated fairly closely to the table Berry had been using before the Goodale mess. Afterwards, however, he took to reducing the drop to avoid any recurrence of that distressing incident, and now erred on the side of over-cautiousness, resulting sometimes in the equally obscene spectacle described by Dr Marshall. At Cardiff, for instance, where Berry executed a man named Roberts, the short drop he gave resulted in the victim's head remaining visible above the trap-doors, and the reporters, as well as the officials present, could see the hooded man's convulsions as he struggled to draw breath. The governor ordered the press men to leave, but Roberts certainly remained alive on the end of the rope for at least three minutes.

The only thing that can have saved Berry from the same fate as Binns in these circumstances was the fact that he was always sober and well behaved, and concerned to do his job as efficiently as possible. He was learning all the time, and was just as upset by mishaps as other witnesses, though he was clearly more distressed when blood was shed than by suffocation of the victim.

The vexed question of the exact drop required to achieve instantaneous death was not to be settled in Berry's time, if at all. So many different versions of the correct drops required have been recorded that it is difficult to sort out who came nearest the truth. Marwood himself had worked out the mathematics which Berry used at first. 'I was slightly acquainted with Mr Marwood before his death, and I had gained some particulars of his method from conversation with him; so that when I undertook my first execution, at Edinburgh, I naturally worked upon his lines.' But Berry claimed to have worked out at least two tables of drops himself, based on his own experience, and in addition to these used the formula recommended by the Aberdare Committee, based on calculations by James Barr, MD, prison surgeon at Kirkdale Prison, Liverpool, who many years afterwards became President of the British Medical Association.

Berry did make several other improvements in the method of carrying out the death penalty. He was conscious, for instance, of the difficulty and fear of a condemned man, sometimes in a state of near-collapse, in mounting steps to the scaffold. Berry was in favour of a sloping ramp to relieve that problem, and this idea was sometimes adopted, but it gradually came to be realised that the built-up scaffold had no scientific basis and was only a tradition, and that the common sense arrangement was to have an execution chamber in which the trap-doors were at floor level with a pit beneath.

Berry was also responsible for the spring-clip device which held the doors in a vertical position when they dropped. Before this innovation, the heavy doors would swing back and strike either the victim or the rope, and when blood or bruises were found on the dead man, inquest juries were apt to conclude that they had resulted from his struggles. If the doors hit the rope, they could displace it and prevent instant death.

Berry introduced the idea of suspending the rope from a *chain* attached to the cross-beam instead of from a bolt or hook. The stretching of the knot necessary to fix the rope to a bolt or iron ring meant that the drop was often slightly longer than calculated, whereas with a chain the length of drop could be adjusted by lowering or raising the chain and there was no subsequent stretching of the rope. 'The rope I use,' Berry wrote in his memoirs, 'is thirteen feet long and has a one-inch brass ring worked into one end, through which the other end of the rope is passed to form the noose. A leather

[96]

washer, which fits the rope pretty tightly, is used to slip up behind the brass ring, in order to prevent the noose slipping or slackening after it has been adjusted.

'In using the rope I always adjust it with the ring just behind the left ear. This position I never alter, though, of course, if there were any special reason for doing so, for instance, if the convict had attempted suicide and were wounded on the side of the throat, death could be caused by placing the ring under the chin or even behind the head.

'The position behind the ear, however, has distinct advantages and is the best calculated to cause instantaneous and painless death, because it acts in three different ways towards the same end. In the first place, it will cause death by strangulation, which was really the only cause of death in the old method of hanging, before the long drop was introduced. Secondly, it dislocates the vertebrae, which is now the actual cause of death. And thirdly, if a third factor were necessary, it has a tendency to internally rupture the jugular vein, which in itself is sufficient to cause practically instantaneous death.'

Berry took to placing the white hood over the victim's head before he reached the scaffold, instead of when he was already standing on it, to avoid the distress to him of seeing the noose hanging ready, but of course it was this action which aggravated the difficulty of the approach to the scaffold, and other executioners did not follow Berry's habit in this respect.

Another practice Berry eventually adopted was to send to the condemned, via the chaplain, a printed poem which read as follows:

My brother – sit and think,
   While yet on earth some hours are left to thee;
Kneel to thy God, who does not from thee shrink,
   And lay thy sins on Christ, who died for thee.

He rests His wounded hand
   With loving-kindness on thy sin-stained brow
And says, 'Here at thy side I ready stand
   To make thy scarlet sins as white as snow.

I did not shed My blood
   For sinless angels good and pure and true;
For hopeless sinners flowed that crimson blood,
   My heart's blood ran for you, My son, for you.

[97]

Though thou hast grieved Me sore,
  My arms of mercy still are open wide,
I still hold open Heaven's shining door.
  Come, then, take refuge in My wounded side.

Men shun thee – but not I.
  Come close to Me, I love My erring sheep.
My blood can cleanse thy sins of blackest dye.
  I understand, if thou can'st only weep.

Words fail thee – never mind.
  The Saviour can read e'en a sigh, a tear;
I came, sin-stricken hearts to heal and bind
  And died to save thee; to My heart thou'rt dear.

Come now: the time is short.
  Longing to pardon and to bless I wait.
Look up to Me, My sheep so dearly bought,
  And say 'Forgive me ere it is too late.'

This excruciating stuff might be almost a greater deterrent to murder than the rope itself. Berry had copied it from a Dorchester newspaper, and used it until one prison governor objected that the chaplain, not the hangman, knew what was best for a condemned man. Berry then dropped this habit.

It was not always felt necessary in Berry's time to employ an assistant for an individual execution. It depended on the circumstances, but when two or three were being hanged together an assistant was essential. In 1886, Berry was called to Carlisle to execute three men known as the Netherby Hall murderers – Rudge, Martin and Baker – who had shot four policemen in the course of a burglary near the Scottish border, killing three of them. When Berry travelled to Carlisle, he was accompanied by an assistant calling himself Charles Maldon. Sharp-eyed newspaper reporters noticed, when the pair arrived, that Maldon seemed particularly well-dressed and, instead of being accommodated in the prison, as executioners invariably were in these times, he went to the best hotel in town. It did not take them long to work out the truth. The assistant was none other than Sir Claude de Crespigny, whose family seat was at Maldon in Essex.

Sir Claude was a magistrate, and he had approached Berry with what seemed to the hangman a perfectly reasonable, and indeed admirable, request. He was quite likely one day, Sir Claude said, to become a sheriff for his own county, and would then be responsible for executions there. He thought he ought to experience the procedure himself before asking other men to carry it out. He gave Berry ten pounds for the privilege of assisting him at Carlisle, and evidently did the job to everyone's satisfaction. But the baronet's involvement in this sordid business broke an unwritten code of class distinction which brought the incident to the notice of Parliament. Was the Home Secretary aware, one Member asked, that a baronet had assisted at a recent execution, and if so, what was his reaction to the disclosure? The Home Secretary replied that a baronet was as entitled as anyone else to assist at an execution provided it were carried out properly.

When Berry went to York to hang James Murphy in November 1886, for the murder of a policeman, he found a man almost indifferent to his own death, and Murphy wrote in his last letter from the condemned cell: 'I am in good spirits the Governor brought your letter to me at dinner time and the hangs man with him. I shaked hands with the hangs man and he ast me to forgive him and I did so. But I eat my dinner none the worse for that.'

Berry was by now replying to his own correspondents on printed notepaper headed 'The Executioner's Office', and he handed out business cards printed 'James Berry, Executioner', with his address. He also had forms printed for the purpose of accepting commissions, stating his terms at £10 per execution plus travelling expenses, reduced to £5 plus expenses in the event of a last-minute reprieve when Berry had already travelled to the prison.

It seems that most executioners liked to think of themselves not merely as public servants but as government agents, which – technically, at any rate – they were not. Berry said after his retirement that he had 'served under four Home Secretaries'. He considered that 'the' executioner ought to be a salaried official with a pension, and early in his career approached his local MP about pressing for this change in Parliament. 'It seems a horrible thing,' he wrote later, 'that I should have to peruse newspaper reports in the hope that a fellow-creature may be condemned to death, whenever I wish to feel sure that "business is not falling off . . .".' But a similar proposal had already been rejected by the Home Office in 1884. When the Aberdare Committee was set up, however, Berry wrote a long letter to its chairman regarding his position.

He pointed out in his memoirs that some previous executioners had been paid retainers by sheriffs, and that Calcraft had received a pension of twenty-five shillings a week (it may actually have been a guinea!). Berry suggested to Lord Aberdare that he should be paid £350 a year as a public official. As Berry's executions averaged about twenty-five a year this figure represented a considerable increase on what he might expect to earn from piece-work, but he justified his claim on the grounds of the 'peculiar social position' he found himself in as executioner – a man to whom no one else would give employment, and who had the expense of sending his children to school away from his home town. As an afterthought, he suggested that if his appeal were turned down, he might be awarded a retainer of a hundred a year by the Home Office in addition to his usual separate fees. In the event, neither of his proposals was accepted, and he had to be content with the status quo.

In fact, although Berry claimed that he could not live on his normal earnings from executions, he had until this time supplemented his income in the traditional ways of the hangman, by selling the ropes he used and other souvenirs, such as the official commission to the hangman to carry out the execution, which was always handed to him by the prison governor immediately before the execution was proceeded with. Berry, like other hangmen before him, had to purchase his own ropes, and sometimes used them more than once, but he was always able to sell them at a handsome profit, particularly if they had been used on especially notorious murderers.

Berry sold some of his ropes – as well as other souvenirs – to Madame Tussaud's, who had his wax effigy standing in the Chamber of Horrors in its new building in Baker Street. (Berry – ever the businessman – charged Tussaud's for the privilege of modelling him from life, unlike Marwood, who sat for nothing.) Unfortunately, some of these relics were lost in a serious fire in the 20s. Berry also gave a white cap he used to a Bradford solicitor, and I have seen a note in which, signing himself as the 'Ex Executioner for the United Kingdom', he explained that he had used the cap on 'over a score' of criminals he had executed at places as far apart as Newgate and Lancaster.

However, these hangman's perks disappeared soon afterwards. It seems that a man with a morbid taste in souvenirs had bought a rope from Berry and brought it out on a train to show it off to his fellow passengers. One of them, at least, was less than charmed by the offensive relic, and wrote to the Home Secretary about this disgusting spectacle, as a result of which a regulation came into force to the effect that all ropes for executions in England would henceforth be supplied by the authorities and remain government property. Each rope was to be used once only and burnt afterwards with the clothes of the executed person, which had also been among the executioner's per-quisites in former times. Executioners travelling to Ireland and Scot-land still had to supply their own ropes.

It was to Ireland that Berry went, accompanied by his wife, in 1887, when he was required to execute Dr Philip Cross at Cork. Dr Cross was a retired army surgeon who lived at Shandy Hall, Dipsey, in County Cork, with his wealthy young wife Laura and their five children. In 1886 Dr and Mrs Cross engaged a twenty-year-old girl, Effie Skinner, as governess to the children, two of whom were epileptic. In no time at all, it seems, Effie became not only the children's governess but the father's mistress, and in due course Mrs Cross insisted on Miss Skinner's dismissal. Dr Cross complied at once, but followed Effie to Dublin on the pretext of business and stayed with her in a hotel for a few days.

Meanwhile, Mrs Cross had begun to have attacks of an illness which Dr Cross diagnosed as typhoid. She experienced repeated vomiting, diarrhoea and an unquenchable thirst. For about five months her condition deteriorated until, one morning in June 1887, Dr Cross informed the servants that his wife was dead. He signed the death certificate himself, specifying typhus as the cause of death, though it was revealed afterwards that he had told his wife at one point that she was suffering from a heart disease. After a hasty funeral, he left for England and on 17 June married Effie Skinner at St James's Church, Piccadilly, where he had married Laura Marriott eighteen years before. Within a month of Laura's death, Effie had been installed as the new mistress of Shandy Hall.

Local gossip, however – not surprisingly in view of Dr Cross's startling indifference to the consequences of his actions – soon led to enquiries by the police, and the body of Mrs Cross was exhumed and found to contain arsenic and strychnine. Cross was arrested and charged with her murder. There was never any doubt about the verdict, and before sentence was passed on him, Dr Cross made a long speech with an apparent coolness which amounted, once again, to total indifference to his fate.

When Berry came face to face with Dr Cross on the gallows and prepared him for the drop, Cross refused to utter a word to the hangman, his social inferior, and turned to face the spectators, in spite of Berry's efforts to turn him the usual way. Berry pulled the lever on the governor's instructions, despite his superstition, inherited from Marwood, that a murderer must not die facing the east. Berry and his wife then promptly left the prison and set off for home without waiting to attend the inquest. The coroner twice adjourned the proceedings, insisting on Berry's attendance, and when the hangman received a letter asking him to return to Ireland, he replied that he would do so only if he was paid ten pounds and his travelling expenses. The upshot of all this was that the inquest on Dr Philip Henry Eustace Cross remains technically adjourned to this day, and he is not officially dead, though if he were alive he would be 162 years old at the time of writing!

James Berry was not the only executioner to take his wife along for the ride occasionally when he went on his journeys, though it is surprising that he took her to Ireland. Sarah Berry must have been made of sterner stuff than even the average Yorkshire woman of the time. She lived in a house filled with constant reminders of her husband's profession, for besides his other souvenirs he kept framed photographs of some of his victims. She suffered the same social ostracism from neighbours and others as her husband and her children, and had to do her best to protect the children from it, though that problem can hardly have been helped by the fact that Berry once took his son Luther to Ireland with him and allowed him to watch while he prepared the scaffold. The couple had six children, but three of them died in infancy. When Mrs Berry went to Cork, she actually stayed with her husband in the accommodation provided in the prison. Perhaps that was the safest place.

Berry wrote late in his life that once he had made the decision to become an executioner, his wife remained loyal and never failed him. But one wonders if she was really the harder of the two, pushing him on when he felt like giving up, constantly reminding him of his duty, though she possibly had his duty to her and her children in mind rather than his duty to his country. Apparently Berry's mother-in-law sometimes supported her daughter in urging James to pull himself together and get on with the job. As Charles Duff succinctly put it, one can imagine Mrs Berry thinking, 'If the jackass doesn't do the job, bang goes my Spring costume.' On the whole, though, Berry and his family did not do so badly. He eventually owned five other houses as well as the one he lived in in Bilton Place.

The execution of a young man at Preston, soon after that of Dr Cross, was a very different matter from the doctor's dignified and silent exit, and one which Berry had good reason to remember. Alfred Sowrey had shot his sweetheart, and Berry recalled afterwards that during the time between sentence and execution 'he became seriously ill through sheer terror, and it was thought that he could not possibly live to the day appointed for the execution. The efforts of the gaol chaplain to bring Sowrey to a calmer and more reasonable state of mind seemed utterly unavailing, the prisoner was too terrified to take much notice of anything that was said to him.' Warders had to carry him to the scaffold crying and screaming, and he landed a kick on Berry's leg which gave the hangman another scar for the rest of his life.

When James hanged Mrs Berry at Liverpool, it was not his wife on the end of the rope but a woman who, though not related, was known to the hangman. He had once danced with her at a police ball in Manchester, and now she was to die for poisoning her young daughter to get the insurance money. She was suspected of having murdered her husband for the same reason, though she was not tried for that. Berry sat with her for a few minutes on the night before the execution, and reassured his old acquaintance that he would, as he put it, 'not keep her alive a moment longer than necessary.' In the event, the woman fainted on the scaffold, and after he had put her to death the hangman added a lock of her hair to his souvenirs.

After carrying out many executions in a period of a few years, Berry, who had started as a teetotaller, was beginning to drink more and more, and reporters who spoke to him noticed that he was no longer the genial character they had once known. His nerves were being affected by his job, and the macabre sense of humour which had often led him to present his business cards to unsuspecting people who had struck up conversations with him now seemed to be deserting him. He had begun to resent the presence of newspaper reporters at executions.

After he had hanged three men in Ireland in 1888, he suffered a mild nervous breakdown and took some weeks to recover. Visits to Ireland by English hangmen were always testing times, since the mob invariably had more contempt for the hangman than for the murderer, and both press and public gave him a hard time there if he was recognised. But when an English magazine *Answers* published an article about him which said that he sometimes went to places of execution disguised as a woman, Berry brought an action for libel. The case was tried before Mr Justice Day at Leeds Assizes, and Mr Waddy, Berry's counsel, described his client as a man 'who has the misfortune, or the fortune, of being the public executioner,' which might seem not to have been an auspicious opening of the case. But Berry won his case against this imputation of cowardice, and was awarded £100 damages by the jury, after the judge had delivered a little homily on the consequences of that 'morbid vanity' which induces people to 'give interviews to newspapers'. *Answers* had, in fact, reproduced an article which first appeared in the *New York Sun* following an interview Berry gave to their correspondent.

Berry may have entertained hopes of numbering Jack the Ripper among his clients in 1889. A story got around that if he was particularly revolted by the murder or murders his victim had committed, Berry would whisper in his ear that he could make the execution very painful for him if he did not fully confess his guilt. This allegation is almost certainly an outrageous piece of journalistic invention. It does not tie in with what we know of Berry's character.

He certainly expected to meet the celebrated Florence Maybrick. He confidently awaited the commission to execute her, and pasted reports of the case, as was his wont, into his voluminous cuttings book. Mrs Maybrick, a young American woman convicted of poisoning her English husband James with arsenic (although he was a self-confessed consumer of poisonous medicines of which arsenic was but one), received anything but an impartial summing-up by the trial judge, who condemned her as much for adultery as for murder and died not long afterwards in a lunatic asylum. She heard the gallows being erected in Liverpool's Walton Gaol before a reprieve was granted in response to public feeling and (no doubt more persuasively) a request from the American President, Benjamin Harrison. Mrs Maybrick was a great-niece of Jefferson Davis, the Civil War leader of the Confederates. So Berry had to cross her out of his appointments book.

The next woman who *did* come Berry's way, as it were, was Mary Eleanor Wheeler, known to history as Mrs Pearcey, though she was not married. She took the name from the man she had lived with for a time, until he left her. She murdered her next lover's wife, Phoebe Hogg, by hitting her with a poker and cutting her throat so savagely that the head was almost severed from the body, and then dumped the corpse, along with that of the Hoggs' baby, in the streets of Hampstead.

Her execution was set for the Monday morning two days before Christmas in 1890, at Newgate. Berry arrived on the Saturday, and was seen by Mrs Pearcey looking through the judas hole in the door of the condemned cell to judge her weight and build. She apparently said to the wardresses: 'Oh, was that the executioner? He's in good time isn't he? Is it usual for him to arrive on the Saturday for the Monday?' At the appointed time on Monday morning, Berry said: 'If you're ready, madam, I'll get these straps round you,' to which the condemned woman replied, 'I am quite ready, Mr Berry.' She went to her death, outwardly at least, with perfect calmness, though she was only twenty-four, and Berry travelled back to Bradford to enjoy Christmas with his family.

Berry never accustomed himself to hanging women. 'It always made me shiver like a leaf,' he said and after he had executed a baby-farmer, Jessie King, in Scotland, he remarked, 'I am inclined to think no woman will ever again be hanged in the United Kingdom.' It was wishful thinking.

Newspaper reporters were excluded from the Pearcey execution by order of the Sheriff of London, but they were present at Kirkdale Prison in Liverpool in the following August when Berry hanged John Conway for the murder of a boy named Nicholas Martin. Berry worked out the drop for the prisoner, who weighed a little over eleven stone and was five feet seven inches in height. Four-and-a-half feet was Berry's calculation, but he was over-ruled by the prison medical officer, Dr. Barr, who said that six feet nine inches was the correct drop according to the scale laid down by the Aberdare Committee. A heated argument then ensued which led Dr Barr to agree to reducing the drop he insisted on by nine or ten inches, after which Berry claimed to have said: 'All right, I'll do as you like, but if it pulls his head off, I'll never hang another.'

As Berry was about to adjust the noose round Conway's neck, the condemned man shouted, 'Hold on, hold on, I want to say something.' 'You can't say anything now,' snapped Berry, 'it's too late.'

The Catholic priest then took Berry's arm, and the hangman said in a temper, 'Get out o' t'way and mind your own business.' But the priest persisted. 'It will make no difference if he lives two or three minutes more,' he said. 'Aw reet then, say what you 'ave to say quick', said Berry, now thoroughly unnerved by these interferences with what he had spent years refining into a smooth and extremely swift procedure. The white cap was lifted from Conway's face and he made a statement thanking the prison officials and forgiving his prosecutors. Berry re-arranged the cap, adjusted the noose and pulled the lever. The spectators immediately heard, above the intonations of the priest, a loud squelch instead of the usual thud in the pit below. The reporters moved forward to look, but Berry shouted, almost hys-terically, 'Take 'em out, take 'em out,' and rushed out of the room himself. It was Dr Barr who saw that Conway's head was hanging from the body by little more than a string of tissue, and that the pit was splashed with blood.

'If the condition of the culprit is such,' the Aberdare Committee's report had stated, 'as to suggest the risk on the one hand of decapi-tation, or on the other of death by strangulation, we have no hesi-tation in saying that the risk of decapitation should be incurred.' It was not what Berry preferred, however. For one thing, it was part of the job of the executioner to go into the pit after an hour and put the dead man into his coffin. As he left the prison, reporters were waiting for him. 'You've made a mess of this one, Mr Berry,' one of them said. 'Nay, I haven't!' Berry replied, and promptly put the blame on the medical men, explaining the difference of opinion he had had with Dr Barr. 'It's all left to t'doctors now. They might as well do t'whole job themselves.' He then went home, having been told he was not required for the inquest, which turned out to be one of those that established the principle of covering up mishaps. The prison gover-nor's evidence was that everything had been conducted 'as usual', and Dr Barr said the execution was 'carried out in the usual way.' When the Coroner asked him if there had been any hitch, he replied, 'No, so far as the execution was concerned.'

The newspaper men were not to be deceived as easily as the jury members, however. They knew what had happened, and reported it fully, coming to their own conclusions as to *why* it had happened. One paper concluded that the priest's interference with Berry's prepar-ations had made him adjust the noose badly. Another threw doubt on

Berry's capabilities by saying that he had been drunk since arriving in Liverpool.

He had in fact been greeted by a large crowd at the Court House Hotel and then followed to the prison, and the Governor of Kirkdale informed the Prison Commissioners that it had 'been the custom for executioners to hold Levées at the Hotel for years past.' It was also officially recorded that Berry had behaved with 'roughness' at the execution, though it was understood that he was irritated by the interference of both doctor and chaplain in his task.

Berry hanged one or two other men in the months following this incident, apparently without mishap, but it was not long before he wrote to the Home Secretary, as follows:

> Dear Sir,
>   I herewith tender my resignation as executioner of Great Britain. My reason is on account of Dr Barr interfering with my responsible duty at Kirkdale Gaol, Liverpool, on the last execution there. I shall therefore withdraw my name now as being executioner to England. Trusting this will be accepted by you on behalf of the Sheriffs of England, I remain, dear sir,
>
> Your obedient servant,
James Berry,
late executioner of England.

Berry was thirty-nine years old. The letter was scarcely necessary, but it recalls Berry's inflated idea of his own importance. In the first place, he was not in the employment of the Home Secretary; in the second, he was not 'executioner of Great Britain', nor even of England. The man who was to succeed him as the sheriffs' first choice, James Billington, was already carrying out executions on his own some years before Berry's retirement.

Berry had been preparing his autobiography, part-ghosted and edited by H. Snowden Ward, and published in Bradford soon after his retirement as *My Experiences as an Executioner*, in which he said that hanging was a real terror to the criminal and a deterrent to murder, and that abolition of the death penalty would be contrary to the Biblical principles of 'An eye for an eye' and 'Whoso sheddeth man's blood, by man shall his blood be shed.' But he now began to put it about that he was in favour of abolition.

It turned out that a certain Mr Leshe, an American, had proposed to Berry that he should undertake a lecture tour in the United States from which he might earn $45,000 for twenty lectures. The talks were to be based on Berry's experiences, but with the theme that the death penalty was a horror which should be abolished. The British public learned with not a little surprise and cynicism that Berry had *always* been opposed to capital punishment, 'in principle'.

In the event, the trip to America never materialised, but Berry did make a start on the entertainment circuit in England, his first appearance being at the Royal Aquarium Theatre at Westminster in March 1892, seven months after the ghastly affair at Liverpool. (This variety theatre was soon to be taken over by Lily Langtry and refurbished as the 'Imperial'.) On the bill with the former executioner was, among others, a singing quartette whose speciality was 'Ta-ra-ra-boom-de-ay'. Berry was to give eleven lectures at this theatre, for which he is said to have been paid two hundred guineas, and then tour the nation. 'James Berry, the Late Hangman,' the advertisements would announce. 'The Man With the Marvellous Experiences – The Man Who Will Entertain You With Exciting Episodes Advocating Abolition of Capital Punishment.'

Berry began his career as an entertainer with a formal lecture which he read standing at a lectern, but as he became more confident and relaxed he was apt to ad lib more, and eventually his talks were accompanied by lantern slides with an accompaniment of piano music and explanations by Berry thought to be amusing to his audience, such as his comment when showing the slide demonstrating pinioning of a prisoner's arms – 'He's tied up so's 'e can't scrat 'is self.' I have seen at Madame Tussaud's about a hundred slides that Berry used in his talks. They were mostly simple painted-glass scenes of prison life, but a few were photographic reconstructions of scenes in the execution chamber. Berry frequently expanded on his scorn for sheriffs. 'If I 'ad my way, I'd make sheriffs do t'job themselves,' he would say. He had elaborate new notepaper printed, now advertising himself as 'Late Public Executioner for Great Britain', and listing the theatres and halls he had appeared in, from the Royal Aquarium and Fulham Town Hall to the Empire, Middlesbrough and the Palace, Aberdeen. He also described himself as 'Phrenologist & Character Reader. Palmistry Explained. Heads Examined.' Beneath all the bluff Yorkshire showmanship, however, Berry was a deeply troubled man.

The affair at Liverpool still preyed on his mind, and at one point he wrote, somewhat belatedly, to Dr James Barr about it, receiving in reply a letter which began, 'In compliance with your request, I have pleasure in giving you a certificate as to the manner in which you conducted the execution of Peter Cassidy in HM Prison, Kirkdale.' Dr Barr went on to confirm the correct and satisfactory conduct of Berry on this occasion, but took advantage of the opportunity to end his letter with the hope that, 'whoever be appointed to the post of Public Executioner may be prohibited from also performing the part of a "showman" to gratify a depraved and morbid public curiosity.' Whether the mistake here was Berry's or the doctor's is not clear, but the victim over whom the dispute had arisen was not Peter Cassidy but John Conway. It is characteristic of Berry and his editor that this letter was included in Berry's book as if it were a vindication of his handling of Conway.

Berry's career in the theatre was short-lived. There was a limit to how much mileage you could get out of the death penalty as entertainment, and there was no audience for endless repeats in those days. So he sought employment elsewhere, becoming a salesman again (for bacon) after having an unsuccessful try at running a pub. He was drinking heavily at times to obliterate his tormenting memories, so it is said, and became increasingly depressed. On occasions he felt suicidal.

This, at any rate, is the story which has been in circulation ever since in published matter – mainly in newspapers and in one full length biography of the hangman. But documents in Prison Commission files show that Berry's departure was not as clear-cut and decisive as has always been believed. In fact, for ten years after his resignation he repeatedly wrote to the Home Secretary asking to be reinstated, but was refused.

As late as March 1902 Berry was making pathetic pleas for his name to be put back on the list, and wrote that he had been persuaded to destroy all the remaining copies of his book – 21,000 out of 40,000 published – 'thinking by taking the advice of my superiors I am taking a step in the right directions'. But in spite of his 'piteous appeal', the Home Secretary saw no reason to consider re-employing a man 'who formerly caused us trouble', and Berry's applications were turned down, especially as there were 'plenty of good men now available.'

One morning in 1904, Berry was sitting on the platform at Bradford railway station when a young man sat down on the same bench and, looking at Berry, whom he did not know, thought he needed help. He spoke to him, and within a few minutes Berry burst into tears as he poured out his story to this sympathetic member of a Christian mission in Bowland Street, Bradford. Berry went to the mission hall with him, prayed there with his new 'brothers and sisters', and 'fully surrendered himself' and 'accepted God's precious gift'.

Berry's wife, though not particularly religious herself, again supported him in the hope that his new convictions would bring him some relief from his troubles, but when some of his religious friends came to his house to hold a prayer meeting, she too broke down and 'gave herself to Jesus'. Berry said that he would never touch alcoholic drink again.

In 1905 another little book was published in which Berry confessed that he had a heavy conscience. He had pursued an ill-considered career as a younger man which had brought him nothing but pain. 'I now hold,' he wrote, 'that the law of capital punishment falls with terrible weight upon the hangman and to allow a man to follow such an occupation is doing him a deadly wrong.'

Berry now embarked on a lecture tour of a different kind, speaking at revivalist meetings all over the country, influenced by the impact of the Moody and Sankey meetings in England, the last of which had been in 1892. Berry's theme was his conversion, but he could only convey the dramatic import of this to his listeners by describing his earlier life as a hangman. For the various horror stories with which he had chilled the spines of his theatre audiences, he now substituted stories of death-cell repentances to touch the hearts of his religious ones. He spoke out with vehemence against the death penalty, from religious convictions now instead of financial considerations.

There can be little doubt that religion saved Berry's life for a few years, though he might have reflected that it had not saved the 134 men and women he had dealt with in the course of a mere eight years as an agent of death.

But mental anguish had taken its toll of his physical health. Late photographs of Berry show a man startlingly reduced in stature from the robust earlier figure as seen in this book. He now looked ema-ciated and considerably older than his sixty years. Berry died at Bradford on 21 October 1913, aged sixty-one. He was buried in the cemetery at Lidget Green. His occupation was given as 'evangelist'.

VII

Dynasty

He did not pass in purple pomp,
Nor ride a moon-white steed.
Three yards of cord and a sliding board
Are all the gallows' need:
So with rope of shame the Herald came
To do the secret deed.

Oscar Wilde
The Ballad of Reading Gaol, 1898

EARLY IN July 1896, when Oscar Wilde was one of the prisoners at Reading, preparations were being made there for the execution of a trooper in the Royal Horse Guards who had killed his wife in a fit of jealousy. His name was Charles Thomas Wooldridge, and his execution was to be the first at Reading for many years.

Wilde saw the victim at exercise in the prison yard, and a grave being dug for him in the grounds. '. . . the shed in which people are hanged,' he wrote in a letter to Robert Ross, 'is a little shed with a glass roof, like a photographer's studio on the sands at Margate.' The execution took place on 7 July, the hangman giving Wooldridge a drop of six feet seven inches. Wilde dedicated his famous poem, inspired by the event, to the memory of the guardsman.

The herald of death on this occasion was one James Billington, a barber by trade from Farnworth, near Bolton. He had been fascinated by hanging, it seems, since he was a boy of ten, and had carried out experiments with dummies on a model gallows in his back yard. When Marwood died, Billington applied for the job (one of the 1400), but Binns was chosen, as we have seen. Billington, however, was given an opportunity to explain his method to the prison authorities at York, and he was appointed to carry out executions at York from 1884, even though James Berry, the Yorkshireman, had soon succeeded Binns as the man favoured by London and Middlesex. They still liked to demonstrate that they had minds of their own in Yorkshire.

A little over-eager to get on with the job, Billington wrote to the Sheriff of Nottingham in July about a prospective victim he had read about:

> Sir I have seen it in the paper to-day that there as been a murder here (Nottingham) and håving been in comunation (sic) with the High Sheriff under Sheriff Chaplin and governor of Armley gaol Leeds in Yorkshire I have been examined with them for the post of hangman and the next that is hung there I have to do it. they could see that my system was better than the last and they was pleased with it. it prevents all mistakes as to the rope catching there arms and it will answer for 2 or 3 as well as one. you will find it to improve on the old system a great deal and I could put it to the old scaffold in about one hour. It is no cumberance and it can be removed with the other part of the scaffold. they engaged me before Berry (?. . .) but it has been kept quiet and I thought if you had not elected one I should be ready at your call – if it was your will. you have no need to be afraid you may depend on me. I shall have no assistance I can do the work myself I don't think it needs two to do the work and as long as they can have a little assistance from the gaol if required. I am a teetotaller ten years and a Sunday school teacher over 8 years, and if you like to see my testimonials if you will write to me I will send them or to Mr Gray he has a copy of them.

Mr Gray was the Yorkshire Under-Sheriff, but the Nottingham authorities did not take Billington up on his thoughtful offer, chiefly because the man he had read about was charged with manslaughter, not murder.

Billington's first execution was at Armley Gaol, Leeds, on 26 August 1884, when he hanged Joseph Laycock, a hawker from Sheffield, for the murder of his wife and four children. He was pleased to get the job, he told reporters, 'as he had made a hobby of this kind of thing, which he could now indulge, without being compelled to confine his efforts to the before-mentioned dummies.' Laycock was crying as Billington pinioned him, and said, 'You will not hurt me?' Billington replied, 'No, thaal nivver feel it, for thaal be out of existence i' two minutes.' The hangman planned a drop of nine feet, but on learning that the prisoner had attempted to cut his throat, reduced it by eight inches to avoid opening the wound. The body twitched a little after the drop, but everyone was satisfied with the new man's work, and he continued to get the hanging jobs in Leeds and York, at Berry's expense.

James Billington was a man of medium height and slight build, but very strong – he had been a collier at one time and, according to one source, a wrestler as well. He had also worked in one of Bolton's cotton mills where he was nicknamed 'Jimmy Armhole', no doubt in reference to his particular job in the textile trade. One of his hobbies was keeping racing dogs, and another long distance walking, for which he wore clogs. He married and had children, and in due course moved from Bolton to Farnworth and set up in business as a hairdresser in Market Street.

He had formerly been noted locally for his singing in the public houses round Oldham and Middleton, but now he signed the pledge and kept it for many years, wearing the blue ribbon of the teetotaller prominently on the black suits he customarily wore. He had a sign in his barber's shop reading: 'Friends, don't swear; it is a sinful and vile habit. You may swear yourselves in hell, but you cannot swear yourselves out of it.' When he was carrying out executions, he habitually wore a black skull cap, which must have given him a forbidding medieval appearance adding to the apprehension of his victims.

Billington had to be content with being second fiddle to Berry until the Bradford hangman resigned, but in 1892 succeeded him as the senior executioner favoured by the Sheriffs of London and Middlesex, as well as Yorkshire and elsewhere. His wife had died in the meantime, and in July 1891 he married again, his new bride being Alice Fletcher, a local grocer's daughter.

He and his first wife had lost three of their children as infants, one of them a girl named Polly, whose school friends bought a little wreath with their pocket-money and delivered it to the house to be placed on her coffin. Billington himself received them at the door, and instantly burst into tears, explaining to the teacher afterwards, 'See, I'd sooner ha' lost five pound than ha' lost her' – a touching sentiment indeed.

Billington had already developed a chronic dread of newspaper reporters, who would often go into his shop for a haircut and try to coax stories of his experiences out of him. He grew to resent these intrusions so much that the moment he suspected his inquisitive customer was a reporter, he would down tools and depart, leaving the customer half shaved or with his hair half cut, and he would not return until the man had left, either after getting himself finished by waiting for an assistant to do it, or by departing unfinished.

But Billington's salon was not the only place where reporters tried to interview him. In December 1892 he was best man to an old friend of his who was getting married at Blackpool, and tried to keep it quiet, but news naturally got round, and he was soon accosted, saying he wanted 'nowt to do wi' any reporters.' The journalist on the *Bolton Journal* was somewhat put out by his attitude, and took the opportunity to say that Billington 'was willing to step into notoriety by the aid of the Press, and then is ungrateful enough to turn his back on his best friends. But for the notice he obtained in these columns, and subsequently in other papers, when he first became candidate for appointment as executioner, he would have had no more chance than the man in the moon. His quarrel with the reporters is, therefore, a little overdone.' This report was not only fanciful but unduly optimistic. It ended with the thought that 'the probability is that he will go down to posterity, assuming that capital punishment is in time to come abolished, as England's last public executioner.'

Unmoved by these arguments, Billington brought an action for libel in July 1893 against a Manchester paper called *Spy* which had published two pieces about him in the previous January and February. The first was a joky article in which the writer said that he had 'just escaped the hands of the executioner. He has had his grisly paws about my swan-like neck, and I have felt his hot baleful breath upon my face . . .' Billington considered that such language was calculated to make people shun him in the street. The second piece reflected on Billington's character and lack of education. 'Although a bit of a 'rum-un' in his early days,' it said, 'he is a changed man now, a Primitive Methodist, a blue ribbonite, and much respected.' This, the plaintiff claimed, meant that he had once been a man of low and disreputable habits, unfit to associate with decent people. He had never given an interview to this paper and did not know the writer. The defendants said the articles were meant to be humorous, but accepted that they were perhaps badly written, and offered to withdraw the statements and pay their own costs. This was accepted under pressure from the judge, who was unwilling to put the case before a jury. Billington retired to lick his wounds.

The pursuit of hangmen by the press was accelerated by the blanket of secrecy which now covered executions, largely as a result of the ghastly bunglings that were being reported in the newspapers in Berry's time. Sheriffs were advised either to exclude reporters altogether or to ensure that their reports were brief and unsensational. In other words, the Home Office wanted to gag the press. Henceforth, what was done on behalf of the British public in this respect was to be done in secret, and prison officials, under threat of the Official Secrets Act, were forbidden to reveal anything other than the most basic facts about executions.

On one occasion Billington received a letter from a poor woman in Italy, forwarded to him by the Home Office. The woman said that her husband was going blind, and she had four young children to keep. She did not know what would happen to them when the family's breadwinner could no longer earn a living. But she had been told that if her husband wore round his neck a length of rope that had been used to hang someone, his sight would be restored. The death penalty had been abolished in Italy in 1889. I do not know how Billington responded to this appeal. He may have obliged. A police officer friend said that he had seen Billington in places of entertainment 'cry like a weeping woman at a pathetic scene, and laugh uproariously at the comic element.'

A month before Billington went to Reading to execute the guardsman who had killed the thing he loved, he was at Newgate to conduct a triple execution. Two of the victims, Harry Fowler and Albert Milsom, had killed an old man at Muswell Hill in the course of burglary. They blamed each other for the murder at their trial, and Fowler made a violent attack on Milsom even while the jury was considering its verdict. The third man was named Seaman, and he had committed two murders at Whitechapel.

For a triple execution, an assistant to the hangman was obviously required, and the man chosen was one Warbrick. Several warders were present in the execution chamber as the three men were prepared, to prevent any repetition of the violence in court, and when Billington glanced round quickly to make sure that all was ready before operating the trap doors, the figure of Warbrick, who was still pinioning one of the victims' legs, was hidden by one of the warders. Billington pushed the lever and Warbrick shot head-first through the trap doors with the three murderers, but had the presence of mind to cling on to the legs of the man he was nearest to, and so saved himself from a nasty accident. This was, as it turned out, the last triple execution to be carried out at Newgate.

Billington did not go home that day. He was required again next morning to execute Amelia Dyer, a highly unbalanced, if not positively insane woman – a baby-farmer convicted of murdering a four-month-old girl in her charge, named Doris Marmon, and undoubtedly guilty of murdering at least six other infants. She had a history of mental illness and suicide attempts, but the jury refused to accept the evidence of expert medical witnesses that she was insane. She was fifty-seven, the oldest woman to be hanged in Britain since 1843. No older woman was to be hanged in Britain, in fact, before the death penalty was abolished.

Billington found himself at the other extreme in 1899, when he hanged Mary Ansell at St Albans, whom many regarded as also insane, if not indeed altogether innocent. She, however, was only twenty-two. Mary was a simple-minded servant girl, and she had a sister, Caroline, who was a patient in the Leavesden Asylum at Watford. There was a history of serious mental illness in the family. When Caroline died, it was alleged that Mary had sent her a cake containing phosphorus in the post, in order to claim about ten pounds in insurance money. Mary's mother said she had been 'silly from the time she was at school.' Another witness testified that she talked to herself, suffered from hallucinations, and would suddenly laugh loudly for no reason. Unimpressed, the jury condemned her on circumstantial evidence, though the foreman remarked afterwards that no one thought she would be hanged. It seems clear, even if Mary did send the poisoned cake, that she had little understanding of the gravity of what she had done.

A scaffold was brought to St Albans from Bedford, and erected in the prison. Neither Queen Victoria nor the Home Secretary responded to appeals and petitions for a reprieve, and James Billington hanged Mary Ansell on a sunny morning in July, whilst a large but orderly crowd outside the prison waited for the black flag to be hoisted just after eight o'clock. Some people were kneeling on the ground in prayer.

No one witnessed the execution except the prison officials, and Mary Ansell's body was buried in the prison grounds. An old lady who remembered the event told the *Herts Advertiser* in 1973: 'I remember feeling sorry for the victim, but I think we all felt she must be guilty as they were hanging her.' It is said that Mary Ansell's brother afterwards confessed to the murder on his death-bed.

Billington was by now a taciturn and morose character who had so

[116]

far abandoned his teetotalism as to retire from the hairdressing business to become licensee of the Derby Arms in Bolton. Whether this new role gave him any respite from the attention of journalists is open to doubt, but he was a changed man if some reports are to be believed. He said that being a hangman was like 'livin' in a bloody cage', and had reputedly ignored his own admonition of late by saying to a man in his barber's chair, 'Th'art axin' a lot o' questions, aren't ta? There's too many nosy buggers round 'ere.' The newspaper men had tended to drop their questioning when the barber had his razor poised over their necks, and they probably found it rather easier to communicate with him now that he was safely behind a bar and drinking as much as they did, if not more. He was suffering from insomnia, and he was in the habit of taking walks round Bolton in the middle of the night. He had become a member of the Royal Antedeluvian Order of Buffaloes, a Freemasons' lodge. He had three sons whom he had brought up to be competent assistant executioners, and the two eldest, Thomas and William, were already assisting their father on occasions.

When Billington went to Ireland in January 1901 to execute Timothy Cadogan at Cork, he got himself into hot water with the authorities there. Cadogan had shot and killed a land agent who had evicted him, and he tried to cut his throat the night before his execution with the iron tip of his boot, but was prevented by warders intervening. Billington hanged him without further incident, as far as we know, but then left the prison without waiting for the inquest, following Berry's precedent. The coroner adjourned the inquest and issued a warrant for Billington's arrest. Billington, however, back in Bolton, said it was not usual for executioners to attend inquests, and he would not return unless compelled to. When the inquest was re-opened, without Billington, the prison doctor testified that the execution had resulted in instantaneous death, but for some reason the jury would not agree on the cause of death, and the inquest was adjourned indefinitely. 'Our executioner', the Bolton paper said, 'has been this week much in the public gaze owing to an execution at Cork at which he was present, and the subsequent inquest at which he was not.'

On the same day that Billington was hanging Cadogan at Cork, a man named Scott was hanging a fellow named Woods in Belfast. We know little about Scott, but he had assisted Berry on more than one occasion, and seems to have got most of his subsequent work in Ireland. He was never a serious threat to the successors of Berry in Britain.

When James Billington went to Newgate in 1901 to execute a Frenchman named Fougeron, the assistant appointed was one Henry Pierrepoint, a man of twenty-four from Huddersfield who had written direct to the Home Secretary, Mr Ridley, for the position. This was his first job, and it was to be one of the last executions to be carried out at Newgate. The old prison, scene of so many horrors, was scheduled for demolition to make way for the new Central Criminal Court. The victim, Fougeron, was an anarchist who had murdered a Clerkenwell jeweller in the furtherance of theft for political funds. Billington spent the night in the room which was customarily occupied by the hangman, and Pierrepoint was consigned to a spare cell next to the condemned cell. Unable to sleep, the young assistant observed the condemned man counting the chimes of St Sepulchre's church clock from two in the morning onwards.

Billington was assisted by his eldest son Thomas in March of that year when he hanged Herbert Bennett at Norwich for the murder of his wife Mary Jane, whose body was found on the beach at Great Yarmouth. Bennett was twenty-two. The couple had been separated for some time, and the appearance of the body suggesting sexual assault, there was some public doubt about the husband's guilt. When the completion of the execution was signalled by the hoisting of the black flag, the flag pole snapped, and this was taken by some as a sign of a miscarriage of justice.

'Bolton is not Titipu,' the local paper proclaimed around this time, 'but like that imaginary Japanese town of Gilbertian creation, it may be said to have a Lord High Executioner. In this instance Billington is his name and not Ko-ko, but unlike that worthy he has not to find victims, they are found for him.' The paper might profitably have quoted the Gilbertian lyrics from *Princess Ida* as well as *The Mikado*:

> We will hang you, never fear,
> Most politely, most politely!

But when Bolton provided the victim as well as the executioner, the papers were beside themselves, particularly as the two chief actors in the drama were well known to each other.

[118]

John Ellis, the long-serving hangman from Rochdale whose victims included some of the most notorious criminals of the century. (*Press Association*)

Dr Crippen in the dock with Ethel le Neve in 1910, en route to the execution chamber at Pentonville. (*Syndication International*)

Sir Roger Casement. His executioner, John Ellis, said afterwards that he 'died like a soldier'. (*BBC Hulton Picture Library*)

Patrick Mahon. This agreeable-looking fellow was hanged by Thomas Pierrepoint in 1924 for one of the most gruesome murders of the century. (*BBC Hulton Picture Library*)

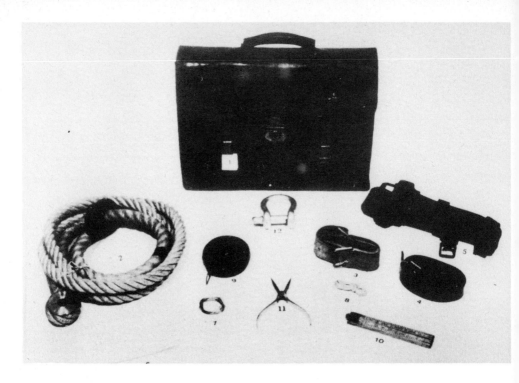

The modern hangman's tackle, as used by Albert Pierrepoint, showing rope, pinioning straps, tape measure, thread, copper wire for measuring the drop, etc. *(Yorkshire Post)*

Irma Grese and Joseph Kramer, most notorious of the thirteen war criminals hanged by Pierrepoint in one day in 1945. *(Keystone Collection)*

Crowds clamouring to read the notice of execution of William Joyce, 'Lord Haw-Haw', outside Wandsworth Prison in 1946. (*BBC Hulton Picture Library*)

Albert Pierrepoint, one of the last hangmen of England, seen here after his retirement. *(Press Association)*

Timothy Evans arriving at Paddington Station in 1949, soon to face a charge that would lead to his execution by Albert Pierrepoint. *(Syndication International)*

Ruth Ellis with David Blakely, whom she shot dead. She was the last woman to be executed, although a death sentence was passed on another woman three years after Ruth Ellis's death.

Harry Allen, one of the two men to follow Pierrepoint, was modelled by Tussaud's and displayed in the Chamber of Horrors in the sixties. *(By kind permission of Madame Tussaud's)*

Patrick McKenna had murdered his wife in a fit of passion, and was deeply repentant, but a petition signed by over 22,000 local people did nothing to save him from the gallows, and Billington was engaged to execute him at Strangeways on 3 December, 1901. McKenna was an old acquaintance of Billington's, if not actually a friend. He had lived in Keston Street, Bolton, where James Billington's father had been in business as a barber during James's youth. One local paper believed that one of James's sons assisted him in the execution, but in fact his assistant was again Henry Pierrepoint. Billington was feeling ill, and Pierrepoint spent the night before the execution playing cards with him in their prison apartment, to help take Billington's mind off his condition. 'Ee, Harry,' he said at one point, 'I wish I'd never ha' come!' But he managed to do the job expeditiously next morning, McKenna sobbing, 'Oh, Lord, help me!' as they launched him into eternity. This piece of information came from Pierrepoint much later, Billington declining to say anything to the reporters who greeted him when he got back to Bolton.

Within a fortnight of this execution, Billington himself was dead. He died on Friday, 13 December, aged fifty-four. The cause of his death was given as a severe attack of bronchitis. He was buried at Farnworth cemetery, in the presence of a crowd drawn there by curiosity, in the grave of his first wife and their three young children. Ten members of the RAOB were there, as well as several beer salesmen and licensed victuallers. Henry Pierrepoint described James Billington later as the best pal a man could have.

'Jimmy Armhole's' achievement had been to execute 147 of his fellow human beings. He left behind him a widow and five children, but not for long. Less than a month had passed before Thomas, James's eldest son, and sometime assistant, died of pneumonia on 10 January, 1902. He was twenty-nine and a widower. He had also assisted his younger brother William at one or two executions, both before and after his father's death.

A newspaper soon afterwards reported an 'official spokesman' as saying that applications for the post of 'public executioner', though there was in reality no such appointment, were coming from people in all walks of life – 'Army pensioners and University men, cotton spinners and weavers, and agricultural labourers . . .'. The article went on to say that 'although the applicants are from all parts of the country the greater number come from Lancashire. This county seems to have a special supply of would-be hangmen . . . Yorkshire comes next, but the other counties are a long way behind these two.'

The 'official spokesman's' information was correct. The Home Office list of approved executioners and assistants in 1901 consisted of James, Thomas and William Billington, William Warbrick, Robert Wade, Henry Pierrepoint and John Ellis. I know nothing about Wade, but of the other six, Pierrepoint was from Yorkshire and the rest from Lancashire.

James Billington's mantle fell naturally on the shoulders of his second well-trained son, William, who was then still living with his step-mother at the Derby Arms, and who sometimes had the assistance of his younger brother John. But early in May 1902, James's widow Alice also died, at the age of forty-four, overcome by the loss of her husband and step-son. It was the third death in the family within six months. The family had by then relinquished its connection with the Derby Arms.

I have had to tread cautiously through a maze of inaccurate information about the Billington family. It is perhaps not surprising that there has been much confusion about them, when even the contemporary local newspapers sometimes got the facts wrong (reporting the death of John Billington as that of William, for instance). Other writers have invented non-existent Billington hangmen, including 'Joseph', 'Joshua' and 'Dick'. One self-perpetuating error is that 'William Billington killed himself and his family in 1925.' It was not only newspapermen and other writers who were confused about the Billingtons. There was some confusion in official circles, too, and if this chapter reads like a comic soap opera, it is not entirely my fault.

When Edward Bell was sentenced to death at Lincoln in 1899, James Billington was engaged to do the job, but William turned up instead, saying that his father was too ill to come, and that he (William) had carried out an execution before. Nonplussed by this situation, the governor allowed him to execute Bell, and when the Prison Commissioners took Billington to task over the matter, he apologised for telling the governor a lie, but pleaded that he had been afraid that, if he had told the truth, 'you would not let me do it'.

Shortly afterwards, the Home Office had occasion to query the employment of William Billington as an assistant at an execution at

Nottingham, as he was not on the official list. The governor reported that he had twice tried to employ Thomas Billington for the job, but his father did not know where Thomas was and had recommended William.

This brings us back to the assistant Warbrick. It appears that he was no more qualified than William Billington to take part in an execution when he had the unfortunate accident, for both men were placed on the list of approved executioners only in 1900. William Warbrick was a Bolton man whose name had formerly been Wilkinson. He had changed it when he discovered that he was born before his parents were married. He was well known to the Billington family. Professional rivalry soon led him to bombard the Home Office with complaints that the Billingtons were preventing him from getting work; that Thomas had run away from home and enlisted; that William was 'only a boy' and 'very fond of drink'. Later in his smear campaign he sent the Home Office a local newspaper cutting reporting that William had been convicted of assault, and Warbrick alleged that he was perpetually drunk. This was not apparently believed, and the Governor of Wandsworth reported that in his opinion William was a more suitable man than his father.

Meanwhile, the Under-Sheriff for London had recommended that more men should be available, as he thought that James Billington was losing his nerve and Warbrick 'not very likely to be thoroughly satisfactory'. So Warbrick's efforts to undermine the reputations of his rivals failed. One is almost inclined to wonder if Warbrick's nasty fall a few years earlier was entirely accidental!

It was William Billington, with Henry Pierrepoint as his assistant, who conducted the first execution at Pentonville Prison on 30 September 1902. The sixty-year-old prison at Islington replaced the demolished Newgate as the scene of executions for north London, and the scaffold used at Newgate, and before that at Horsemonger Lane, was moved there, being regarded by the hangmen of the time (if not necessarily by their clients) as the finest in the country, equipped for hanging three victims side by side. It was also from this time that the practice of raising a black flag on the prison roof was discontinued, the public outside being notified that an execution had taken place by the tolling of a bell instead.

Another Bolton criminal – Harry Mack – fell into William Billington's trap in December at Strangeways, but there is no evidence that the two men were acquainted. Mack had murdered the woman he was living with at Oldham. At the inquest, the doctor said that death was due to dislocation of the neck between the third and fourth vertebrae, and that the execution had taken only seventy-five seconds from the moment the condemned man left his cell.

In January, Billington was in Ireland, at the beginning of what was to be a peak year for executions in recent times, twenty-seven people in all being hanged in Britain. Billington's job in Ireland was to hang two people, a week apart from each other, for the same murder. Joseph Taylor was put to death at Kilkenny for the murder of John Daly, and a week later Mary Daly, the victim's wife, who had been having an affair with Taylor, was hanged at Tullamore as an accessary.

On 3 February William Billington and his assistant Henry Pierrepoint conducted the first execution at Holloway Prison. It was a double execution involving two baby-farmers, Annie Walters and Amelia Sach. The younger of the two, Sach, had taken infants from their mothers, on payment to procure good homes for them, and then passed them on to Walters who murdered them.

Early in March, Billington was in London again, this time to execute Edgar Owen, alias Edwards, at Wandsworth. He had been found guilty of the murder of a Mr and Mrs Darby and their baby. He had gone to the grocery shop which the couple were advertising for sale and battered them and their child to death. Then he had dismembered their bodies and buried them in a garden at Leyton, stolen the cash box from the shop and some of the goods and furniture, explaining to the locals that the Darbys had 'gone up north'. Edwards was reported to have said as he approached the scaffold, 'I've been looking forward to this a lot.'

Billington did not leave London until midnight, catching the 12.05 train from St Pancras to Manchester. He sat in an empty carriage, but another man joined him just before the train departed. Billington buttoned up his overcoat and went to sleep. After nearly an hour, as the train was approaching Luton, his sleep was disturbed and he woke to find the stranger unbuttoning his (Billington's) coat. When asked what he was up to, the man said he was buttoning it up because he had noticed Billington shivering. Billington told the fellow he had better leave him alone, and threatened to pull the communication cord. The man then said, 'Oh, it's a fight tha wants!', and grabbing the hangman by his coat, threw him against the carriage door, which flew open, and Billington fell out on to the line, sustaining injuries to his face, arms and a leg, and lay there unconscious for an hour.

This unlikely story seems to have been generally swallowed at the time, but there is reason to suspect that there is not a word of truth in Billington's dramatic tale. Henry Pierrepoint told his son, Albert, when the latter was a boy, how on one occasion in London he and William Billington had spent the day, after carrying out an execution in the morning, at the Crystal Palace, then made their way to St Pancras to catch the midnight train, and called at a pub in Euston Road for a drink. Eight youths came in, provoked the two strangers into a quarrel, and then drew knives. But the executioners, aided by the bartender, were more than equal to the young thugs, and gave them a beating, emerging 'without a scratch' according to Pierrepoint's account, before going to catch their train.

I have no evidence that this adventure, if it is true, occurred on the day of Owen's execution at Wandsworth, but it seems quite likely that Billington told the story of being pushed off the train to explain the bruises which were still very evident when he appeared in court a few days later to answer a summons in connection with his separation from his wife and the sale of some of their property. A local reporter at the County Court wrote that Billington 'showed unmistakable signs of the severe shaking he got after falling from the train. One side of his face was quite twice its natural size and his wrist had been badly damaged.'

Most executioners have been keen to get home as quickly as possible after an execution, partly to avoid being recognised in the locality. Henry Pierrepoint is well known to have preferred hanging around for drinks with his mates, but it is not clear whether on this occasion he led Billington astray, or vice versa. 'Billie' Billington, at any rate, was no teetotaller as his father had once been, and *any* story would have been less likely to put his career in jeopardy than admitting that he had got into a fight in a pub after an execution.

Perhaps William Billington's career as a hangman reached its climax in the following month when, on 7 April 1903, he executed 'George Chapman' at Wandsworth. Henry Pierrepoint was again his assistant. 'Chapman' was a Pole, his real name being Severin Klosovski. He had been a barber-surgeon in Poland and worked as a barber's assistant at Whitechapel when he first came to London in

[123]

1888, and lived with a Polish woman whom he married bigamously, having left a wife in Poland. After spending two years in America, he came back to England leaving his second wife behind also, and then lived with a woman named Annie Chapman, thereafter assuming the name George Chapman. Then he turned his attention instead to a Mrs Mary Spink, who was sufficiently well-off to help her new partner to open a barber's shop at Hastings, where she played the piano for the entertainment of customers whilst they were having their hair cut. But the couple soon decided to return to London, where they became licensees of the Prince of Wales Tavern off City Road. On Christmas Day of the same year, Mary Spink died, apparently of consumption.

Chapman took on a barmaid named Bessie Taylor, and they lived together, Chapman, after a spell at Bishop's Stortford, taking a lease on the Monument Tavern at Southwark. In February 1901, Bessie died of 'exhaustion from vomiting and diarrhoea'. Chapman's next barmaid and mistress was Maud Marsh, and she died in October 1902. Maud's mother, however, had been ill after drinking a brandy and soda which Chapman had poured for Maud on one occasion, and her doctor had seen Maud and warned Chapman's doctor that she was being poisoned. When Maud's death occurred, Chapman's doctor refused to sign a death certificate, and Chapman was arrested after an autopsy revealed the presence of antimony in her body. He was accused at first of the murder of Maud Marsh, but subsequently the murders of Mary Spink and Bessie Taylor were added to the charge after their bodies had been exhumed and found to contain antimony. Chapman was thirty-seven. While in custody, he referred to Edgar Edwards, whom Billington and Pierrepoint were to execute in a few days. 'Edwards is a hot 'un', he said. Chapman's trial lasted four days, but the jury needed only eleven minutes to find him guilty, and he was stricken with terror as the death sentence was pronounced.

The infamy of George Chapman was increased far beyond his merits as a sordid philanderer by the suspicion, which has still not been entirely dispelled, that he was Jack the Ripper. The suspicion was based chiefly on the facts that he was living in Whitechapel at the time of the Ripper murders, and that he had been a surgeon's apprentice as a young man in Poland. The police officer who arrested Chapman was Chief Inspector Godley who, fourteen years earlier, had worked with the officer investigating the Ripper murders,

Inspector Abberline. The latter remarked to Godley when Chapman was arrested, 'You've caught the Ripper, then?' But the overwhelming argument against identifying Chapman with Jack the Ripper is that a man who was possessed by a sadistic sexual mania can hardly have turned into a patient and calculating poisoner.

Chapman's failure to secure a reprieve led to his collapse, and warders kept a close watch on him as it was feared he would attempt suicide. He wrote to some friends in his imperfect English: 'I cannot express my sorrow to you of my posision, but yet I wish it was over as the time is dredful long waiting for it . . . If I was guilty I would say. But I am not, therefore I must insist upon to my last, as I cannot accuse myself of which I am innocent of . . . My dear friends, be human to all living (creatures) as I have been . . . Good bye for ever from yours faithfully Frent – George Chapman.'

He was almost in a state of collapse on the morning of the execution, but Billington did his work speedily, warders supporting Chapman until the trap fell. Chapman's body was said to have been buried in the prison grounds between those of Kate Webster and Dr Lamson. It was Wandsworth's forty-fifth execution.

Early in July Billington hanged Samuel Dougal at Chelmsford for the murder of Camille Holland. Dougal was a Cockney and another philanderer. He had been married three times, his first two wives having died in Nova Scotia, where he had been serving as a soldier. He had a good military record and a bad criminal one. Miss Holland was a wealthy spinster in her mid-fifties, hitherto a woman of Victorian virtue, who went to live with Dougal at a farm she bought at Clavering in 1899. After a few weeks she disappeared, and a younger woman moved in with Dougal in her place. This turned out to be Dougal's third wife, whom he had married in Dublin. Dougal became wealthy on the proceeds of Miss Holland's property and her bank account, becoming the first man in the area to own a motor car. Meanwhile, he had paid his attentions to an assortment of women and servant girls, and was once seen giving cycling lessons to a naked girl in a field. Four years after Miss Holland's disappearance Dougal was arrested for forgery, and a long search of the farm eventually revealed Camille Holland's corpse in a ditch. She had been shot in the head with Dougal's revolver. He denied murder, claiming that the victim had been shot accidentally. As Billington prepared him for the drop, and was almost ready, the chaplain, Rev. Blakemore, waved the executioner aside and demanded 'Are you guilty or not guilty?', and repeated the question twice before Dougal said 'Guilty' through the white hood over his face, just as the trap fell. Questions were asked in the Commons about the behaviour of the chaplain, and the Home Secretary took steps to prevent any recurrence of this incident.

Billington was engaged in Manchester and Durham during the first week of December 1903, but at the end of that week it was announced that he was thinking of retiring, two years after succeeding his father and elder brother, because his frequent absence from his hairdressing salon in Great Moor Street, Bolton, was having an adverse effect on the business. 'It is not expected,' the *Bolton Journal* reported, 'that the present assistant hangman will seek the position his brother is about to vacate.'

John Billington was William's partner in the barber-shop. The younger man was a teetotaller and assistant organist at the local Spiritual Hall. He had assisted at a few executions, and on 29 December carried out one himself at Liverpool, hanging Henry Starr for the murder of his wife Mary at Blackpool. This may have been John Billington's first execution as principal, his brother having been engaged to execute a couple named John Gallagher and Emily Swann at Leeds on the same day. William had as his assistant a young man named John Ellis, who had assisted him once before in a double execution at Newcastle.

In another double execution at Walton Gaol, Liverpool, in May 1904, Billington and Pierrepoint executed William Kirwan, a sailor who had killed his sister-in-law, and Pong Lun, a Chinese who had shot a man in a gambling quarrel. Pierrepoint alleged, many years later, that Billington had said to the latter, 'Come on, Ping Pong,' and that Lun bridled at this, but laughed helplessly as he entered and looked round the execution chamber, unable to believe that he was going to be done to death with this weird English contraption.

William Billington's resignation did not come as soon as he had threatened, for the two brothers were in action again at different prisons on 17 August of that year, when William hanged John Kay at Leeds for the murder of his mistress, Jane Hirst, and John Billington hanged Samuel Holden at Birmingham for the murder of *his* mistress, Susan Humphries. It was said that the latter walked to the gallows smoking a cigar, but generally speaking, the only information given to the press by this time was the name of the executioner and the

[126]

prison governor's standard statement that the execution had been carried out 'without a hitch' (or 'any untoward incident') and that 'death was instantaneous'.

Soon after this double family event, William Billington seems not only to have resigned as an executioner, but to have relinquished his interest in the hairdressing business as well, leaving it in the hands of his brother; and Henry Pierrepoint began to carry out executions with Ellis as his assistant for a short time until Ellis, too, became a senior executioner in his own right. For the sake of clarity, however, I will complete the story of the Billington dynasty before moving on to their successors.

On 20 July 1905, William Billington was charged with failing to maintain his wife and two children. They had been admitted to the Bolton Union Workhouse for a month in February. There was a separation order against Billington for sixteen shillings a week, but not a penny had been paid so far that year. Billington claimed that his wife was living with another man, but the relieving officer said that she was in fact living with her sister in Burnley. Billington then explained that he had been out of work for four months, but having just got a job in Manchester he could now pay a small sum monthly. The magistrates sent Billington to prison for a month with hard labour.

At the end of October, John Billington died, at the age of twenty-five. An attack of rheumatic fever had been followed by dropsy. He was buried at Heaton Cemetery, and left a young widow and baby. It was the fourth Billington death in as many years, and left William as the sole male survivor.

Hardly a month had passed before William was in court again, charged once more with neglecting his wife and family. They had again spent some time in the Bolton workhouse, and had received none of the money Billington had promised to pay. (We may wonder how the local magistrates expected him to pay when they had committed him to prison instead of allowing him to earn his living.) The prisoner was described as a blacksmith and hairdresser. He said he had done his best to get work since leaving prison in August. He had also signed the pledge, and had not tasted drink since he came out of prison (nor since he went in, presumably!). He had now opened a shop, and offered to send his wife two pounds straight away, as well as her railway fare, as he wanted her and his children to live with him again. This was accepted by the magistrate, and the case was adjourned for two months.

William's promises were empty ones, however. He sent a letter to his wife, but it bore no stamp and contained no money. The case was re-opened on 8 February, and it was stated that Mrs Billington and her children were still in the workhouse. Billington was not in court, and he was sentenced to another month's imprisonment in his absence. I am not sure if he served this further sentence, or what happened to his wife and children. William Billington lived on until March 1934, when he died in his early sixties.

When both William and John Billington had been removed from public service by resignation and death, the executioner's crown, or at any rate his noose, fell for a while to the founder of another family firm, the erstwhile assistant Henry Albert Pierrepoint, or Pierpont as it was often spelt then. But before we move on to that famous and lengthy incumbency, it will be well to deal with the other heir to the Lancashire monopoly, John Ellis.

VIII

For Whom the Bell Tolls

The long-term ill effects upon the character balance of those who
participate in legal homicide are not to be underestimated.

A. Hyatt Williams
Consultant Psychiatrist, 1969

ONE OF THE first of the cotton mills you used to come to if you
travelled into Rochdale by the road from Oldham was the Eagle Mill
in Queen Victoria Street, opposite the Grammar School for Boys. It
was at this mill, the home of the Eagle Spinning Company, that
young John Ellis was put to work when he left school, for the family
lived close by.

He was the eldest of his parents' four children, and had two sisters
and a brother. Joseph Ellis, his father, was a hairdresser, and his wife
Sarah bore him their first child on 4 October 1874. Joseph was a
respected man in the neighbourhood, who had done well for himself.
He carried on his business further down the Oldham Road, past the
canal and the London Midland and Scottish Railway. He had invested in property in the district, and owned 'a tidy number of houses'.

His prosperity was as much due to his ruthlessness as to the general
well-being of the town at the time. He made one of his daughters,
Helen, work in the shop as a lather girl, much against her wishes, to
save himself expense. He was a sturdily built man of medium height,
and a very strict disciplinarian; Liberal in politics and more than a
trifle illiberal in other matters. He was a Methodist and a fundamen-
talist, and the family attended a chapel in Oldham Road known as
the Red School.

John Ellis, an undistinguished pupil, left school and went to work
in the Eagle Mill as a stripper and grinder. When he was twenty, he

[129]

was married at Middleton parish church to Annie Beaton Whitworth, one of the girls who worked at the mill. The bride was twenty-two, and the ceremony took place on 20 April 1895. The young couple set up house in Balderstone, and settled down to what one might have predicted would be the routine life of an average working man's family. But things soon took an unexpected turn.

One evening John Ellis knocked at the door of his foreman, Mr Hopkins, who lived near the mill in Queen Victoria Street, and asked him for a reference. Mr Hopkins learned with not a little surprise that the young man wanted to apply for the post of executioner. He wisely told Ellis to go home and think about it for a week and discuss it with his family, and then come back if he still wanted to apply. A week later, Ellis returned and repeated his request, and in due course, he sent off to the Home Office, with his letter of application, no less than three good references. Few applicants went to this amount of trouble, and the Home Office was suitably impressed. A confidential report from the Chief Constable of Rochdale confirmed that the testimonials were genuine and that Ellis seemed to be a man of good character.

Annie Ellis was far from happy about her husband's decision, but he was determined, and there was nothing she could do to stop him. But when Joseph Ellis heard about it, he raised the roof. Such an idea must have stunned him and threatened his position as a respected businessman. His wrath only subsided when he had 'played hell all round' and cut his son off without a farthing. John Ellis, however, was unrepentant, and awaited a reply to his letter.

He is reported as telling a newspaperman who asked him why he had chosen such a career, 'I hardly know, but it wasn't through influence. I applied with other young men for a post that was vacant as assistant hangman, and I suppose I was lucky. I think what first suggested such a profession to me was when some friends and I were reading about an execution, and one of them said to me, "You would never have the nerve to hang a man." I said I would – and did.'

This is hardly an adequate explanation, and perhaps the real reasons were largely unrealised by Ellis himself. He was no introvert preoccupied with self-examination. The Home Office used to receive an average of five applications a week from men wanting to be hangmen, though the post was never advertised. Most of them came from cranks, of course, and though some applicants were more suitable than others, and may have developed a strong sense of duty later – as Ellis did – none was inspired purely by a selfless desire to serve the community.

More or less on his own admission, Ellis had the average morbid interest in sensational crimes, and like Berry, studied press accounts of trials very carefully throughout his career. He obviously knew that one of the executioners at the time was Billington from just up the road at Bolton, and this must have made some impression on him, even if he had not met him, which would explain Ellis's obscure reference to 'influence', as well as his knowledge of a vacancy. I have not found any evidence, but it seems likely that Ellis knew one or more of Billington's sons. Perhaps they met at a local hairdressers' convention.

Ellis, at any rate, was not satisfied to be one of the crowd making their dismal way down the cobbled streets every morning to the call of the factory whistle, and he did not have long to wait for results. His letter was one of those picked out as promising, and he was invited to go to Strangeways Prison for an interview with the governor, who was sufficiently impressed to recommend him for a week's training at Newgate. Ellis was one of the last executioners trained at this prison before its demolition. He proved to be a satisfactory trainee, and returned home to Rochdale at the end of the week, in May 1901, confident that he was to be placed on the list of official killers issued to county sheriffs.

By this time all approved applicants were issued with a memorandum of conditions they were expected to conform to, including a prohibition from 'giving to any person particulars on the subject of his duty for publication.' So when the *Daily Mail*, in its issue of 14 December 1901, published the news of Ellis's appointment as an assistant, Ellis was promptly warned that failure to comply with the standards of behaviour expected of him could lead to his removal.

Ellis's career as an executioner began in that year at Newcastle, where he assisted William Billington at the double execution already referred to. He suffered from what we might call 'stage-fright' throughout his career, and his first real execution must have been a nerve-racking experience, even though he only had to pinion the legs of the prisoners. But all, apparently, went well.

He remained an assistant for seven years, during which time he helped William Billington again in executing Mrs Emily Swann and

John Gallagher at Leeds in 1903, hanged together for the murder of Mrs Swann's husband. This was the first of three experiences Ellis had of executing women. Mrs Swann was in a state of collapse on the morning of her death, but was revived with brandy to such an extent that she said, 'Good morning, John' to Gallagher as they stood back-to-back on the trap doors. Gallagher responded with, 'Good morning, love,' and Mrs Swann replied, 'Goodbye. God bless you.' Such evident composure was disconcerting to young Ellis and, combined with a deeper psychological motive, contributed towards a life-long repugnance to the capital punishment of women.

Ellis assisted at three executions on consecutive days in 1905. The first victim, one Edge, had murdered the child of his landlady when she had turned him out of his room, and being temporarily if not permanently insane, was wrongly hanged at Stafford on 27 December, Ellis's Christmas holiday being cut short by the necessity to travel on Boxing Day. On the twenty-eighth, a man named Smith was hanged at Leeds, and at Derby on the twenty-ninth, the victim was a man named Silks.

Ellis's first job as a senior executioner came on New Year's Day, 1907, when he went to Warwick, new Gladstone bag in hand, to hang one Davis. Ellis said in his memoirs that he had been delighted to receive the offer, and had accepted it with alacrity. Having calculated a drop of seven feet nine inches, he was challenged by the Under-Sheriff, who thought it was too long and said, 'I have seen more executions than you have, and I consider that a most unsuitable drop.'

'Very possibly,' Ellis claims to have retorted, 'but seeing an execution is one thing and performing one is distinctly different.' The Under-Sheriff persisted in his disapproval, until Ellis said, 'If you will take the full responsibility for whatever happens, I will adopt your suggestion,' whereupon the official agreed to let Ellis please himself. Ellis proudly reported that death was instantaneous, and 'there was not even a quiver of the rope'.

In 1910 (two years after the death penalty was abolished for those under sixteen years of age), Ellis was again involved in three executions on consecutive days, and the second of these brought him the first of his encounters with criminals of national notoriety, Dr Crippen.

On 22 November, Ellis hanged Henry Thompson at Liverpool for the brutal murder of his wife. Ellis regarded Thompson as the most callous man he ever met, noting with disgust that he had to be woken up on the morning of the execution, saying he had slept 'better than at home'. He also remarked, 'Well, I shall be senior to Crippen in the other shop.'

Dr Hawley Harvey Crippen was an American living in England, and was sentenced to death for the murder of his wife Cora, a former music-hall artiste known as Belle Elmore, who had discovered to her great annoyance that her husband had a mistress. Consequently, she was preparing to leave him. This would have suited the doctor admirably, no doubt, were it not for the fact that he found she was planning to take their joint savings with her. In view of this, he took urgent steps to keep her at home.

Suspicions were aroused when Crippen's mistress, Ethel le Neve, was seen wearing Mrs Crippen's jewellery, and especially when she and her lover departed for America. Police found the remains of Mrs Crippen under the cellar floor, and Crippen and Miss le Neve were chased across the Atlantic and arrested on board ship.

Crippen was executed at Pentonville at nine o'clock on 23 November 1910, and death was instantaneous, as the saying goes. On this occasion, Ellis adopted a practice which he used invariably afterwards. Instead of heading the procession to the execution chamber, he walked quickly to the gallows by himself and awaited the arrival of the prisoner there. He seems to have thought this routine less distressing for the prisoner.

A large crowd had gathered outside the prison, and the first intimation they had that Crippen was dead was the posting of the notice on the gates, as there were three other men awaiting execution at the time, and the customary tolling of the bell was dispensed with, out of consideration for their feelings. Ellis remarked to a friend in the 'local' later that if he had been allowed to keep the rope, he could have sold it for £5 an inch! But ropes were now supplied by the Home Office to prevent such dealings in macabre relics.

In July 1911, Ellis was at Leicester to dispatch William Palmer, who gave the hangman what he described later as 'the most exciting execution in my long career'. Palmer was fifty, and had murdered an aged widow who lived alone in a Leicestershire village. He protested his innocence to the last, comparing his 'ill-deserved' fate with that of Jesus Christ, and crying out on the night before his death, 'I'm going to be murdered in the morning.'

When Ellis and the officials arrived at his cell door, Palmer shouted, 'Are you going to let these fellows murder me?' and leapt at the warders, who fell to the floor with him in a struggling heap. Four warders eventually got him under control, and Palmer went the forty yards to the gallows cursing and wrestling violently.

Less than a year after the death of Crippen, another notorious murderer was hitting the national headlines. This was Frederick Henry Seddon, who lived within a few minutes' walk of Crippen's house. Seddon murdered his lodger, Miss Eliza Barrow, an extremely unpleasant but fairly wealthy woman of doubtful mental stability. He killed her with the arsenic from threepenny packets of fly-papers for financial profit he did not need.

Ellis, who – according to one of his friends – 'read everything he could find in the newspapers about murders, and always made his mind up about the verdict beforehand', attended part of Seddon's trial. Since Ellis belonged to the Royal Antediluvian Order of Buffaloes, it did not escape him when Seddon, declaring his innocence, made the Masonic sign. It was not lost on the judge either, who happened to be the Provincial Grand Master of Surrey, and touchingly regretted, in passing sentence, that he had to condemn a fellow member to death.

Seddon walked calmly to the execution chamber on 18 April 1912, and Ellis claimed a record time of twenty-five seconds in carrying out the sentence, but interest in Seddon's execution was eclipsed by the nation's preoccupation with the Titanic disaster, which had occurred four days before.

At Stafford on 10 March 1914 Ellis earned a reprimand from the Home Office. Experience had led him to exceed by a few inches the length of drop specified in Home Office instructions (a practice justified shortly after his retirement when Sir Bernard Spilsbury recommended an increase of three inches in the specified drop on 'humanitarian grounds'). Owing to a small error in marking the rope, Ellis gave his victim, one Davies, a longer drop than he had intended, with the result that the rope grazed the man's skin. The prison doctor made a formal complaint about this, and Ellis was instructed not to exceed the regulation drop in future.

On 12 August 1915 he travelled to Maidstone to execute George Joseph Smith, the 'Brides in the Bath' murderer, at eight o'clock on the following morning. Smith was certainly the most despicable visitor to Ellis's threshold. A vulgar and illiterate scoundrel variously known as art dealer, land agent and junk-shop owner, he surprisingly possessed a talent for making women fall for his doubtful charms, whereupon he cheated them of their money in the pretence of protecting their interests, and briskly absconded.

On at least three occasions Smith found it necessary to resort to marriage; all three being illegal since he was married already. The three rather stupid and unfortunate women involved in these contracts came to untimely ends in their baths, their feet having been jerked upwards suddenly to cause drowning from shock. The first victim was Beatrice Mundy, to whom Smith was known as Mr Williams, and who met her death at Herne Bay in July 1912. Next was Alice Burnham, who died at Blackpool in December 1913; and finally Margaret Lofty, who knew Smith as Mr Lloyd, and died at Highgate in similar manner in the following year. It is said that on one of these occasions, Smith bought a cheap tin bath from a local store on the day of the murder, and returned it a week later, having no further use for it, and asked for his money back.

When Smith stood in the dock at his trial, he conducted himself in his customary rude and self-assertive manner, frequently interrupting the proceedings, and during the judge's summing-up he provided the only light relief in the whole sordid affair by shouting, 'It's a disgrace to a Christian country, this is. I am not a murderer, though I may be a bit peculiar.'

When the sentence of death was passed, however, his confidence deserted him, and he nearly collapsed in the dock. His terror was great, and he had to be dragged and half-carried screaming along the prison corridors to the execution shed, where Ellis's assistant Pierrepoint and the warders had to hold him up on the trap doors whilst he was prepared for the drop. In the report of the execution in *The Times*, the only hint to the world outside that any untoward incident had occurred was casual mention that six warders were present in addition to the usual officials.

With the possible exception of Crippen, Ellis's most famous victim was Sir Roger Casement, an Irishman in the employ of the Foreign Office, who was knighted for his selfless service to oppressed peoples in 1911 and, one might argue, hanged for it five years later. His execution may fairly be regarded as Ellis's *magnum opus*.

Casement won fame, honour and respect from the British people by his thorough exposure of the unspeakable atrocities then being visited on the natives of the Belgian Congo and in the Putumayo basin of Peru. At the outbreak of war in 1914, however, his devotion to the cause of Irish freedom led him to flee to Germany, where he attempted to persuade Irish prisoners of war to form an Irish Brigade on the side of the Kaiser, and also to get the German government to send arms and ammunition to Ireland for a revolt. Both efforts failed, and Casement was arrested by the British authorities when he landed in Ireland from a U-boat. Tried at the Old Bailey for treason, he was found guilty and sentenced to death.

In the meantime, a disgraceful smear campaign was being carried out against him on behalf of the government, by the circulation of his private diaries to influential people – particularly American journalists. The diaries contained references to Casement's homosexual practices, and on the grounds that anything is permissible in war, the campaign was organised in order that his execution should not make a martyr of him in Ireland and America, and thus alienate those countries from the British cause. The diaries were even shown to King George V, lest His Majesty should feel inclined towards clemency. One of the most enthusiastic hawkers of the diaries was Sir Basil Thomson, Assistant Commissioner of Metropolitan Police, who was himself arrested for an offence in Hyde Park some time later!

Vigorous efforts were made to save Casement by many prominent people. Bernard Shaw drew up a petition to the Home Secretary, Mr Herbert Samuel, which has been described as one of the most sagacious pieces of writing Shaw ever produced. Another petition was directed to Prime Minister Asquith by Sir Arthur Conan Doyle, bearing the signatures of Arnold Bennett, John Galsworthy, C. P. Scott and the Bishop of Winchester, among many others. This was always somewhat optimistic, Asquith having been Home Secretary at the time of the Oscar Wilde affair. The efforts of Casement's sympathisers failed to triumph over the government's determination to hang him, and Ellis (who, in a burst of patriotism – as his friends thought – had declared that he would give £10 to charity for the chance to hang Casement), was called to Pentonville to carry out the execution on 3 August 1916.

Some 200 people gathered outside the prison, and there were cheers when the bell was tolled at nine o'clock. Casement, who was fifty-one, walked to the scaffold with impressive dignity, towering above the warders and officials, responding to the priest's words of the litany for the dying.

A slight adjustment to the drop was necessary owing to Casement's height. The pit was not deep enough to allow the man to hang without his feet touching the floor. He insisted on facing Ellis, who entered his victim's last words in a little notebook he kept for the purpose. An article in the *Catholic Bulletin* attributed the following statement to Ellis: 'The impression will ever remain on my mind of the composure of his noble countenance, the smile of contentment and happiness, as he willingly helped my assistant . . . the steady martial tread of his six feet four inches and soldierly appearance adding to the solemn echo of his answers to the Roman Catholic chaplain while marching to his untimely doom. Roger Casement appeared to me the bravest man it fell to my unhappy lot to execute.'

While it is clear that this eulogy is not the language of a Lancashire barber, there is no reason to doubt that it reflects Ellis's true feelings, for he wrote afterwards, 'Casement may have been a traitor, but he died like a soldier.' It was the first execution for treason in Britain for more than a century. 'Don't let my body lie in this dreadful place,' Casement had pleaded in Pentonville. 'Take me back to Ireland.' But his remains did lie in that dreadful place for nearly half a century until, in February 1965, Prime Minister Harold Wilson agreed to allow their return to Ireland, where they were reburied in Dublin's Glasnevin Cemetery.

The war years naturally brought a temporary reduction in the crime rate and, consequently, in the number of executions. In the four years 1915-18 inclusive, there were thirty-six executions in England and Wales, compared with fifty-nine in the preceding four years and fifty-eight in the succeeding four. Business soon picked up, however.

One of Ellis's occasional visits to Scotland took him to Glasgow to execute Thomas McGuinness in March 1917. The prisoner was in a state of collapse, but refused brandy on the grounds that, despite his name, he was a teetotaller. The apparatus at Glasgow was very ancient, and in his hurry to drop McGuinness before he collapsed, Ellis very nearly dropped his assistant too, who leapt aside just in time.

At Pentonville in March 1918, Ellis hanged a Frenchman named Louis Voisin. Voisin was a butcher, and had made a professional-looking job of carving up a young woman, Emilienne Gerard, and distributing the pieces, wrapped in brown paper, in a public garden in Bloomsbury, where they were discovered by a horrified postman. Owing to the wartime shortage, Ellis was asked to bring his own meat and other rations for his prison meal, for which he was paid on arrival.

During the troubled years in Ireland after the war, Ellis carried out a number of executions there which involved him in some personal danger. On one occasion he hanged six members of Sinn Fein 'before breakfast' at Mountjoy Prison, Dublin. Two were executed at six o'clock, two at seven and two at eight. 'That was a terrible day', Ellis remembered, 'and the strain was dreadful.' The executioner's job had traditionally been a trifle perilous in Ireland, as we have seen. Ellis's life was threatened on one or two occasions, and he carried a revolver, had police protection, and travelled to and from Ireland in a cargo vessel, dressed as a warder and wearing dark glasses. He was once threatened by Sinn Fein when it became known that he was to execute three men in Londonderry for complicity in a murder, and a police patrol was put on his house. But when he was on his way to Belfast, he was informed that the three had been reprieved. On arrival back at Liverpool, he was recognised by a steward, who said, 'They haven't shot you yet, then!'

It is perhaps much to the credit of the Irish that they had to employ an English hangman. Ellis claimed that he hanged every one of the Sinn Feiners executed during the troubles. But he was rarely recognised. When he turned up at Liverpool for an execution one day, a man outside the prison approached him and said, 'Has Ellis, the executioner, arrived yet?' 'I really don't know,' Ellis replied.

In appearance, Ellis was undistinguished and, as one newspaper put it, 'never looked what he was'. He was about five feet nine in height, slightly built, and beginning to stoop a little by this time. He had pale blue eyes and a pale complexion. His head was going bald, but he had a bushy auburn moustache.

After a number of years in his father's hairdressing business, Ellis tried his hand as 'mine host' at a public house in Middleton with the name 'The Jolly Butcher'. This was not a success, and he returned to hairdressing, opening a new shop half a mile away from the old one, also in Oldham Road, Rochdale. Like his parents, he and his wife had four children – three daughters and a son – and the family lived in Kitchen Lane, Balderstone.

Ellis's hobbies were always concerned with animals. He put his hand to the profitable North Country hobby of poultry breeding, and had quite a considerable farm at one time. He usually had a bulldog or two around the house, and apparently once had a parrot, as well as rabbits. Latterly, the bulldogs were replaced by whippets.

He was fond of sport, and had a portrait of his favourite boxer, Jim Driscoll, on the sideboard at home. He supported the Rochdale 'Hornets' Rugby Football Club, and knew some of the players well. He was also a gambling man, and a friend who occasionally placed bets for him told me that Ellis used to receive tips from R. S. Seivier, the newspaper proprietor and racehorse owner, who sent tips to selected people on the understanding that winners would make contributions to a hospital fund he ran. I gather that Ellis had few winning tips from him, but no doubt Mr Seivier received a donation or two all the same, Ellis being generous with his money. He subscribed to various charities and deserving causes, and in later years helped to provide an annual treat for local army veterans.

Ellis's health was not good, however. He suffered from neuritis, and drank quite a lot, which can only have aggravated the disease. Many independent witnesses have testified to this; how he liked two glasses of beer before lunch, and how he was 'a genius at persuading landlords to serve him after hours', and sat playing dominoes or telling stories to his friends. To them he was 'just one of the locals' in spite of his calling, and was treated like everyone else. A typical tale told to me by one of his friends concerned an argument Ellis had overheard in a pub one night. The two men had made a bet and agreed to write to a newspaper to settle it. 'No paper settling for me', said Ellis to my informant when having his hair cut one day. 'I were once in a pub,' the barber continued, 'when a fellow said, "Eh, Jack, how long is it since tha did that theer job in Ireland?" I said midnight such a day such a year, when another chap said "I'll bet thee a pound tha didn't". I thought to meself, easy money. I ought to know; I did the job. Anyhow, I left it to them and they wrote up to a paper, but I lost, because summer-time weren't in Ireland then. But anyhow, the same thing occurred again a while after. The same question came up, so naturally, another pound at stake. Again they wrote to a paper, and again I lost, for these last lot wrote to a different paper and they answered as I had said the first time.'

Relatives of Ellis have told me that he *never* talked about his jobs. It seems to be true that he never talked about them to his family, and Ellis said in his memoirs that his wife learned, like Mrs Berry, never to ask questions about them. But it is equally certain that he did talk about them on occasion to his closer friends, especially when he was in his cups. He always avoided the words 'hanged' and 'executed' when referring to his victims, and used the expression 'put them away' instead. It would be going too far to say that he betrayed the trust the authorities had invested in him, especially as it has not been clear what the position of the executioner was in regard to 'official secrets', the Home Office remaining stubbornly non-committal on the subject. Ellis published a long series of articles, running every week from April 1924 to February 1925, about his experiences, without – as far as I know – any official action being taken to suppress them; but Albert Pierrepoint, in *his* autobiography, refers specifically to being subject to the Official Secrets Act. I shall return to this point in the last chapter.

The temptation for Ellis to talk to *some* people may have been reinforced by the sense of social ostracism he felt on other occasions. 'Conversations cease suddenly when I am about,' he confessed, 'and I can feel people eyeing me as if I am some exhibit in the chamber of horrors. They will avoid shaking hands with me when they are introduced – they shudder at the idea of grasping the hand that has pinioned murderers and worked the gallows lever. Socially it is a bad business being a hangman.'

On 12 April 1920, Ellis travelled the short distance from his home to Manchester to execute Lieutenant F. R. Holt at Strangeways. Holt's girlfriend, Kathleen Breaks, had been found riddled with bullets on the sands beween Blackpool and Lytham St Annes on Christmas Eve, 1919, and Holt had been sentenced to death for her murder. Owing to his background – his mother had died in a mental hospital – and his excellent war record, there was a good deal of sympathy for Holt, and many signatures were acquired on a petition for a reprieve, which failed. Holt gave a lot of trouble in prison, and Ellis noted, typically, that he showed no signs of gratitude for the efforts of his friends to save him.[1]

S. J. Coe, who was then a crime reporter on the *Rochdale Observer*, described in his book *Down Murder Lane* how he interviewed Ellis at

[1] It is perhaps worth noting that Holt was in no way deterred from his crime by the fate of George Joseph Smith, who had committed one of his murders in the same locality six years earlier.

his home two hours after Holt's execution: 'The hangman admitted me to his cosy fireside, and when I asked him how the murderer met his doom, he brushed his red moustache with the back of his hand, tapped his pipe on the copper kettle steaming on the hob, his blue eyes searched the sky for a picture of the scaffold, and then he said, "Oh, aw reet, tha knows!" I might have been asking how his rabbits were, judging by his casual answer.'

This picturesque little story is, however, false in detail if true in substance, because Ellis did not return home that day. The governor of Strangeways paid for a taxi to take him straight to the railway station, to catch the 9.30 a.m. to Cardiff, where next day he hanged a negro, Tom Caler, who had cut the throats of a woman and her baby. Ellis and his wife celebrated their silver wedding anniversary in the following week.

On 30 May 1922, having again been on duty at Strangeways that morning, Ellis caught the ten o'clock train from London Road Station to Gloucester, where he was required to execute Herbert Rouse Armstrong. His assistant on this occasion was one Edward Taylor. Ellis said in his reminiscences that on arrival at Gloucester he had been told that he had backed a 'dead-heater' at Epsom at 100-8. This evidently made his day for him.

Armstrong was a solicitor and had been a major in the army. He had poisoned his wife Katie, who was a tyrant in the home, with arsenic from a weed-killer, having drawn up a will on her behalf which left everything she had to him. Fifty-two years old, Armstrong had won some sympathy from the prison officials by his gentle manner and good behaviour, and a warder asked Ellis to be gentle with him, to which Ellis replied indignantly, 'If I don't know my business after twenty-one years' experience, it's time I got out of it.'

Armstrong had not been weighed for three weeks, and Ellis refused to prepare for his execution until his weight had been taken again. He was a slightly built man of only 115 pounds, and Ellis gave him what turned out to be the longest drop he ever used – eight feet eight inches.

Just after midnight, Armstrong woke and asked a warder what time it was, and said, 'It's hard to wait to die.' A few seconds before eight, the prison governor asked Armstrong if he had anything to say, and he replied, 'I am innocent of the crime for which I have been condemned to die.' Ellis, undeterred, pinioned his arms, and gave him his customary advice: 'Please look straight at me when you get there and it will soon be over.'

Ellis noted that the governor and chaplain had been 'much affected' after saying goodbye to Armstrong. Standing erect on the trap doors while Ellis adjusted the noose, Armstrong said loudly, 'I am coming, Katie', and died instantly. Ellis afterwards met a Rochdale Hornets player in the town, and spent a pleasant hour with him before catching his train, arriving home just in time for tea.

The years 1920 and 1922 were 'good' ones for English executioners. There were twenty-one executions in England and Wales in 1920, and twenty in 1922, compared with only five in 1921, a particularly bad year. The average number of executions a year during Ellis's twenty-three years of hanging was fifteen. Ellis's own average was between eight and nine a year, but some of these were in Scotland and Ireland. It was in 1922 that the death penalty was abolished for infanticide.

On 13 March of that year, Henry Jacoby, eighteen years old, killed a resident at Spencer's Hotel in London's West End, where he worked as a pantry boy. The victim, Lady White, was the widow of Sir Edward White, a former Chairman of the London County Council. Jacoby killed her in her bed with repeated blows to the head with a hammer.

The boy claimed at his trial that he had thought she was a burglar. He had made various statements which, according to his defence counsel, were extracted from him by the police using third-degree methods. The jury found Jacoby guilty but put in a strong recommendation for mercy which was, however, ignored. His execution was fixed for 7 June 1922 and Ellis was engaged to carry it out. There was a great deal of criticism of the Home Secretary, Edward Shortt, for not granting a reprieve to this lad who, though by no means mentally defective, was a bit of a simpleton.

Major Blake, the Governor of Pentonville, recalled in his reminiscences some years afterwards that Jacoby behaved like a 'thorough little gentleman' in prison, and everyone – even Ellis – was considerably upset by his execution. An article in the *Empire News* in 1934 reported Ellis as saying of Jacoby, 'I saw t'poor lad the day before his death. He was nobbut a child. It was t'most harrowing sight I ever saw in my life. And I'ad to kill him t'next day.' (Ellis saw Jacoby playing cricket with other prisoners in the prison yard.)

[142]

There is no doubt that Ellis was upset by this execution. Many people have said so, and some considered that this hanging had more effect on Ellis than any other. It is said that he talked of resigning after it. He related in his own memoirs that Jacoby, towards the end, had said to one of the prison warders, 'I've told all my friends to buy up all the ropes there are, so that Ellis will have to use a rubber one tomorrow. So I shall bounce back and have a look at him again.'

On the way to his execution, Jacoby turned to Major Blake and said, 'I want to thank you, sir, and everybody here, for all your kindness to me.' Ellis said to Major Blake when it was over, 'I hope that everything was satisfactory, sir.' The governor reported that Ellis spoke in a husky voice and that his eyes were red.

Major Frederick Wallace Blake was a remarkably humane prison officer of long experience. He was appointed Governor of Pentonville in 1919, and witnessed eleven executions. In support of his conviction that the death penalty is indefensible, he wrote: 'Why is it that we feel a horror, as if we are about to commit a crime, when a man is going to be hanged? Why is it that we feel something unholy, something not clean? It is not only my own feelings, but those of the warders, who have to assist in the hanging, are the same. They are given spirits to help them pull themselves together. I shall be glad when this awful form of punishment no longer exists. It is frightful suffering, because one feels deeply the mind of the stricken man, and his thoughts seem to vibrate through the prison and give us some of the terror through which he is passing. And every prisoner in his cell seems to look very white and lined; his nerves are on edge. There is not a sound in the prison until the wretched man has found his last home and gone to a higher Judge.'

On the morning of 4 October 1922, shortly after midnight, Mr Percy Thompson, a shipping clerk, was walking home in Ilford with his wife Edith when a young man named Frederick Bywaters approached them and, after a brief verbal exchange with Thompson, stabbed him twice in the back of the neck and ran away. Mrs Thompson, in great agitation, ran for a doctor, but by the time he arrived, Thompson was dead.

Mrs Thompson and Bywaters were arrested and charged with the murder, and their joint trial began at the Old Bailey on 6 December. The case against Bywaters was a clear and simple one. He admitted that he had stabbed Thompson, but said that he had done so in self-defence because Thompson had threatened to shoot him – a claim that was neither supported by the evidence nor believed by the jury. Mrs Thompson was charged as a principal in the first degree. That is, she was accused of being an accessory before and during the fact, having incited Bywaters to commit the crime and assisted him in doing so.

At the time of the trial, Edith Thompson was an attractive woman of twenty-eight. She had married Percy Thompson in 1915, but her love for him was short-lived; he was an unimaginative and disagreeable character who sometimes ill-treated her. There were no children. Bywaters, who was twenty, had known Edith for some years. He was a ship's writer on a P&O vessel, and during one of his leave periods he stayed with the Thompsons at their Ilford home. He interfered in a quarrel between them when he saw Thompson strike his wife, and afterwards left the house.

He and Edith Thompson became lovers, and when he was away at sea they kept up a regular correspondence. Mrs Thompson faithfully destroyed all the letters written to her by Bywaters, but he kept hers, thus unwittingly killing the thing he loved, for they were produced in devastating evidence against her. Some contained extraordinary reports of what appeared to be attempts on Mrs Thompson's part to poison her husband, and she occasionally enclosed newspaper cuttings describing murders by poisoning, and asked Bywaters for his advice on what to do. From the Crown's point of view, this was evidence enough of her trend of thought, even though Sir Bernard Spilsbury, who had performed an autopsy on the exhumed corpse of Thompson when the letters were discovered, had found no trace of any poisons or their effects. The case for the prosecution was fortified by indications of impatience in the letters, which were taken to refer to a conspiracy to get rid of Thompson.

The defence counsel invited the jury to believe that the references to poisons being administered were products of Mrs Thompson's vivid imagination, and that neither she nor Bywaters took them seriously. Mrs Thompson, unwisely going into the witness box herself, said that she wrote the letters only to convince Bywaters that she would do anything to keep his love, and her impatience referred to their plan to go away together, since Thompson would not hear of a divorce.

The jury of eleven men and one woman retired to consider their verdict during the afternoon of the fifth day, and after two hours and eleven minutes found both defendants guilty of murder. When the judge passed the sentence of death on them, Mrs Thompson cried out, 'I am not guilty; oh, God, I am not guilty!'

The trial was far from being a legal classic in any respect. The Crown's use of the letters was highly questionable, as was the whole procedure of the joint trial – the defence being hampered by the need to say nothing in favour of one prisoner which might be prejudicial to the other. The judge's summing-up was appallingly misleading. He omitted to mention Spilsbury's very significant evidence, and gave full expression to his personal distaste for the couple's illicit love affair, as if they were on trial for adultery. Above all, if Mrs Thompson had not insisted on going into the witness box herself, against the advice of her counsel, it is doubtful if Bywaters could have been convicted of more than manslaughter, and she would then have been acquitted.

There are some grounds for believing that the passages in the letters from which a conspiracy to murder was inferred, were in fact concerned with measures to counteract the effects of sexual intercourse, and it has been suggested that Sir Henry Curtis-Bennett, Mrs Thompson's counsel, was well aware of this, but dare not bring it out in court as it would brand his client not only as an adulteress but also as an abortionist, and do her case more harm than good.

However that may be, Mrs Thompson was condemned to death. The appeals of both prisoners were dismissed on 21 December and the executions were provisionally fixed for 2 and 3 January 1923. Ellis agreed to carry out both executions, but at that time, having followed the case with his customary zeal, he fully expected Mrs Thompson to be reprieved.

Public opinion was sharply divided in its reaction to the verdict and the sentence. England was going through what Macaulay called one of its 'periodical fits of morality' after the horrors of the war, and many people felt that Edith Thompson was justly condemned as a wicked scheming woman who had corrupted the innocent young Bywaters and led him to commit this terrible crime. On the other hand, a large body of opinion believed her plea of innocence, and even to some of those who thought her guilty, the thought of her execution was abhorrent, for no woman had been executed in Britain since

Rhoda Willis, fifteen years before. A petition for Mrs Thompson to be reprieved, containing thousands of signatures, was sent to the Home Secretary, but to no avail. The popular image of justice as an eye-for-an-eye avenger prevailed over the view that the execution would be an act of retrogression.

Edith Thompson, as Rebecca West wrote at the time, 'dreamed the wrong dreams. . . . Humanity has its need to dream. And if you do not give humanity the good music, the good pictures, the good books that will set it dreaming right . . . it will dream bad dreams that lead to lies and death.'

Ellis, meanwhile, had received a further communication from the Essex Sheriff's office at Chelmsford, informing him that both executions would probably take place on the same day at different prisons, 'in which case it will be necessary to employ two executioners. We should be glad to know whether you would be prepared to act at the execution of Mrs Thompson on Tuesday the 9th January at Holloway, or on Friday the 5th January at the same place.'

It is chilling to reflect that a woman's life depended on the hangman's convenience. After pondering on the matter for some hours, Ellis's sense of duty, supported to some extent, no doubt, by the prospect of £10 plus expenses, overcame his distaste for hanging women, and he confirmed that he would arrive at Holloway on Monday 8 January. If he had planned to take his whippets out on the Tuesday, Mrs Thompson might have been 'put away' four days earlier. It might have been a mercy for her.

In the twenty-nine days between her sentence and execution, Edith Thompson became a mere shadow of a human being. It was said that her last hours in the shadow of the gallows were passed in a state of near-collapse.

Half a mile away at Pentonville, Governor Blake had formed a good impression of Bywaters, and talked with him for a while on the evening of the eighth. During the course of their conversation, Bywaters, who showed little concern for his own fate, swore to Major Blake that Mrs Thompson was innocent. (After his retirement through ill-health in 1926, Major Blake reported the conversation in his reminiscences in the *London Evening News*. He was promptly charged with an offence under the Official Secrets Act and fined £250. The Crown's case was summed up by *The Times* as follows: 'In this case Bywaters was represented as saying that the woman was innocent. It was undesirable to make such a statement public, for there are always persons who believe that what a man said just before he died must be true, and great uneasiness might be caused by the publication of such an assertion.')

Ellis, meanwhile, had received a few angry anonymous letters. One writer said: 'If you go and pull that lever and take a woman's life, Government ain't to answer for it. God'll send the bill to you.' And another: 'Dear Sir, – Be a man and don't hang a woman. You know you have to die yourself in a few years. Just think.'

But hangmen are not distinguished for their thinking, and undeterred, Ellis decided to try air travel for the first time. On 8 January he flew from Manchester to Croydon. The flight cost him two pounds five shillings. I have not been able to discover if this expense was borne by the Sheriff in question – the rail fare from Manchester to London in 1923 was only two pounds six shillings *return*. But Ellis heard later that the aircraft had crashed on its return flight, killing the pilot and two passengers.

Two assistants had been appointed, named Phillips and Baxter, and one of them met Ellis in the city and they went to Holloway together. There were some armed police on duty outside to prevent a threatened Sinn Fein raid on the prison to rescue a woman convicted of hiding firearms at Woolwich. Dr John Morton, who was both prison governor and medical officer, spoke anxiously to Ellis about Mrs Thompson's condition, and asked what he would do if she fainted. Ellis asked him to have a chair ready in case, and advised him to give her a stiff dose of brandy five minutes before the time.

Next morning, Ellis made his final adjustments to the apparatus and peered into the condemned cell, where he saw the wardresses 'fastening Mrs Thompson's suspenders', as he reported in his memoirs, though – anxious to preserve the image of his essential respectability – he added that he immediately went away, 'not wishing to spy on a woman getting dressed.' It was a dismal wet morning, but a fairly large crowd had gathered outside, and mounted police had been called out to keep the roads clear. Opponents of capital punishment mingled with cranks drawn there by morbid curiosity. A few women were kneeling in prayer.

At three minutes to nine, Ellis took up his position and heard a low moan from the cell. The chaplain, Rev. Glanville Murray, and two wardresses, were trying to console Mrs Thompson. She was, however, nearly unconscious and a dreadful sight. Ellis walked off to the execution chamber. Two officers picked up Edith Thompson and carried her in. Ellis remarked later that she looked as if she were dead already. Her head was sunk on her breast and she seemed to be oblivious to the proceedings. He thought she had been doped with brandy at intervals instead of being revived with it at the proper time as he had requested. The officers held her up on the trap doors while Ellis placed the bag over her head and adjusted the noose. He quickly pulled the lever and Edith Thompson's troubles, at any rate, were over.

The practice of tolling the prison bell had ceased by this time, and outside in the cold and damp January air, the solemn crowd stood silently waiting for the notice of execution to be posted on the prison gate.

At Pentonville, meanwhile, Frederick Bywaters had been executed at the same time. Tom Pierrepoint has been credited with doing this job (by his nephew Albert among others), but it seems also to have been claimed by one William Willis, whose career was mostly as an assistant. He wrote in his diary, apropos of Bywaters, 'I told him, "Look at me and you'll be all right." He walked firmly, but not too quick. Death instant.' This Willis carried out an execution at Strangeways on 15 December 1925, when he hanged one Johnson, using as his assistant the same Phillips who was Ellis's second assistant in the Thompson execution. Willis assisted at over a hundred executions, but I have reason to believe that he subsequently committed suicide. My efforts to find official confirmation of this have so far failed.

Everyone directly involved in the Thompson execution was considerably distraught by the horrible scene they had witnessed. The chaplain, who had asked for a chair to be placed for him as he was prone to spells of dizziness, suffered a serious nervous breakdown, and resigned. He afterwards declared that 'the impulse to rush in and save her by force was almost too great for me.' Rev. Murray also told the Select Committee on Capital Punishment in 1930 that 'no one can leave the slaughter shed without a deep sense of humiliation, horror and shame.' Other prison officials present retired or resigned within a short time. Miss Margery Fry, in a statement to the Royal Commission on Capital Punishment in 1950, said that she had 'never seen a person so changed in appearance by mental suffering as the governor appeared to me to be'. Dr Morton's deputy, Miss Cronin, told Miss Fry that in her opinion, if Mrs Thompson had been spared, she could have become a very good woman.

Mr Beverley Baxter, MP, speaking in the House of Commons on 14 April 1948, said: 'Two of the warders who had taken part in that execution came to my office, and their faces were not human. I can assure you, Sir, they were like people out of another world. Edith Thompson had disintegrated as a human being on her way to the gallows, and yet somehow they had to get her there. . . . Those two warders . . . said to me, "Use your influence; never again must a woman be hanged."' Ellis himself described the affair as the most nerve-racking experience he had ever had.

He had not finished with women yet, however. On 10 October of the same year, he hanged the first woman to be executed in Scotland for more than half a century. Mrs Susan Newell was sentenced for the murder of a schoolboy of twelve. The trial had created a sensation, revealing that she had wheeled the dead boy's body in a go-cart eleven miles in broad daylight in order to dispose of it, with her eight year-old daughter sitting atop the bundle. No motive for the murder was ever found, and the woman was doubtless insane and should not have been hanged.

Although the execution was carried out without any trouble at Duke Street Prison, Glasgow, and Mrs Newell met her death 'unflinchingly', Ellis's nervousness – understandable this time – led him to pinion her arms insecurely, and she got her hands free and objected to the white bag. Ellis's explanation of the incident was that he thought she was going to be awkward and merely wound the strap round her wrists instead of fastening it properly, in order to get it all over the more speedily. His assistant on this occasion was the man named Baxter from Hertford who had also assisted at the Thompson execution.

Ellis's health was now deteriorating. He was suffering more from neuritis and was having many sleepless nights. At last he decided to retire, and sent a letter of resignation to the Prison Commissioners in March 1924 in which he said: 'In severing a connection with your Department which has extended over a period of twenty-three years, I would like to express my deep appreciation of the courtesy, civility and assistance that has always been extended to me by prison officials all over the kingdom whenever I have been brought into contact with them for the purpose of carrying out the law's decree.

'I have felt honoured, too, on numerous occasions, by your confidence in my discretion, a trust which I hope you will agree that I on my part have always faithfully endeavoured to justify. If at any time in the future you should find any need for my services in an advisory capacity, I shall be glad to render any aid that lies in my power.'

His resignation being accepted, Ellis carried out his last execution at Leeds. He had served the same length of time as the immortal Jack Ketch. Only four hangmen up to that time had exceeded his twenty-three years. He had carried out 203 executions, some of them in Scotland and Ireland. In Scotland, the executioner's fee was higher than in England – £15 plus expenses. It is therefore probable that he had received an average of about ninety pounds a year during his sixteen years as an official executioner, and made in all a figure approaching £2,000 for putting his fellow men and women to death. Not that his income from hanging ended with his retirement. But for the time being, he now attempted to settle down to a more peaceful life of haircutting and whippet breeding.

Peace did not come so easily, however. His barber's shop had become something of a tourist attraction, and people stared into it for a sight of the hangman. He received many letters from people wanting to know how to get his job, one such coming from as far away as Bombay. He was inundated with requests of this kind and with offers for his memoirs or invitations to lecture. He was once offered £1,000 for a series of lectures on Crippen.

Ellis agreed to write his reminiscences for Thomson's *Weekly News*. The first of his articles appeared in April 1924 under the general title 'Secrets of My Life Revealed'. He lost no time in demonstrating that he was just an ordinary bloke who liked 'a bob on the 'osses' and supported Rochdale Hornets. A photograph of him appeared with each week's article, sometimes fondling a dog, or standing in the garden with his wife; his high collar and big moustache his permanent distinguishing features. As *Weekly News* readers were settling down in their armchairs to absorb his revelations, however, the author was lying in Rochdale Infirmary recovering from a severe face wound, self-inflicted.

Mrs Ellis had been woken up on the morning of Sunday 24 August, at about one o'clock, by a loud bang, and going downstairs, she found her husband lying on the floor of the living room, bleeding fiercely from the neck, and with a revolver beside him. She bandaged him up and called a policeman, who found Ellis sitting in a chair with his face bandaged and his shirt covered in blood. He managed to say to the constable, 'I have shot myself. I am sorry. I shall say no more.' He was taken to hospital and treated for a fractured jaw; the bullet having entered his neck under the chin and come out over the jawbone.

When Ellis had sufficiently recovered, on the following Wednesday, he was taken to Rochdale Magistrates' Court and charged with attempting to commit suicide. He appeared in the dock heavily bandaged, with three days' growth of beard, and was very pale and drawn. He leaned wearily on the side of the dock during the hearing. After listening to the evidence, the chairman of the magistrates asked Ellis if he had any reason to offer for doing this foolish thing, and Ellis replied that he had not. It was stated that he had been drinking on the night before the attempt.

The chairman then procured two promises from Ellis – neither of which he kept. The first was that he would give up intoxicating drink, and the other that he would not repeat his attempt to kill himself. The chairman also delivered himself of the following observations: 'I am sorry to see you here, Ellis. I have known you for a long time. If your aim had been as true as some (sic) of the drops you have given, it would have been a bad job for you. Your life has been given back to you, and I hope you will make good use of it, and lead a good life in atonement.' So saying, he bound Ellis over to keep the peace for twelve months and discharged him, and Ellis went home.

When Thomas Pierrepoint heard of the incident, he remarked to his nephew Albert, with more than a hint of professional jealousy, 'Bloody hell, Ellis has tried to commit suicide! He should have done it bloody years ago. It was impossible to work with him.'

After more than twenty years of travelling and excitement, Ellis's ideas of the good life had perhaps become a little obscured. At least, the uneventful life of a hairdresser was not sufficiently attractive to prevent him from considering various offers from the entertainment business, and he soon found one to his liking.

On Monday, 12 December 1927, he sent the *Daily Express* into one of its customary fits of hysterics:

HANGMAN ACTS IN A PLAY
Crowds rush to see real executioner
Ellis
Gruesome death cell scene

Gravesend, Monday

A professional hangman became a professional actor tonight at the Grand Theatre, Gravesend. What the Actors' Association will say about it and what the public will think remain to be seen.

He was John Ellis, the barber, of Rochdale, who was the official executioner for many years, and retired in 1924. Ellis appeared as the hangman in a new melodrama, 'The Life and Adventures of Charles Peace', produced for the first time. He had to execute the king of burglars and murderers, Charles Peace, and carried it through in the full sight of an enthusiastically excited audience with the promptness and expedition that comes from long practice. Mr Thomas Morris, who took the part of Charles Peace, was the actor well and truly hanged. I saw Ellis in his dressing room beneath the stage a few minutes before he made his debut. His conversation was more than a little gruesome. 'I am feeling more nervous now than at any real execution,' (he said). 'I hope it all goes all right. If Mr Morris complains afterwards he will be the first one that I have handled who has ever done so'. . . .

The play brought storms of protest from individuals all over the country, as well as from official bodies. A question was drafted for the House of Commons asking the Home Secretary 'whether his attention has been drawn to the play which is now being performed at the Gravesend Theatre in which John Ellis, an ex-hangman, appears in the role of executioner and gives a presentation of an execution on the stage, and whether he will take steps to prevent the continuance of this demoralising spectacle.' The manager of the company saw the Lord Chamberlain for half an hour on 15 December, but would not disclose the results of the interview to reporters outside.

But faced with such an uproar, the curtain had to come down after a very short run, and Ellis's exit as an actor followed hot on the heels of his début. All the props, with the exception of the scaffold, were sold, and Ellis gave his share of the proceeds to a poor children's fund in Manchester. As for the scaffold, he had it taken home and stored in a nearby garage. It might come in useful some time.

Charles Duff told me that Ellis collected press cuttings about himself ('only the best ones, though') and that one evening he was sitting by the fire reading them, and thinking over old jobs, when he fell asleep and let his precious records fall into the fire, and they were all destroyed.

Ellis assured Mr Duff in an interview that he had never bungled an execution. 'We don't make mistakes nowadays,' he said; 'it's all taped and worked out, and even if there should be some slight mishap, the whole government machine goes all out to save the hangman's face. *They have to.*'

Ellis soon found himself in the limelight again. His retirement had passed practically unnoticed, and his attempted suicide had been played down as much as possible, but he seemed to have a genius for attracting attention to himself, and now the sensation-hungry reporters buzzed round him like wasps. Ellis took the opportunity to say a few things that were on his mind.

'It is often rumoured', he said, 'that my retirement in 1924 was the outcome of the Mrs Thompson case. It was nothing of the kind. My reasons were altogether different. Mrs Thompson was the first woman I actually hanged, and it was my most upsetting experience, but there was another after that – Mrs Newell at Glasgow.'

He also gave his views about the executioner's pay, echoing Berry of Bradford: 'Hangmen are not paid as they ought to be, and there is no pension. Today the pay is the same as twenty years ago, though the assistant gets a guinea more. But the executioner should have a salary. I have been as long as nine months without an execution to deal with. I had to carry on another business – I am a barber – because there was not a living in it.'

But there was money in the entertainment business, and Ellis's next venture took him on tour round some of the country's seaside resorts and fairgrounds, where he gave lectures on his working methods, illustrated by a model scaffold (rescued from storage) and demonstrations of its operation. Needless to say, he did a roaring trade. Eager holiday-makers and sightseers flocked in at sixpence a time for the doubtful privilege of witnessing this exhibition.

Ellis accepted an offer to take his show to Southall Faiground in London for a fortnight at £20 a week, but at the end of the first day he broke down with congestion of the lungs, and had to spend a week in bed. After that he had an eight days engagement in Redcar, and

[153]

received numerous offers from Blackpool and other places, often turning them down if the money offered did not satisfy him.

When his touring ended, Ellis had the scaffold erected in his back garden – a macabre decoration of the landscape, adding to the misery of the slump, which was then at its height. All over the north of England queues of unemployed and miserable men stood in the rain outside the labour exchanges. This reflected on Ellis's business as a barber, and he now found it hard to earn an adequate living from hairdressing. It came to the point when he had to take a spare-time job selling counter-cloths to public houses. His health was becoming worse. He was drinking heavily, and friends and neighbours have reported that he began to behave rather strangely at this time.

A Mr Frederick Bowman was negotiating with Ellis for the publication of his memoirs in book form. On 18 September 1932, Ellis wrote to him: 'Dear Mr Bowman, – Many thanks for letter. Please excuse delay in answering. I do not close till 8 o'clock and do all my writing at home. This week I have been busy, as we are holding our harvest festival, yesterday and today, belonging to a lodge I am a member of, the RAOB. . . .'

On Tuesday the twentieth, Ellis was later than usual arriving home. He had his tea and went into the parlour for a smoke. He had been drinking. At a quarter past seven he sat down at the table and had a cup of tea and a little to eat. Mrs Ellis and her daughter Ivy were in the kitchen. Suddenly Ellis jumped up from his chair, pulling at his collar, and rushed into the kitchen. He seized a cut-throat razor from a shelf and shouted 'I'll kill you.' His wife ran out of the house. His alarmed daughter asked him what was the matter, and Ellis, lurching forward, shouted, 'I'll cut your head off.' She also ran outside, and then her brother appeared on the scene.

He went into the house and saw his father, with the razor still in his hand and two savage gashes in his throat, sinking to the floor. When a policeman arrived, he found Ellis lying face downwards in a spreading pool of blood. The executioner had done his last job.

At the inquest Mrs Ellis said that her husband, who was fifty-eight, had been depressed by ill-health for eighteen months, and had threatened suicide more than once when he had been drinking. Relatives said that he had not had a good night's sleep for many years. The coroner gave his opinion that Ellis took his own life in a sudden frenzy of madness, and recorded the customary verdict, Suicide while of Unsound Mind. One newspaper reported that the Prison Commissioners had known Ellis as one of the 'coolest and most self-possessed hangmen ever known,' but Billington, who had known him rather better, once said that he wondered how Ellis stuck it so long, 'being so nervous and anxious about everything going OK.'

It has been popularly believed ever since that Ellis's suicide was a direct result of his execution of Edith Thompson, but although this experience undoubtedly had a bad effect on him, as indeed it did on everyone present, there is no real evidence that it was the chief contributor to his depressed state of mind, even though his son told a newspaper that the family 'all knew what prevented him from sleeping. I do not think it was the memory of the 200 executions he had taken part in but the recollection of hanging two women that drove him to suicide.'

We can safely ignore the sentiments attributed to him by the well-meaning but eccentric Mrs Violet Van der Elst, a wealthy campaigner against capital punishment who was regularly to be found holding her vigils among the crowds outside prison gates on the mornings of executions. She alleged that Ellis would afterwards 'sit alone for many hours, his eyes staring in front of him, and when anyone spoke to him he used to whisper "I wish I hadn't done it, I wish I hadn't done it." And if pressed to tell what he had done, he would say "Hung an innocent woman."' There is nothing to suggest that Ellis thought Mrs Thompson innocent, and we can judge Mrs Van der Elst's reliability by her assertion that at the time of Ellis's first suicide attempt, he tried to hang himself. I am not sure if Mrs Van der Elst was the source of the story that Edith Thompson's hair turned white between her sentence and execution. The same story has often been told about condemned prisoners (George Joseph Smith, for example), but such a phenomenon is in fact impossible. No doubt there was a great deal of exaggeration. There was even one allegation that the drop had caused some of Mrs Thompson's internal organs to fall out. But the government could hardly complain at ill-founded rumour if it insisted on concealing the facts.

It has also been argued frequently that the execution of Henry Jacoby had a permanent effect on Ellis's mind. The truth is more probably that Ellis's long experience of death-dealing precipitated the birth of a mental state which had been in embryo for some years and was conceived, perhaps, quite early in his career. His heavy drinking aggravated his ill-health and depression, and the drinking, as with so many other executioners, was a result of the fearful responsibility, which he had taken on as a thoughtless young adventurer, becoming too great a load for his mind to bear.

IX

A Family Affair

No doubt the ambition that prompts an average of five applications a week for the post of hangman reveals psychological
qualities of a sort that no State would wish to foster in its
citizens.

Report of the Royal Commission
on Capital Punishment, 1953

HENRY ALBERT PIERREPOINT was born, doubtless of Huguenot stock,
at the village of Clayton, near Bradford. He conceived the idea of
becoming an executioner when he read, as a boy, of the appointment
of the local man, James Berry, to succeed Marwood and Binns.

Henry, or Harry as he was invariably called, was one of his parents' ten
children, of whom four died young. He went to work, at the age of twelve,
in the worsted mill at Clayton. Later, he started a carrier's business in the
village, but eventually moved to Huddersfield when he married a girl
from Manchester, and worked in the Huddersfield gasworks, leaving the
carrier's business in the hands of his older brother Thomas.

Henry Pierrepoint was twenty-five when he wrote to Home Secretary Ridley, and was asked to go to Strangeways for an interview with
the governor, Mr Cruikshank. When he arrived there, he was too
embarrassed to tell the warder at the gate what he had really come
for, so muttered something about a post in the prison service. He was
promptly marched off for a thorough medical, stripped, weighed and
measured, and packed off home as being too short. He wrote to the
governor saying that he had been turned away without his interview,
and after sorting out this confusion satisfactorily, he was sent to
Newgate for a fortnight's training.

His wife had had their first child by this time – a daughter. Like
Berry's wife, Pierrepoint's tried hard to persuade her husband
against taking such a job, but he was determined to do it. At Newgate,

he was put in the attic where hangmen stayed when engaged for executions there. He found their various initials carved in the woodwork. He completed his training, and discreet enquiries were made in Yorkshire about his character and the people he associated with. His first offer of a job came soon afterwards, but the condemned man in question was reprieved, and as we have seen, the first execution Pierrepoint attended was as James Billington's assistant when Marcel Faugeron was hanged at Newgate in 1901. After the execution had been carried out, the prison doctor took Pierrepoint's wrist and felt his pulse, saying, 'You'll do.' A few days later, he received a letter from the Prison Commissioners saying that he had been placed on the Home Office list of approved executioners. In the first fifteen months, he took part in the execution of fifteen people, assisting both James and William Billington, but also carrying out executions as principal himself. 'I was very ambitious for duty,' he wrote later. 'I loved my work on the scaffold.'

It was only for about five years though, between the beginning of 1905 and 1910, that Harry Pierrepoint held the 'number one' position among the appointed executioners. By the later date, it is clear that John Ellis took precedence. This was undoubtedly due to Ellis's greater discretion, at least in his early years. Their rivalry was such that Pierrepoint remarked later, 'If I ever meet Ellis, I'll kill him – it doesn't matter if it is in the church!'

Ellis was Pierrepoint's assistant at an execution at Swansea early in May 1909, and it seems likely that there was some undisclosed friction between the two on that or a similar occasion. There are dark hints in Albert Pierrepoint's book of hangmen undermining the reputations of their rivals, and there was clearly a lot of professional jealousy in the business. (In the rivalry between Yorkshire and Lancashire in producing hangmen, Lancashire may be said to have won by a neck.) Henry Pierrepoint undoubtedly felt aggrieved that he was not senior to Ellis, having begun as an assistant in the same year, and having carried out executions himself before Ellis.

The Yorkshireman's trouble was that he had a weakness for alcohol. He was, as his son Albert confirmed, a sociable fellow and an easy talker. Whether he was easily led or was himself the leader is open to question. He would leave home to do a job somewhere and not return until he was 'skint', having gone off on a binge with friends, sometimes for as long as a week.

Harry Pierrepoint, like most executioners, kept a diary of his jobs, but as well as recording names, dates and prisons, he noted the age, height and weight of his victims and details about their necks – whether they were thick, flabby, or thin and weak, and so on. He also noted his travelling expenses. He invented a special pinioning strap for a condemned man who had only one arm, and was also noted for his unorthodox habit of putting the white hood on the victim's head *after* the noose was in position. It was generally accepted in the 'trade' that if the cap were put on first, it would be less distressing for the victim, because he would not be so acutely aware of the noose being adjusted round his neck. The noose also prevented the cap from coming off at the moment of the drop and revealing the man's face to the official onlookers. There seems to have been more than a hint of sadism in Pierrepoint's practice, because there was no logical reason for it.

Harry Pierrepoint had been an executioner for only a few years when he persuaded his brother Thomas, his senior by six years, to become one too. He trained Tom himself in the stable at Clayton, near the Black Bull and the triangular village green with its horse-trough. When Tom went to Pentonville for his official training, his instructor said to him after a few days, 'You don't want any more. Your Harry's been teaching you.'

Thomas Pierrepoint was a different sort of man from his impressionable brother. Steadier and stronger in character, he was also more reserved, and would not talk about his experiences, except eventually to his nephew Albert, to whom he once said, 'If you can't do it without whisky, don't do it at all.' Tom continued to run the carrier's business at Clayton and also ran the village general store with his wife. Hanging was not his only sideline – he was a bookie as well.

Though he remained on the Home Office list for over forty years – one of the longest periods on record – he never wrote his memoirs, unlike his brother and his nephew, who described his uncle in old age sitting at home 'champing at his pobs'. (For those unfamiliar with northern feeding habits, I ought to explain that 'pobs' are pieces of white bread soaked in warm milk, usually given to sick children or to adults who have lost their teeth or need easily digestible food in times of illness.)

It was Henry Pierrepoint who hanged Arthur Devereux at Pentonville in August 1905, for the murder of his wife and their twin sons;

and Thomas Pierrepoint who assisted Ellis at the execution of George Joseph Smith in 1915.

On 14 August 1907, Harry Pierrepoint, with Thomas as his assistant, executed Rhoda Willis at Cardiff. There was a widespread rumour at the time that Ellis had been offered this job and, because of his reluctance to hang a woman, had refused. There would be a hangman's strike, it was said, and the woman would have to be reprieved. The Home Office is said to have received several offers from private citizens to do the job, including one from a woman. (Pierrepoint said in his memoirs later that he met one woman once who offered him a financial inducement to get her on the list of official executioners.) Other executioners, however, did not share Ellis's scruples, and the brothers Pierrepoint went to Cardiff to see the woman off.

Rhoda Willis, said to be a beautiful woman, was also known as Mrs Leslie James. She had taken a one-day-old baby from its unmarried mother on payment of £6, then smothered it on a train. It will not have escaped the notice of readers that many of the women executed around this period were baby-farmers. There are fashions in crime, dictated by social conditions and attitudes. Rhoda Willis was hanged on her forty-fourth birthday. Her execution was the last involving a woman for over fifteen years, and she was the last woman executed by Harry Pierrepoint, who wrote long afterwards: 'I was attracted and fascinated by the blaze of her yellow hair, and as she left her cell and walked in the procession to the scaffold the sunlight caused her hair to gleam like molten gold. I had hanged women before but never one so beautiful. . . .'

In the following year Harry and Tom did a job together not far from home when they hanged John Ellwood at Armley Gaol in Leeds for the murder of a cashier.

1909 was a good year for the chief hangman, putting a few extra pounds in his pocket to be spent in the pubs wherever he happened to find himself. Among his victims was Madar dal Dhingra, an Indian student who had shot Colonel Sir William Wylie and Doctor Cowas Lalcaca, for political reasons, in the vestibule of the Imperial Institute in Kensington. The Parsee assassin weighed only 100 pounds, a featherweight unprovided for in Home Office calculations. Pierrepoint gave him eight feet three inches.

Near the end of that year Harry Pierrepoint was called to Durham to execute one Abel Atherton, a miner who had murdered his former landlady, Mrs Patrick. She had evicted him because of his unwonted attentions to her fifteen-year-old daughter. The execution is of interest because the authorities at Durham held out longer than most against government pressure to exclude newspaper reporters from executions, and the hanging of Atherton was described by a local journalist.

Pierrepoint's own account related how he went to the condemned cell and, tapping the terrified young man on the shoulder, said, 'Keep your pluck up, my lad,' as he pinioned him. The reporter described how the ritual procession walked into his view as the first stroke of eight o'clock sounded on the Assize Court clock. 'On the drop,' he continued, 'there was the ankle strap lying ready for use, and across the drop there were two stout boards with foot-pieces, ready for the attendant warders to render Atherton assistance if required.

'At the door the Chaplain stepped aside, and the remainder of the procession passed inside. The moment the threshold had been passed, Atherton's cap had been removed from his head, and the executioners urged him forward to the mark in the drop. The assistant instantly dropped onto his knees and fastened the ankle strap, and while Pierrepoint was adjusting the noose, Atherton in a husky voice cried out: 'Yer hanging an innocent man.' Pierrepoint whipped the white cap from his pocket, drew it over the condemned man's head, stepped aside and pulled the lever, and Atherton shot from view before – incredible as it may seem – the clock had ceased striking. Atherton was given a drop of 7 feet 3 inches, and death was absolutely instantaneous. As the Press representatives stepped forward and looked into the pit the body was hanging perfectly still.'

One of Henry Pierrepoint's jobs came to him in Jersey. It was the first execution in the Channel Islands for over thirty years, and the previous one had been carried out in public. Tom Connan had murdered his brother-in-law. Hundreds waited to see Pierrepoint arrive, and after the job was done the local authorities, according to his own evidence, feted him and sang 'For he's a jolly good fellow' when he was entertained for dinner.

It was Ireland, however – as always – that provided Pierrepoint with some of his most memorable experiences. At Armagh he prepared to hang a man whom he thought innocent of the murder for which he had been sentenced. (One may well ask why he accepted the job, in that case.) As he was about to pinion the man's legs, the prisoner shouted 'Executioner!' Pierrepoint carried on, adjusting the noose. 'Executioner!' the man said again, then exclaimed 'Guilty!'

'I was staggered,' Pierrepoint recalled, 'never expecting to hear a confession, the prisoner having carried himself so firm and collected. My blood was up. I pulled the lever violently. I felt I could have pulled it from its bearings. Never in all my career was I so much deceived by a condemned culprit.'

Harry Pierrepoint resigned in 1914, after about eleven years as an executioner. He had taken part in the execution of more than a hundred people. (Pierrepoint himself laid claim to 107 executions, rather less than the 142 attributed to him by some reports.) His son Albert hinted in his autobiography that his father's resignation may have had something to do with Ellis.

Harry and his wife now had five children, and he was still working at the gasworks in Huddersfield. But his wife had never really felt at home in Yorkshire, and during the First World War the family moved to Failsworth, near Manchester. By this time Harry had written his reminiscences for Thomson's *Weekly News*. But he was a sick man. Towards the end of 1922, he rewrote his memoirs for *Reynolds Newspaper*, which advertised the forthcoming series by describing the ex-hangman as a man of 'tremendous strength. His nerves are like unto finely-tempered steel. He can talk with equanimity about a grim scene he has witnessed when a soul was on the threshold of another world.' But about a month after his final article appeared, he died, early in December, aged forty-eight. Neither the contemporary newspapers nor his son Albert indicated the cause of death, and I have been unable to trace his death certificate.

Meanwhile, brother Tom carried on, and in fact remained on the list of executioners for thirty years after Harry's resignation. He sucked sweets during executions, and clearly took the gruesome task in his stride more than some of his immediate predecessors and contemporaries. He hanged Jack Field (nineteen) and William Gray (twenty-nine) at Wandsworth in 1921, for the murder of a seventeen-year-old typist in the course of robbing her at Eastbourne; and Albert Burrows (sixty-two) at Nottingham in 1923, for the murder of Hannah Calladine (a woman whom he had married bigamously) and three children, one a boy of four whom he had sexually assaulted before throwing him down a mine-shaft.

In March 1924, when Ellis retired, Tom Pierrepoint became the undisputed 'number one' hangman, and in August that year he executed Jean Pierre Vacquier, the so-called 'Byfleet murderer', at Wandsworth, for poisoning with strychnine his lover's husband, Alfred Jones. Tom Pierrepoint had already taken part in about twice as many executions as his brother, and still had a long way to go. Nearly a month later, young Albert Pierrepoint's Aunt Lizzie told him that his Uncle Tom was 'doing that Mahon at Wandsworth'.

Patrick Mahon was another Eastbourne operator, and one of the most notorious murderers of the period between the wars. He killed Emily Kaye, one of many women with whom he had affairs, after inducing her with false promises of marriage to hand over most of her savings, whilst she was staying in a bungalow he had rented for his foul purpose at the Crumbles. Mahon, who was already married, cut Miss Kaye's body into pieces, burning the head and legs in the sitting-room fireplace, boiling other pieces in a pan, and throwing others from a train. He said at his trial that he put the head on the fire during a thunderstorm, and the eyes opened just as there was a flash of lightning, which made him rush from the room in terror. He put the torso in a trunk, and when it was found, Sir Bernard Spilsbury established that Emily Kaye had been pregnant when she was murdered.

Four jurors in turn were taken ill during the course of the trial and had to be replaced. Mahon was visibly shaken when a clap of thunder was heard in court. The jury did not believe his claim that Emily Kaye had died accidentally when they had quarrelled and she had attacked him. When Tom Pierrepoint had prepared the condemned man on the trap doors and drew the bolt, Mahon jumped, but his body merely hit the back edge of the trap as he fell, and his death was said to have been instantaneous.

Baxter, the man from Hertford and sometime assistant to Ellis and the Pierrepoints, carried out an execution himself in 1928, when he and another occasional assistant of Tom Pierrepoint between them hanged Frederick Browne and Pat Kennedy, at Pentonville and Wandsworth respectively, for the murder of PC Gutteridge in an Essex lane. They were middle-aged car thieves, and having shot the policeman when he stopped them, one of them, probably Browne, shot him in both eyes at close range as he lay on the ground moaning.

In that same year, when Tom Pierrepoint had executed a man at

Lincoln in January, the coroner asked the prison governor how long had elapsed between the executioner entering the cell and the prisoner being dropped, and was told: 'I am not allowed to say anything except that a very short interval elapsed.'

'Are you allowed to say how long the body remained hanging?' the coroner asked.

'No, sir, I am not.'

The list of approved executioners in January 1929 was as follows:

> Thomas Pierrepoint
> Robert Baxter
> Robert Wilson
> Thomas Phillips
> Henry Pollard
> Lionel Mann
> Alfred Allen

Only Pierrepoint and Baxter had conducted executions at this time. The others had acted as assistants. Pierrepoint was from Yorkshire, Baxter from Hertford, and Allen from Wolverhampton. The other four were Lancashire men.

Alfred Allen had been a Provost Sergeant in the First World War, and put up as his chief qualification for the job that he had been present at military executions by firing squad. He was thirty-nine years old and worked for the Sunbeam Motor Company. But at his first execution, when he assisted Baxter in the hanging of Trevor Edwards at Swansea in December 1928, he fell into the pit when Baxter pulled the lever. He was not seriously hurt, and no blame was attached to anyone for this repetition of the Billington/Warbrick incident. The prison governor reported that Baxter was 'quicker than anyone I have seen', and Allen was just too slow getting clear, having 'a defect in one eye.'

The Secretary of State noted ruefully on the file that they did not seem to be having much luck with their recent recruits, Allen having 'nearly executed himself', and one Rowe resigning almost immediately after his appointment. Rowe was a former Coldstream Guardsman who had evidently had quite enough after his first execution. Another man, Edward Taylor, had also been deleted from the list after only a few months in the job.

None of the assistants at that time appear to have presented any challenge to the two top men, but it is clear that rivalry existed between Pierrepoint and Baxter, for they were both officially warned in 1928 that 'touting for business' could lead to their names being removed from the list.

One of Tom Pierrepoint's innovations in the technique of hanging was to improve the washer which prevented the noose from slipping. It was possible in certain circumstances for a plain leather washer not to hold the brass ring firmly in place, and Pierrepoint invented a rubber washer which was cut to form claw-grips on the rope, which would not slip in any circumstances.

1930 was a bad year in the execution business. Not only were there only five hangings in Britain during that year, but a House of Commons Select Committee, appointed to consider whether another penalty should be substituted for the sentence of death, recommended the abolition of the death penalty for an experimental period of five years. The Committee had concluded that capital punishment could be abolished 'without endangering life or property, or impairing the security of society.' This view was ignored by the government of the day, but in the following year pregnant women were given immunity from the death penalty. The movement for abolition was gaining ground, and threatening the hangmen's income.

At Bedford prison in March 1931, Alfred Rouse visited 'Uncle Tom's cabin'. Rouse had murdered an unknown victim and burnt the body in his (Rouse's) car at Hardingstone, Northamptonshire, in order to fake his own death, having made promises of marriage to several women who bore his children, and being financially embarrassed by maintenance orders against him.

In May 1934, two men, Frederick Parker and Albert Probert, were hanged at Wandsworth for the murder of an elderly shopkeeper at Portslade, Sussex, in the course of stealing £6 from his till. The execution was the last at which a newspaper reporter was allowed to be present, the Sheriff of Sussex having invited a crime reporter from the Press Association to witness the hanging. At the inquest on the two bodies, the coroner asked the governor if he had any objection to the name of the executioner being published, and was told that it was not usual.

In December, Pierrepoint was the hangman when Ethel Major was executed at Hull, for poisoning her husband with strychnine, and in April 1936 Tom Pierrepoint, with his young nephew Albert as his assistant, hanged Dorothea Waddingham at Birmingham's Winson Green Prison. Waddingham had poisoned a bedridden inmate of the old people's home she ran at Nottingham, after the victim, Ada Baguley, had made a will leaving all her property to the 'Nurse' who in fact had been only a workhouse ward orderly, and had a criminal record.

Then, in July, Tom Pierrepoint hanged Charlotte Bryant at Exeter with Albert as his assistant again. Bryant was an illiterate Irish woman who poisoned her husband Fred, a farm labourer, at Coombe, near Sherborne, Dorset, so that she could marry her current lover, a gypsy named Parsons. She seemed indifferent to her fate in court, chewing caramels throughout her trial, and met her end with apparent bravery – the Catholic priest who attended her said that her last moments were 'truly edifying'.

This little crop of female victims was the first for several years, and certainly gave the apprentice Albert some useful experience, for a number of women were to come his way in due course. Tom Pierrepoint alarmed his nephew on some occasions by accepting appointments at different places for the same day. His experience and shrewdness told him from his reading of the newspapers that one or the other of the murderers would either be reprieved or that the execution would be postponed because of an appeal, and he was not going to sacrifice £10 and expenses by refusing an engagement and ending up without a job at all on the day in question. 'There'll come a bloody day,' he said, 'when they'll all be reprieved.' It was not, however, to be in Tom Pierrepoint's lifetime.

In 1938, the Commons carried a motion to suspend the death penalty for five years, but it was again ignored, and when a similarly phrased amendment to the Criminal Justice Bill came up in the following year, it was defeated. Tom's sideline was safe, and his nephew's future assured.

Albert Pierrepoint has been credited with hanging more criminals than any other English executioner. The claim is not proven, and is almost certainly ill-founded. Nevertheless, despite the secrecy surrounding executions by his time, Albert Pierrepoint became one of the most famous of executioners, as well as one of the longest-serving, and was proud of what he claimed as his family's 'unique tradition of service to the State'. It was hardly that. Apart from the Billingtons, we have noticed the Brandons and the Otways, and there have almost certainly been other 'family firms' in the past – Shakespeare makes a reference to 'hereditary hangmen' in *Coriolanus*.

Albert was eleven when he learned what his father, recently retired, had been doing when he was away from home so often. Reading Henry Pierrepoint's memoirs in the *Weekly News* in the autumn of 1916, he conceived his own ambition. When a school-master set his class an essay on 'What I should like to do when I leave school', Albert began: 'When I leave school I should like to be the Official Executioner . . . .'

Born in March 1905 at Clayton, Albert was the middle one of Henry Pierrepoint's five children, and his eldest son. When the family moved to Huddersfield, he still went to Clayton frequently to visit his Uncle Tom and Aunt Lizzie, and helped with the horses as well as feeding the chickens and milking the goats. He related in his autobiography *Executioner: Pierrepoint*, how he used to taunt the billy-goat to charge him, knowing that before it reached him it would be brought to an abrupt halt by the length of chain with which it was tethered.

When he was twelve, after the family had moved to Newton Heath near Manchester, he started working half-time at a local cotton mill, going to school in the mornings or afternoons of alternate weeks until his thirteenth birthday, when he left school and worked as a piecer at Marlborough Mills. He was seventeen when his father died. After a few years he left the textile industry to work as a delivery man for a wholesale grocer, using a horse and dray at first and then, having learned to drive, a lorry. In due course he became manager of this business.

Meanwhile, he had applied at the age of twenty-five to become an executioner, writing to the Home Secretary. ('Whatever you want done for you, lad,' his father had said, 'go to the top of the tree.') The reply he received said there were no vacancies, but about a year later he was informed that a vacancy had now arisen and if he was still interested he should go to Strangeways for an interview with the governor. He found that he was one of ten applicants being inter-viewed there that day. When the governor asked him why he wanted to be an executioner, Albert replied that he knew from what his father had said that it was 'something to take pride in'. He was subsequently called to Pentonville for a medical examination and a week's training, and left without knowing if he had qualified. But at the end of that year – the year in which Ellis committed suicide – Uncle Tom asked

Albert to go with him as his assistant for an execution he had been asked to carry out in Dublin.

Albert was proud of his light baritone singing voice, and sang Irish songs on the boat going over – the image of the hangman in Brendan Behan's *The Quare Fellow*, a northern English publican who sings 'The Rose of Tralee'.

His first independent appointment as an assistant came in the following year, 1932, when the governor of Winson Green Prison invited him to Birmingham to assist at an execution there. Uncle Tom was again the executioner, and from then on Albert frequently partnered his uncle in executions all over the country, though the appointment of his assistant was never up to Tom except in Ireland. Executioners were selected by county sheriffs; assistants by prison governors. But the Pierrepoints became a well-known and efficient team, and jobs naturally came their way, especially as, at one period, they were the only two qualified hangmen in the country, two of the listed assistants having died and another resigned within a short time. (Albert Pierrepoint wrote later that many eager trainee assistants were shaken out of their ambition by this first experiences of actual executions, and that others who passed this final test of their nerve left 'with monotonous rapidity' after two or three executions because of their memories, dreams and fears. This, of course, is to their credit, though Albert did not seem to think so.)

Soon after Winston Churchill became Prime Minister in May 1940, Albert Pierrepoint got his first job as chief executioner. He was thirty-five. His Uncle Tom was still 'Number One', as they called it in the trade. Albert's job was to hang a gangland killer at Pentonville, and the assistant appointed was a Doncaster man named Steve Wade, who worked regularly with the younger Pierrepoint from then on. Wade was older than Pierrepoint – he had served in the First World War.

In his first ten years as an executioner, Albert Pierrepoint had worked as an assistant for three guineas a time whilst the executioner's fee was still £10. The fees had remained the same for decades, as we have seen, and all executioners seem to have groused about the reward they received for killing their fellow human beings. Pierrepoint himself clearly regarded the Home Office as 'tight' with money. He claimed that as soon as he became a chief executioner *he* got the fees raised by 50 per cent, so that henceforth he received £15 a time, and assistants five guineas. The fees were not paid all at once. Half was paid at the time, and the rest sent after two weeks if the men's conduct at the execution had been satisfactory.

Pierrepoint kept a diary or log-book like his father, but left out the physical details about the victims' necks, which he said he found 'distasteful to record', and added the name of his assistant on each occasion. It was Steve Wade who, on one occasion during the war, apparently bluffed Pierrepoint into believing that they were both required to attend the post-mortem on a young Burmese man who had killed his wife, and whom Pierrepoint and Wade had just executed at Wandsworth. Dr Keith Simpson was the pathologist, and Pierrepoint was startled to see a blonde girl sitting beside the naked corpse, taking notes as Simpson sawed off the cranium. She was Simpson's secretary, Molly Lefebure, who subsequently wrote in her book *Evidence for the Crown* that Pierrepoint had said, as he walked in, 'If you don't mind I'd like to take a look at my handiwork.' Pierrepoint denied that he said this. But he saw the actual physical effects of his work – a fracture dislocation between the second and third cervical vertebrae was reckoned to be the quickest and cleanest way of producing 'instant' death.

In 1943 Thomas Pierrepoint retired. Newspaper reports said that he had been asked to retire by the Home Office, and that he was reluctant to do so, though he was in his mid-seventies. He told one local reporter in Yorkshire: 'I cannot tell you whether I am retiring or not. I am not allowed to speak – the Home Office, you know. I cannot even tell you my own name. I don't know whether it's Thomas, William, Henry or anything else.' He was credited with more than 300 executions.

Meanwhile, in August 1943, Albert Pierrepoint married Anne Fletcher, who also lived at Newton Heath. He was thirty-eight. They went to Blackpool for their honeymoon, and soon afterwards Albert was flown to Gibraltar where he was required to hang two saboteurs. He was now the unchallenged 'Number One.'

He said in his autobiography that one of the things that attracted him to adopt his father's extra job was that it provided the opportunity for travel! The Second World War gave Albert Pierrepoint more travel than he had bargained for, and considerably increased the total number of executions he was able to lay claim to by the end of his career, which would otherwise certainly have been lower than those of other executioners over a similar length of time. Probably about half of all those executed by Pierrepoint A. were men (and a few women) convicted of war crimes in Germany and Austria, and in addition, he executed a number of spies in this country, as well as several American soldiers – sentenced to death by courts martial – at the military prison at Shepton Mallet.

Among the fifteen enemy spies he hanged in Britain was one who gave him what he described as his 'toughest session on the scaffold'. The victim was a German who had parachuted into Britain during the blitz, landing near London Colney in Hertfordshire. He was quickly caught and sentenced to death. The execution took place at Wandsworth, but the prisoner 'kicked up rough' and fought warders and Pierrepoint in hopeless desperation to escape his fate.

Late in 1945, Pierrepoint went to Germany under military auspices, with the honorary rank of Lieutenant-Colonel, to execute thirteen war criminals. Eleven of them were former officials at the Belsen concentration camp, including the commandant, Josef Kramer, the notorious 'Beast of Belsen'. There were three women – Irma Grese, Elizabeth Volkenrath and Juana Bormann. Kramer was a year younger than Pierrepoint himself. He had served at Dachau and Auschwitz before being appointed commandant at Belsen in 1944. His was the responsibility for the camp which, when the British entered it in 1945, contained 13,000 unburied corpses and 40,000 barely living, another 13,000 of whom died within a matter of weeks. Some were reduced to cannibalism for survival. The only drinking water was from a pond which had corpses floating in it. At the Belsen war crimes trial Kramer denied everything, saying it was all untrue and that he found it difficult to believe that any of his staff had ill-treated prisoners. One of his staff, however, was the twenty-two year-old Irma Grese, who had been a nurse prior to war service at Ravensbruck, and then Auschwitz, before ending up at Belsen, where her brutality was a by-word. They had all, of course, merely been obeying their orders.

Pierrepoint executed this tribe on Friday the thirteenth of December, 1945, at Hameln – the women one at a time, Grese first, and then the ten men two at a time. His assistant was a British Army warrant officer.

Three weeks later, on 3 January 1946, he hanged William Joyce at Wandsworth for treason. Joyce was a scar-faced Irish-American who had spent much of his life in England and carried a British passport when he went to Germany at the beginning of the war. He began broadcasting Nazi propaganda to Britain on German radio, invariably beginning his talks with the announcement, 'Jairmany calling, Jairmany calling.' His broadcasts were regarded as comic rather than menacing by the British public at large, and he was quickly nicknamed 'Lord Haw-Haw'. Nevertheless, he was arrested in Germany and sentenced to death as a traitor after much soul-searching by Britain about its right to try him for treason at all, since he was not, strictly speaking, a British citizen.

Joyce's wife was brought over from Germany and allowed to visit him every day until he received a new visitor – Albert Pierrepoint. About three hundred people had gathered outside the prison, and police had to control the crowd which rushed forward to read the notice of his execution when it was posted on the prison gate. Pierrepoint did not go home that day. He was required at Pentonville next morning to hang another traitor, named Schurch.

Having given up his job with the wholesale grocer during his busy war years, Pierrepoint decided early in 1946 to take on a public house. The one he chose was at Hollinwood, not far from his former home, on the Oldham Road from Manchester. Its name was 'Help the Poor Struggler', a source of constant and understandable mirth which, notwithstanding Pierrepoint's declared refusal to talk about executions to his customers, he must have known from the outset would bring him plenty of business born of morbid curiosity.

As well as executing the traitor John Amery, Pierrepoint was going back and forth to Germany for some time after the war to execute war criminals. On one occasion he hanged twenty-seven in less than twenty-four hours, and twice hanged seventeen in a day. This is probably some kind of record in man-to-man slaughter. Altogether he hanged about 200 war criminals, and it must have been galling when the major Nazi leaders did not come his way after the Nuremberg trials.

The International Military Tribunal passed death sentences on Goering, Ribbentrop, Keitel, Kaltenbrunner, Streicher, Jodl, Frank, Rosenberg, Frick, Seyss-Inquart and Sauckel. Goering cheated the gallows by swallowing poison in his cell, but they hanged his corpse anyway – a sorry little glimpse of ritual savagery worthy of the Nazis themselves. The others were hanged in Nuremberg prison in October

1946, but not by Pierrepoint. The task was deputed to Master-Sergeant John C. Woods of the US Army, and he badly bungled the job. It was reported in the press that the trap was not big enough for the men to fall through, so that the heads of some hit the edges as they dropped and their noses were torn off; and that they died from strangulation through the drops being too short. Some if not all of them took up to twenty minutes to die. Streicher was reported to have shouted out, just before the trap doors fell, 'The Bolsheviks will hang you one day!' Keitel was said to have lived for more than twenty minutes after the drop. And Woods was approached with an offer of £600 for the rope that hanged Ribbentrop.

They were Master-Sergeant Woods's last hangings. He said, 'I've had enough of it,' and pointed out to a French reporter how the British hangman's work had 'made an old man of him.' Woods said, 'He is all broken up and one gets the impression that his head and hands are about to fall off. That is the result of the terrible nervous tension to which the hangman is subjected.' He was referring to Tom Pierrepoint, who *was* an old man of seventy-three when he retired in 1943. He was severely disabled by arthritis, but lived until 1954 when he was eighty-five – exceptional longevity in the killing field. Three weeks after the Nuremberg executions, Albert Pierrepoint wrote to the Home Office to say that the American United Press Association had sent him official photographs of the hangings and asked him to say why he thought they had been bungled, with particular reference to Keitel and Frick. Pierrepoint asked the Home Office to return the photographs to the senders as he did not want to enter into corre-spondence on the subject. The Prison Commissioners thanked him for his discretion, and returned the pictures with a letter to the effect that Mr Pierrepoint's conditions of service precluded him from making any comments.

Albert Pierrepoint was asked to train Austrian executioners in the British method, since they were still using the old technique of giving a short drop and clinging to the victim's legs. They knew no better there, for capital punishment had been abolished as long ago as 1919, and was only reinstated by Hitler. They did not follow Pierrepoint's teachings for long – the death penalty was abolished again in 1950.

Pierrepoint also trained an executioner for the Republic of Ireland at Strangeways, and went to Dublin to assist him in his first job, but

[172]

had to take over himself when the new man went to pieces. Pierrepoint always carried a revolver on his trips to Germany and
Ireland.

As well as the war criminals he hanged in 1946, Pierrepoint executed the murderer Neville Heath, after one of the most sensational
post-war cases in Britain. Heath, a former Borstal boy with a long
criminal record, had been a pilot in the RAF, but was dismissed the
service for bad conduct in December 1945. He murdered Margery
Gardner, aged thirty-two, in London and Doreen Marshall, aged
twenty-one, at Bournemouth, in the course of savage sexual attacks in
which the women's bodies were mutilated. There was never any
doubt about his guilt, but his defence was insanity. He was a sadistic
psychopath and a sexual pervert, but was not considered insane in
legal terms by the jury, and was convicted and sentenced to death for
the first murder, being hanged at Pentonville on 26 October. It is said
that he asked for a whisky just before his execution, adding, 'I think
I'll make it a double.'

In February 1947, Walter Rowland was hanged at Strangeways in
disquieting circumstances. He had been convicted of the murder of a
prostitute, Olive Balchin, whose body had been found on a bomb-site
with a leather-dresser's hammer which had been used to deliver fatal
blows to the head. Rowland had previous convictions for violence –
he had killed his two-year-old daughter thirteen years before and
been sentenced to death for that, but had been reprieved. He was
over-talkative when arrested, but admitted that he had been with
Olive Balchin and thought he had contracted VD from her, though
he denied killing her. He was found guilty and sentenced to death,
whereupon he said: 'Somewhere there is a person who knows that I
stand here today an innocent man. The killing of this woman was a
terrible crime, but there is a worse crime being committed now, my
lord, because someone with the knowledge of this crime is seeing me
sentenced today for a crime which I did not commit . . . the day will
come when this case will be quoted in the courts of this country to
show what can happen to a man in a case of mistaken identity.'

Then a prisoner at Walton Gaol, Liverpool, David Ware, confessed that *he* had killed Olive Balchin. When he was interviewed by
police, he said hardly anything that could not have been gleaned from
the newspapers and from local knowledge of Manchester, and he
subsequently withdrew his confession, saying that he had made it to

gain publicity. Three witnesses at Rowland's trial had spoken of a man with dark or black hair. Ware's hair was dark, Rowland's fair. One of the three – the man who had sold the murderer the hammer – had failed to pick Rowland out in the magistrates' court. Ware claimed that Olive Balchin had stolen a ten-shilling note from his pocket whilst they were making love on the bomb-site. A ten-shilling note and some small change were found on her when the body was discovered. But Rowland was hanged. Four years later, a man went to the police in Bristol and said, 'I have killed a woman. I don't know what is the matter with me. I keep on having an urge to hit women on the head.' The woman, who survived, was a prostitute. The man was David Ware. He was found guilty of attempted murder but was pronounced insane and sent to Broadmoor, where he committed suicide in 1954.

In April, 1947, Pierrepoint was walking along Charlotte Street to keep an appointment at the War Office regarding yet another imminent visit to Germany, when he saw a crowd of people gathered round a man lying in the road. Assuming it was the victim of a road accident, he did not stop, but realised later that the man was Alec de Antiquis, a motor mechanic who had been shot dead whilst trying to foil a jewel robbery. Three young men were arrested and duly charged with murder. They were Christopher Gerachty, Harry Jenkins and Terence Rolt. Because Rolt was under eighteen, he was ordered to be detained at His Majesty's pleasure, but Jenkins and Gerachty were sentenced to death and were hanged by Pierrepoint at Pentonville in September. Gerachty was the one who fired the fatal shot, but Jenkins was condemned as an accessory in an armed robbery.

There was much public agitation over this affair, and a growing call from a minority for the abolition of the death penalty. In 1948 Sydney Silverman, MP, introduced a Bill to the House of Commons to suspend capital punishment for an experimental period of five years. It was passed by the Commons with a narrow majority of twenty-three votes, but in June was thrown out by the Lords, the bishops being well to the fore in arguing against the Bill. Lord Schuster said that he did not feel inclined to take part in 'an experiment which may be at the expense of the lives of every policeman and every warder in the country', and Lord Goddard, the Lord Chief Justice, went one better by saying that the experiment 'must mean gambling with the lives of the people'. Shades of Lord Ellenborough and the Black Act!

Meanwhile, a man sentenced to death for the murder of his wife had been reprieved in April because it was thought unsafe to hang him. William Gray had shot himself, fracturing his jaw, after shooting his wife, and medical opinion was that his injuries were such that it would be 'impracticable to carry out the execution.' Pierrepoint would either have to give Gray a drop so short that he would die of strangulation in extreme agony, or so long that it would pull his head off.

A job nearer home came the hangman's way in November 1948, when Pierrepoint went to Walton Gaol to execute Peter Griffiths, a young ex-guardsman who had murdered three year-old June Devaney after abducting her from a children's ward at Queen's Park Hospital, Blackburn, and raping her. Griffiths had swung the child by one leg to smash her head against a wall. This shocking case was remarkable for the success of a massive fingerprint operation in which 46,000 sets of prints were examined – those of nearly all the adult male residents of Blackburn. Griffiths' prints matched those found on a bottle of water under the child's hospital bed.

In January 1949, Pierrepoint's first woman client in Britain walked with him to the execution chamber at Strangeways. She was hardly the sort of beauty that had made his father's heart flutter at Cardiff, but Margaret Allen was the first woman to be hanged for more than twelve years. She was a lesbian and a former 'clippie' on the buses, who claimed to have undergone a sex change and called herself Bill. She had battered an old woman to death with a hammer, apparently in the furtherance of theft. Although Mrs Van der Elst was outside the prison on the morning of execution, along with about three hundred other people, there was little local sympathy for the woman, whose temper showed to the end when she kicked her last breakfast over the walls of the condemned cell.

In May of that year, the government appointed a Royal Commission, under the chairmanship of Sir Ernest Gowers, to consider whether capital punishment for murder should be limited or modified. The Prime Minister, Clement Attlee, asked the Commission to consider also if any change was needed in the *method* of carrying out the death penalty. But the Commission's terms of reference did not allow it to recommend total abolition.

On 10 August, Pierrepoint the third was present at Wandsworth to execute John George Haigh, the so-called 'Acid Bath Murderer'. Haigh was the son of a Yorkshire colliery foreman and his wife, who were both Plymouth Brethren and brought their son up in the strict isolation of that sect. But when the boy broke free of this regime in his later school years, he slowly turned to persistent crime, and came to spend much time in prison. At the age of thirty-nine, he inveigled himself into the confidence of a rich widow, Olivia Durand-Deacon, and in February 1949 he shot her in the head and, after removing all the valuables from the body, submerged it in a vat of sulphuric acid he had all ready for the purpose. But the lady's disappearance and police suspicions of Haigh eventually led to the discovery of traces of a body in the sludge left when Haigh had emptied out the drum of acid, and Haigh was arrested. He admitted to several other murders in similar fashion, and in what the jury took to be feigned insanity, declared that he had killed his victims in order to drink their blood. In fact he had clearly also killed them for financial gain. He had said to a police officer when he was arrested, 'What are the chances of getting out of Broadmoor?' He was never to find out. Pierrepoint hanged the 'vampire' after the jury had taken seventeen minutes to find him guilty as charged.

Pierrepoint used on Haigh a special pinioning strap of calf leather which he reserved for executions in which he had what he called 'more than formal interest'. 'Deciding whether or not to use it has been the only sign of personal involvement in an execution which I have permitted myself to show.' He made a red ink entry in his diary when he used it, as he did on Josef Kramer and Neville Heath.

He did not use it in March of the following year when he went to Pentonville to execute the insignificant Timothy John Evans. Twenty-five years old and mentally subnormal, Evans had been arrested for the murder of his wife, Beryl, and their baby Geraldine, in the previous November. He was tried for the murder of the child, after police had elicited confessions from him, and was sentenced to death on conviction, though he maintained his innocence during the trial and afterwards. Pierrepoint had no more reason than most other people at the time to believe that Evans *was* innocent. So Pierrepoint hanged Evans on the morning of 9 March 1950. Evans had slept well during the night, and probably had not the imagination to realise fully what was happening to him. He was a thin little fellow, and Pierrepoint killed him with a relatively short drop.

Pierrepoint told the story in his autobiography of a thin, sad-faced man who used to come into his pub on Saturday nights with a married woman who was not his wife, and sang songs over his beer. He and landlord Pierrepoint greeted each other as 'Tish' and 'Tosh' from a catch-phrase of the time. The couple left Albert's pub one Saturday night in 1950, and next morning her naked body was found in a hotel room at Ashton-under-Lyne, five miles away. She had been strangled, and the word 'Whore' had been scrawled across her forehead. Three months later Pierrepoint was called to Strangeways to execute her murderer. 'Hallo, Tosh', the man said as Pierrepoint entered his cell. 'Hello, Tish,' Pierrepoint replied, 'How are you?' And then he hanged this man whose name, he wrote, 'it is my privilege to withhold'. It is mine to reveal it. It was James Henry Corbitt. He was a 37-year-old toolmaker, and his unsuccessful defence had been insanity.

Meanwhile, Pierrepoint had been called upon to give evidence to the Royal Commission. He was also asked to carry out a dummy run-through to demonstrate the method of carrying out an execution. He did this in the execution chamber at Wandsworth for the male members of the Commission. The two women on it, Dame Florence Hancock and Elizabeth Bowen, were not present. Nor were they present when Pierrepoint sat down before the Commission to answer questions, but he was 'very much put out' by having to sit near a female secretary who was making a shorthand transcript. He was sensitive about speaking of his job in the presence of a woman. This attitude derives from northern working-class puritanism, and was mistaken even then. The voices of women were shrill in their demand for corporal as well as capital punishment, and it would have been proper for them to be made fully aware *exactly* what spokeswomen in parliament and elsewhere were advocating.

At one point the hangman was asked: 'You must in so many executions have had things go wrong occasionally?' 'Never,' Pierrepoint replied, but he admitted when pressed about 'awkward moments' that he had once hanged a foreign spy 'who had to be carried to the gallows strapped to a chair', and eventually admitted to 'probably three more' occasions when he had been faced with 'a faint at the last minute or something like that, but it has not been anything to speak about'.

'What happens if a prisoner faints at the last minute?' asked Sir Alexander Maxwell.

'They carry him to the scaffold . . .'

'But what happens if he gets on to the scaffold and then faints?'

'He has to go just the same. They pull the lever and away he goes,' Pierrepoint answered.

It became clear that the Lord Chief Justice, Rayner Goddard, was in favour of hanging almost anybody, as long as he was not required to do the job himself. He was in favour of hanging women, thought too many condemned criminals were being reprieved, and had no qualms about hanging the insane, though that was, quite properly, against the law in every civilised country in the world. Nothing in all the evidence given to the Royal Commission is more chilling to read than the words of the Lord Chief Justice.

Mr W. Bentley Purchase, the North London Coroner, told the Commission that Sir Bernard Spilsbury had once recommended an increase of three inches in the standard drops given, for humanitarian reasons, and that when his recommendation was adopted, remarkable consistency of dislocation between the second and third cervical vertebrae followed. But Pierrepoint denied later that Spilsbury had any influence on the drops he gave.

Whilst the Royal Commission was in session, in December 1951, a nineteen-year-old Nottingham clerk, Herbert Mills, was hanged at Lincoln for the murder of a woman, apparently to draw attention to himself, a lonely cripple. The medical officer stated, at the inquest after the execution, that the man's heart had continued to beat for twenty minutes after the drop. This phenomenon has become well known, and has been observed even in cases of beheading, when the blood spurts in a pulsating rhythm with the continuing heart-beat.

Albert Pierrepoint's most often quoted words to the Royal Commission are those he gave in reply to the question: 'Have you had any experience of judging what the general opinion of ordinary people in England is about capital punishment? I imagine that people must talk to you about your duties.' 'Yes,' Pierrepoint answered, 'but I refuse to speak about it. It is something I think should be secret, myself. It is sacred to me, really.' He was disturbed at having to reveal information to the Commission which he knew would soon be in all the newspapers, when he had spent half his life avoiding saying anything, 'under legal duress' as he put it. He was mistaken in this view, of course. Capital punishment was carried out on behalf of the people, and it was right that the people should be made fully aware of what was being done in their name.

What was being done in January 1953, before the Royal Commission's report was published, was that Pierrepoint was at Wandsworth killing Derek Bentley, aged nineteen and mentally deficient, for a murder which he did not commit, and which was committed whilst he was under arrest and out of sight. The case caused widespread agitation and undoubtedly increased support for abolition of the death penalty.

In November of the previous year, two young men had been seen clambering over the gates of a warehouse in Croydon. Police chased them over the roof, and Bentley was caught. The other burglar, Christopher Craig, drew a revolver and shot a police constable, Sydney Miles, in the head. The two were charged with his murder and found guilty. Craig could not be sentenced to death because he was only sixteen. The jury added a recommendation to mercy in Bentley's case, but he was sentenced to death by Lord Chief Justice Goddard, who had made reference to 'Bentley's precious skin' in his summing up. Two hundred MPs protested at the Home Secretary's refusal to advise the exercise of Her Majesty's mercy. 'I didn't kill anyone,' said Bentley, 'so why are they killing me?' Around five thousand people were outside the prison gates on 28 January, many of them singing 'Abide with me.' When the imperturbable Pierrepoint had done his job, the notice of Bentley's death was posted as usual, but the hostile crowd tore it off and destroyed it.

Meanwhile, in June 1952, Pierrepoint had given up helping poor strugglers and had taken a pub with a less provocative name, the 'Rose and Crown' at Hoole, near Preston. A regular assistant to Pierrepoint by this time was Harry Allen, also a publican, whose hostelry was called the 'Rope and Anchor'.

In July 1953, Pierrepoint went to Pentonville to hang John Reginald Halliday Christie, who had been the chief prosecution witness against Timothy Evans three years earlier. Christie had been convicted of the murder of his wife Ethel, and had confessed to the murder of five more women whose remains had been found in the house and garden of 10 Rillington Place. The bodies of Beryl and Geraldine Evans had also been found there, the Evans family having lived at the same address. Christie had killed his six acknowledged victims over a period of ten years. The two women buried in the garden were already there, unknown to anyone but Christie, when Evans was brought to trial in 1950. All the victims, including the two Evans, were strangled. The nation was now faced with the fact that there had almost certainly been a serious miscarriage of justice. Could there have been two murderers in the same house, at the same time, murdering young women by the same method, both dumping their victims temporarily in the outside wash-house? What was immediately obvious to anyone with any common sense was that if the jury at Evans's trial had known that Christie had murdered two women, they could not have considered Evans's guilt proven beyond reasonable doubt, especially as Evans had accused Christie of murdering Beryl. It took two official enquiries, many books and articles, and thirteen years from the time of Christie's trial, to get a free pardon granted to Evans, not that it did him any good.

The Royal Commission's report was finally presented in September 1953, four and a half years after it was appointed. Among its recommendations was the suggestion that Pierrepoint's responsibilities should be delegated so that other qualified executioners were always available. Hence it did not foresee the imminent abolition of the death penalty. It also recommended that the bodies of executed persons should henceforth be taken down immediately after death had been certified rather than being left hanging for an hour. It had been part of the hangman's responsibility before taking a body down to measure the distance between its heels and the trap doors. The measurement was always greater than the drop the hangman had given, because the hour's hanging stretched the flesh of the victim's neck.

Louisa Merrifield's neck was stretched in that same month, before the Commission's recommendation was adopted. This forty-six-year-old woman was hanged by Pierrepoint at Strangeways, for the murder of Sarah Ricketts, a widow who employed Mrs Merrifield as her housekeeper at Blackpool. The case is of little interest except as one of a series of executions of women by Pierrepoint. He said he hanged 'around a score' of women in his career, and another of them came in December 1954 at Holloway. She was Styllou Christophi, a fifty-three-year-old Cypriot living temporarily with her son and daughter-in-law in London. She had a jealous hatred of her son's wife, and strangled her and then tried to burn the body with newspaper and paraffin.

It was only four months later when a twenty-eight-year-old night club hostess, Ruth Ellis, shot her former lover, racing driver David Blakely, in a *crime passionel* that once again had the whole nation thinking about the death penalty. Ruth Ellis had suffered a miscarriage shortly after Blakely had left the apartment they shared. There was widespread agitation and several petitions for a commutation of the death sentence passed on her, but to no avail. Pierrepoint said that someone sent him a cheque for £90 as a bribe not to execute her. But he did hang her at Holloway on 13 July 1955.

Professor Keith Simpson, the pathologist, remarked at the inquest that there was a strong smell of brandy about her body. This suggests that she was in a state of collapse when she was executed, and a sinister note was added by a letter to the medical journal *The Lancet* from Dr I. H. Milner, in which he suggested that Mrs Ellis was made to change into canvas underclothing on the morning of the execution. She was the last woman to be hanged in Britain. In effect, two people were killed in revenge for the murder of David Blakely, one of whom was certainly innocent. Twenty-seven years after her death, Ruth Ellis's son, who was only a child of eleven when she was hanged, committed suicide.

We have seen how some of the modern executioners are supposed to have reacted to the hanging of women. And even if there were not a grain of truth in any of the assorted rumours, which is unlikely, there is significance in the very fact that such rumours gained currency. There was clearly much public disquiet about the execution of women, and obviously some nervousness or distaste on the part of executioners from Berry onwards. Since they all came from Yorkshire or Lancashire, it seems likely that the social climate in which they were brought up had much to do with it. There was bound to be much soul-searching and psychological tension, amounting to considerable stress, in steeling themselves to the execution of those whom these working-class lads had been bred to regard as tender beings they were obliged to protect from violence and harm.

Pierrepoint claimed to have been above all this, though he did testify to the Royal Commission on the appalling effects of the execution of women on female prison officers. He pointed out, however, that women warders did not witness actual executions, being replaced by men just before the victims entered the execution chamber.

Pierrepoint himself thought that women were often braver than men in going to the scaffold, and explained that, as far as he was concerned, the only difference between hanging men and women was that he had to alter the position of the ankle strap for women, 'for the sake of decency during the drop'. Not everyone shared his view, however. Rev. Joseph Walker, the chaplain at Strangeways, resigned from the prison service after the execution of Margaret Allen, telling the *Daily Mail* afterwards that he had been taking three grains of pheno-barbitone a day to blot out his memory of the scene. He had had severe heart attacks a few months after the execution. He also knew two other officials who were still sick men years after their experiences in execution chambers.

On 23 February 1956, Albert Pierrepoint sent his resignation to the Prison Commissioners. He was fifty-one, and had been an executioner for nearly twenty-four years, eight of them as an assistant. He wrote later that the Home Office asked him to stay on, and that he was the only executioner who was asked to reconsider his decision to resign. This claim is as ill-founded as some of his others. What about James Foxen, for example? When Pierrepoint refused, he was asked not to reveal the reason for his departure. Rumour instantly had it that his resignation was connected with the execution of Ruth Ellis. Pierrepoint categorically denied this. In fact, he had been deeply offended by a dispute over expenses to which he felt entitled after travelling to Manchester to execute a man who was reprieved at the last minute. He had been sent £4 as recompense for his trouble, and thought this mean, considering his length of service and experience, and wrote in high dudgeon to the Home Office requesting 'removal of my name from the list of executioners forthwith'. Although it cannot have cost Pierrepoint more than a few shillings to get from Preston to Manchester and back, executioners had customarily expected half their normal fee, as well as travelling expenses, in the event of a reprieve. Nevertheless, it seems a fairly trifling affair to resign over, at the age of fifty-one, and I think Pierrepoint had really had enough, and was just looking for the excuse this incident presented him with. It is evident that several executioners had realised in due course that their youthful bravado had been a mistake, but were too proud to admit it. Few of the established 'number one' hangmen got out as early as Pierrepoint.

Pierrepoint retired to his new pub, and after eighteen years published his autobiography, in which, after he had made his tidy sum as an executioner (and the death penalty had already been abolished), he wrote:

> I now sincerely hope that no man is ever called upon to carry out another execution in my country. I have come to the conclusion that executions solve nothing, and are only an antiquated relic of a primitive desire for revenge which takes the easy way and hands over the responsibility for revenge to other people.
>
> I have seen prison officers faint on the scaffold, strong men weep, and women prison officers sobbing helplessly. I have known prison doctors who could not examine the body after execution because the beat of their own heart was obliterating anything they could distinguish. I have felt overpowering sorrow for the victims of crime, for little children murdered, for the families of all concerned, for the special worry which policemen's wives always suffer and for the tragic occasions when it is justified. Yet I have had many friends in the police and in the prison service who also feel very strongly against capital punishment.
>
> It is said to be a deterrent. I cannot agree. There have been murders since the beginning of time, and we shall go on looking for deterrents until the end of time. If death were a deterrent, I might be expected to know. It is I who have faced them last, young lads and girls, working men, grandmothers. I have been amazed to see the courage with which they take that walk into the unknown. It did not deter them then, and it had not deterred them when they committed what they were convicted for. All the men and women whom I have faced at that final moment convince me that in what I have done I have not prevented a single murder.

He emphasised the point in a preface: 'The fruit of my experience has this bitter after-taste: that I do not now believe that any one of the hundreds of executions I carried out has in any way acted as a deterrent against future murder. Capital punishment, in my view, achieved nothing except revenge.'

Pierrepoint appeared on television in this and other countries after his autobiography was published, plugging the book without giving away any of the secrets he had always guarded so carefully. He and his wife eventually retired to a Lancashire resort. One Yorkshire newspaper reported the ex-hangman's death 'in the middle Seventies', but at the time of writing he is still alive, an old man with his sacred memories and records, apparently believing that God chose him to be a hangman.

X

Redundant Hangmen

I hope we have seen the last of that obscene public servant, the
hangman.

Charles Irving, MP
House of Commons, 1974

'EVERYTHING IS conducted with decorum,' James Berry had written,
and the Royal Commission of 1949 was provided with a memorandum by the Home Office which attempted to reinforce this impression. But how can any human being in his right mind apply the word
'decorum' to the process of what amounts to a ritual sacrifice? Of the
actual execution, the memorandum said this:

> Some 20 minutes before the time fixed for the execution the High
> Sheriff, or more usually the Under Sheriff, arrives at the prison, and a
> few minutes before it is due, proceeds with the Governor and medical
> officer to the place of execution.
>
> The executioner and his assistant wait outside the condemned cell,
> with the chief officer and officer detailed to conduct the prisoner to the
> execution chamber. On a signal given by the Sheriff they enter and the
> executioner pinions the prisoner's arms behind his back. He is escorted to
> the drop with one officer on either side. The Sheriff, the Governor and the
> medical officer enter the execution chamber directly by another door.
>
> The prisoner is placed on the drop on a marked spot so that his feet
> are directly across the division of the trap doors. The executioner
> places a white cap over the prisoner's head and places the noose
> round his neck, while the assistant pinions his legs. When the execu-
> tioner sees that all is ready he pulls the lever.
>
> The medical officer at once proceeds to the pit and examines the
> prisoner to see that life is extinct. The shed is then locked and the
> body hangs for one hour. The inquest is held the same morning.

Burial of the body takes place in the prison graveyard during the dinner hour. The chaplain reads the burial service.

These clinical government words are, to coin a phrase, economical with the truth. The reality was, as we have seen, an obscene ritual in which, as one authority put it, 'dislocation of the neck is the ideal aimed at.' It is doubtful if, in modern times, many complete bunglings have taken place, to the extent of decapitating a victim or slowly strangling him to death, but that is not the point. The process by which two men were employed to do a man or woman to death in the presence of officials representing the Church, the Law and the medical profession was an obscene act authorised by the State on behalf of the people, and a disgrace to a country that purported to be civilised.

Among the things which that brief and sanitised Home Office evidence did not make clear was what happened *between* the body hanging for one hour and the inquest being held the same morning. It was the executioner's job to take the corpse down, strip it of its clothing (regardless of its sex), clean it up and place it in a coffin or on a stretcher for the post mortem. Pierrepoint explained this in reverent tones, but what neither he nor any other executioner, witness or Home Secretary has been willing to spell out is the condition the corpse and the clothing might be in.

The condemned wore his or her own clothes on the morning of execution rather than prison uniform, and in the present century the clothes were burnt afterwards, along with the rope. It is not at all uncommon for the bowels and bladder of *anyone* to be evacuated at the moment of death, and this involuntary physical reaction is all the more likely at moments of extreme terror, as when one was suddenly to drop into space to one's death. Such a result is said to be especially common in cases of asphyxia – hence the old euphemisms: the hangman was the 'crap merchant' and being hanged was 'pissing when you can't whistle'. Victims of judicial hanging were dressed in their own clothes because prison uniform could be reissued to someone else after laundering, and the authorities did not want it soaked with urine, splattered with excrement and, sometimes, stained with blood.

The stretching of the victim's neck (and the marks of the rope on the flesh) were ended by adoption of the Royal Commission's recommendation that the body should be taken down immediately death had been certified. But the reason for its always having been left hanging for an hour, up to that time, was that the heart would continue to beat for as long as twenty minutes after the drop, and no one was too certain that death had occurred. Mr H. N. Gedge, the Under Sheriff of London, had been challenged by the Royal Commission to admit that 'the longer the drop the lower the fracture of the neck occurs, and the lower the fracture of the neck the less certain one can be that death is instantaneous?'

'I do not know that as a fact,' Mr Gedge had replied. 'All I can say is that so far as I can see death is instantaneous. I have now and again found some twitching and I am told that it can be a mechanical and muscular reaction, in the same way as you can cut a chicken's head off and it will still run round.'

As I understand it, in a 'perfectly' done execution, the medulla is separated from the pons at the base of the brain and causes death as instantly as it can possibly be measured.

Albert Camus wrote that 'the man who enjoys his coffee while reading that justice has been done would spit it out at the least detail.' The truth of this was amply demonstrated by the letters of protest to newspapers which described the execution of Caryl Chessman in the electric chair at San Quentin in May 1960. The Home Office still refuses to answer any question about individual executions, executioners, or the business of execution in general, in this country. Government and Civil Service, like all the rest of us, are fully paid-up members of the British league of hypocrites. The process carried out on behalf of the people, and supposed to deter by example, had to be cloaked in official secrecy because the details would be so repellent to modern society as to make the process self-defeating.

After Pierrepoint's retirement, two former assistants were appointed to succeed him, neither claiming precedence over the other. This was also in line with the Royal Commission's recommendations. One of them was Harry Allen, another publican ('Rope and Anchor'!), who had assisted Pierrepoint on numerous occasions. Between them, these two carried out thirty-four executions in the next seven years.

Four months after Pierrepoint retired, the Commons gave its third reading to Sydney Silverman's Bill to abolish the death penalty, but the real debate was tactically delayed by a move to introduce a clause reintroducing whipping as an alternative. This was easily defeated, but those Honourable Members voting in favour of flogging included three women and eleven former military men who still used their ranks, as well as such then well-known reactionaries as Cyril Osborne and Gerald Nabarro. The Bill for abolition was again thrown out by the Lords, and by a huge majority, provoking a famous outburst in the *New Statesman*, which described their lordships as coming from the hills and forests of darkest Britain, 'the halt, the lame, the deaf, the obscure, the senile and the forgotten – the hereditary peers of England united in their determination to use their medieval powers to retain a medieval institution.'

No one was hanged in Britain during 1956, all convicted murderers being reprieved because it would have been indefensible to hang people whilst the law by which it was done was under review. To the two new hangmen, it must have looked for some time as if they would never get a chance to show their skills.

But in March 1957 the Homicide Act came into force – an ill-advised compromise which made five categories of murder capital offences, including murder in the furtherance of theft. This meant in theory that a cold-blooded killer who murdered a woman after raping her could not be hanged, but if he stole a shilling from her handbag as well, he would be sentenced to death. The first victim of the new law was John Vickers, who was hanged at Durham on 23 July 1957 for the murder of an elderly shopkeeper whilst committing a burglary.

It is arguable that Vickers was hanged through a misleading statement of the law by the judge in his summing-up. It was the first execution for nearly two years, and a silent vigil was held throughout the night at the Quaker headquarters in Euston Road, organised by Christian Action and the National Campaign for the Abolition of Capital Punishment. Six Members of Parliament were present.

A woman was sentenced to death for capital murder a year later. Mary Wilson, sixty-six years old, was convicted at Leeds of the murder by poisoning of two of her three husbands, Oliver Leonard and Ernest Wilson, in order to gain their property. The sentence was commuted to life imprisonment, presumably on account of her age. If she had been hanged, one wonders if anyone would now remember Ruth Ellis.

By this time, the sinister secrecy of the act of putting a man to death had gone so far that notice of an execution was no longer being posted on prison gates. There was merely an announcement from the Home

Office that so-and-so had been executed at such-and-such a prison on a certain date.

It has been said that after Berry's book appeared in 1892, the government invoked the Official Secrets Act to prevent hangmen from publishing details of their experiences. The Home Office refused to say whether executioners had been subject to the Official Secrets Act, although Pierrepoint said specifically that he was. As far as I know, no action was taken or contemplated against him or his father, or against Berry or Ellis, for publishing their memoirs, but action has been taken under the Act against prison governors, which would suggest that hangmen were not required to sign it, possibly because of the technical difficulty that they were not employed by the government. I am now able to clear up this little mystery, once and for all. A Home Office memorandum was always issued to executioners and assistants when they were officially listed, laying down the expected standards of conduct. Until 1932 it was considered a sufficient restraint on them in itself, warning them (since they were in it for the money) that if they broke the rules in any way their names were liable to be deleted from the list.

In 1933, however, shortly after Albert Pierrepoint's name was added to a list consisting of eight men, all the executioners and assistants were required to enter into an Agreement and a Bond in the sum of £50, to ensure that they complied with the conditions on which they were engaged, both during and after their periods of employment. In particular, they were to continue to observe the condition that they should not make any unauthorised disclosure of information about executions, not publish or take part in any 'displays etc., concerning or representing executions'. There was a particular reference to 'lectures and performances, dramatic or otherwise'.

This legal restraint was first mooted in 1932 and arose from the case of a man 'formerly employed as an executioner having given demonstrations of executions at fairs'. Clearly Ellis's misdeeds reflected on his successors. Everyone on the official list in 1933, from Tom Pierrepoint at the top to his nephew at the bottom, signed the new Agreement and Bond, and it was clearly this that the young Albert Pierrepoint took to be the Official Secrets Act.

In 1959, Ronald Marwood, a twenty-five-year-old scaffolder, was hanged at Pentonville for the murder of PC Summers, who had intervened in a gang fight outside a dance hall. Marwood, who was drunk, had stabbed him, though he later denied being in possession of a knife. Despite the fact that there was little if any doubt about Marwood's guilt, there were several petitions for a reprieve, including one from 150 MPs, and a noisy demonstration by prisoners inside Pentonville on the night before the execution. There was no suggestion of premeditated violence on Marwood's part; he was not connected with the gangs whose fight he became involved in; and his only previous conviction was for theft when he was fourteen.

Nearly 1,000 people demonstrated outside the prison on the morning of 8 May, some shouting 'savages', 'beasts' and 'murderers' at the mounted police who were called in to disperse them. It was a bit like the old days at Tyburn and Newgate. But the important aspect of the case was that it raised again the absurd anomalies of the Homicide Act, and moved Sydney Silverman to table another motion in the Commons for the abolition of the death penalty. This came to nothing, and the hangings went on, although there is clear evidence that, as in the time of the Bloody Code, juries were becoming reluctant to convict on charges of capital murder. There were seven executions in England in 1960, but the number went down to four in 1961, and to two in each of the following three years. The annual average in the twelve years up to 1960 had been about ten.

In April 1962 James Hanratty was hanged at Bedford for the so-called 'A6 Murder'. He was accused of the shooting to death of Michael Gregsten, and shooting Gregsten's girl friend Valerie Storie, whom he also raped, after forcing Gregsten at gun-point to drive from Windsor to the lay-by on Deadman's Hill in Bedfordshire. The trial was the longest murder trial in English history up to that time, lasting twenty-one days, and the jury members took nine and a half hours to reach their verdict. There was much confusion about Miss Storie's identification of Hanratty.

After he had been hanged, one of only two men to be executed in that year, a man named Peter Alphon, whom police had temporarily suspected in the first place, confessed to the murder, and several books were published disputing Hanratty's guilt. The argument for Hanratty's innocence was not as convincing as that for Evans had been in the previous decade, but the circumstances were sufficiently disquieting to draw the attention of the nation once more to the fact that innocent men and women had been hanged in the past and could be hanged in the future. The National Campaign for the Abolition of

Capital Punishment, led by the publisher Victor Gollancz and the future Lord Chancellor, Gerald Gardiner, QC, was gaining momentum. A great many distinguished men and women in all walks of life – even the Church – had given the campaign their support. A sprinkling of bishops now joined with royalty (the Earl of Harewood), philosophers (Russell, Popper, Ayer), noblemen, politicians, scientists, artists, men of letters, judges, barristers and many others on the campaign's Committee of Honour, in a concerted effort to force the unconscionably protracted debate to a successful conclusion.

On 13 August 1964, two men were hanged at different prisons for the same crime. Peter Anthony Allen and Gwynne Owen Evans were found guilty of murdering a laundry-van driver, John West, in the furtherance of theft. Allen was hanged at Liverpool (possibly by his namesake), and Evans at Manchester. *The Times* thought this event hardly worthy of mention on the following day, but as it turned out, Allen and Evans were the last two people to be executed in Britain.

Just before Christmas, Sydney Silverman's final Abolition Bill was passed by the House of Lords, if you please, for an experimental period of five years. Towards the end of that period, in December 1969, Commons and Lords approved total abolition of the death penalty for murder. Britain had at last taken the decisive step toward civilisation that most other western nations had taken well ahead of it. There was no increase in the murder rate. The number of executions in England and Wales from the turn of the century to the end of capital punishment was 748, an average of nearly a dozen people a year whose executions had been 'justified' by the stubborn conviction that murder would increase rapidly if they were not hanged.

This was the belief also in 1865, when the murder rate in proportion to the population was higher in Britain than it has ever been since – even though Calcraft was then busy strangling people to death in front of large crowds as a deterrent.

In 1974, when the House of Commons debated bringing back the death penalty for acts of terrorism, those voting in favour numbered 217 of our Members of Parliament, and included the Prime Minister, a well known supporter of full employment for executioners. The move to reintroduce capital punishment was comfortably defeated then, and has been again since, but 218 MPs, again led by Mrs Thatcher, still voted for its return in 1988. The proposal will recur from time to time, and unless the government of the day seriously contemplates killing criminals by lethal injection, and turning doctors into executioners, hanging is the method being proposed whenever the subject of the death penalty is raised.

It is not part of my purpose in this book to rehearse the overwhelming arguments against hanging – I hope the history of our executioners has made most of them pretty clear. But the one most relevant to this book has never really been given enough emphasis. It has been expressed mildly by the psychologist W. J. H. Sprott: 'it is indecent to require anyone to carry out such an act.' Can anyone seriously argue with that? I hope the pages of this sorry catalogue of public servants have made the point well enough.

The fact is that these men were given public part-time employment which, in most cases, resulted in the permanent maiming of their personalities. The weakness for publicity that Charles Duff observed in hangmen and drew to my attention many years ago has been amply demonstrated. Applying for a job as an executioner was an idiot's route to fame, if not fortune, but I think that those who served as executioners (or assistants) for many years sought to satisfy through publicity a kind of craving for confession. They needed some sort of reassurance, through public interest, that they had not been doing dreadful wrongs all these years after their youthful bravado, thoughtless and unimaginative, had made them ritual manslayers, naturally shunned by the public at large, even when the public in its ignorance supported the death penalty.

Albert Pierrepoint frequently used a curious phrase in his autobiography, when referring to one of his victims. 'I had to hang Derek Bentley,' for instance, and 'I had to execute Mrs Louisa Merrifield.' The plain truth is, of course, that neither Pierrepoint nor any other modern executioner *had* to hang *anybody*. They were freelance agents, and there is no way in which any of them could have hidden behind the familiar Nazi claim that they were simply 'obeying orders'. They were never *under* orders. They were *invited* to carry out executions, and they did so for money. They were free to refuse and were in any case always ready to shift the responsibility onto someone else. Not that they were alone in this. It was always the Law which was responsible for killing murderers, an abstract concept absolving judges, juries and everyone else from any personal involvement in death-dealing. For the executioners, however, this proved not to be enough. Une-

[192]

ducated working men are not at home with abstractions, and what they *knew* was that they had accepted payment for killing their fellow men and women. It is quite clear that, as older men, when they reflected on this fact, most of them found it difficult to live with. The need for self-justification became acute. Several sought religious absolution; others cerebral abdication. One or two, like Ellis, found a more complete escape from their sense of guilt.

If one tries to make a just and dispassionate distinction between murderers and executioners, one is surely forced to conclude that, psychologically, executioners have frequently been – generally speaking – of a lower order of humanity. The vast majority of murders are committed on impulse, in the heat of the moment, and in domestic circumstances. Jealous rages, drunken quarrels and other sources of stress within or close to the family circle are responsible for most of the deaths classified as murder in this country. They are not premeditated. I have described some of the more atrocious and exceptional murders in this book partly because the perpetrators have inevitably become the most famous victims of the hangmen of England, and partly because I do not want, by ignoring the ghastliness of many murders that were notorious, to call upon myself the absurd and insulting charge which has been levelled so often against abolitionists – that they have more sympathy for murderers than for their victims. To be opposed to the death penalty is not in any sense to condone murder, of course, which must always be paramount among the worst crimes of humanity and properly incur the severest penalties. But for any man to enter into regular contracts to kill men and women in prison slaughterhouses for financial gain seems to me the worst kind of outrageous obscenity that a peacetime government could possibly encourage.

When the Royal Commission was in session, in 1950, there were twenty-six 'establishments with execution apparatus'. I do not know how much of this 'apparatus' remains inside prisons. There is a genuine gallows in the Chamber of Horrors at Madame Tussaud's, and a former execution chamber remains at Devonport Dockyard, once used, presumably, after naval courts martial. There may be others kept as museum relics here and there. But there is, at Wandsworth Prison in south London, an execution chamber, kept intact because the death penalty remains on the statute book for treason. That, at any rate, is the received wisdom – the Home Office will neither confirm nor deny it. It follows that there is, somewhere in Britain, at least one man (presumably not a woman, but who knows?) trained to carry out an execution if need be, and quietly awaiting the opportunity. This has been the story of that man's predecessors in office, and let us hope he is proud of them, or if he is called upon to put his training into practice, he might throw down his rope in disgust, and say, 'No free man in a civilised country should be asked to do this job.' One or two previous executioners *have* said this, in effect, but alas, it was always when their careers as hangmen had ended.

Lord Denning, who had in his time pronounced many death sentences, told John Mortimer some years ago that he now considered the death penalty wrong and, agreeing that his reasoning was based on the concept of a constant moral imperative, had to admit that, if the death penalty is unethical now, it must *always* have been unethical.

None of us who are old enough to have paid taxes before 1965 can evade our share of the responsibility for this disgusting ritual of revenge, the mathematical logic of which is $1 + 1 = 0$. We cannot wash our hands of it by saying individually that we were always morally opposed to capital punishment. *All* of us helped to purchase the ropes and pay the hangmen's fees.

Although I have been against the death penalty ever since I was old enough to think about it seriously, I feel a sense of shame in belonging to a society which, calling itself civilised, failed for so long to realise that civilisation and capital punishment are mutually exclusive. Does it not denote a desperate want of courage and imagination when a country in twentieth-century Europe should still have relied, only twenty-odd years ago, on a method of dealing with criminals that feudal barons were using in the Dark Ages? We have no moral justification for sitting in judgement on a murderer when, by sanctioning premeditated killing, we reduce ourselves to the murderer's level. If this book should help, even a little, to ensure that Margaret Thatcher's deplorable 'Victorian values' never return, in this respect at least, the personal defilement I feel in dwelling for so long on the subject will have been well worth while.

Sources

1. Books

Andrews, William	*Old Time Punishments*	(Andrews & Co., 1890)
Anon	*The Groans of the Gallows, or the Lives and Exploits of William Calcraft and Nathaniel Howard, the Living Rival Hangmen of London and York*	(C. Elliot, 1855)
Ash, A. & Day, J. E.	*Immortal Turpin*	(Staples Press, 1948)
Atholl, Justin	*The Reluctant Hangman*	(John Long, 1956)
Aubrey, John	*Brief Lives*	(Penguin edition, 1972)
Berry, James	*My Experiences as an Executioner*	(Percy Lund, 1892)
	Thoughts above the Gallows	(Parker Bros., 1905)
Birkett, Sir Norman (Ed.)	*The Newgate Calendar*	(Folio Society edn., 1951)
Bland, James	*The Common Hangman*	(Ian Henry, 1984)
Bleackley, Horace	*The Hangmen of England*	(Chapman & Hall, 1929)
Blom-Cooper, Louis (Ed.)	*The Hanging Question*	(Duckworth, 1969)
Browne, Douglas G. & Tullett, E. V.	*Bernard Spilsbury: His Life and Cases*	(Harrap, 1951)
Buchanan-Taylor, W.	*Shake the Bottle*	(Heath Cranton, 1942)

Camus, Albert	*Resistance, Rebellion and Death*	(Hamish Hamilton, 1961)
Chapman, Pauline	*Madame Tussaud's Chamber of Horrors*	(Constable, 1984)
Chesney, Kellow	*The Victorian Underworld*	(Temple Smith, 1970)
Coe, S. J.	*Down Murder Lane*	(W.H. Allen, 1945)
Collins, Philip	*Dickens and Crime*	(Macmillan, 1962)
Duff, Charles	*A New Handbook on Hanging*	(Andrew Melrose, 1954)
Eddowes, Michael	*The Man on Your Conscience*	(Cassell, 1955)
Elst, Violet Van der	*On the Gallows*	(Doge Press, 1937)
Foot, Paul	*Who Killed Hanratty?*	(Cape, 1971)
Fraser, Antonia	*Mary Queen of Scots*	(Weidenfeld & Nicolson, 1969)
Freud, Sigmund	*Totem and Taboo*	(Routledge & Kegan Paul, 1950)
Garmonsway, G. N. (Trans.)	*The Anglo-Saxon Chronicle*	(Everyman's Library, 1972 edition)
George, M. Dorothy	*London Life in the Eighteenth Century*	(Penguin edn., 1966)
Griffiths, A. G. F.	*The Chronicles of Newgate*	(Chapman & Hall, 1884)
Hale, Leslie	*Hanged in Error*	(Penguin Books, 1961)
Hall, J. W. (Ed.)	*The Trial of William Joyce*	(William Hodge, 1946)
Hay, Peter, et al	*Albion's Fatal Tree*	(Allen Lane, 1975)
Honeycombe, Gordon	*The Murders of the Black Museum*	(Hutchinson, 1982)
Hyde, H. Montgomery	*Oscar Wilde: The Aftermath*	(Methuen, 1963)
Kennedy, Ludovic	*Ten Rillington Place*	(Gollancz, 1961)
Koestler, Arthur	*Reflections on Hanging*	(Gollancz, 1956)
Koestler, Arthur and Rolph, C. H.	*Hanged by the Neck*	(Penguin Books, 1961)
Longford, Elizabeth	*Victoria, R.I.*	(Weidenfeld & Nicolson, 1964)
Lyons, F. J.	*George Joseph Smith*	(Duckworth, 1935)
Macaulay, Lord	*History of England*	(London, 1848-61)
MacColl, Rene	*Roger Casement*	(Hamish Hamilton, 1956)

Mandeville, Bernard de	*An Enquiry into the cause of the frequent executions at Tyburn*	(J. Roberts, 1725)
Marks, Alfred	*Tyburn Tree; Its History and Annals*	(Brown, Langham & Co., 1908)
Mortimer, John	*In Character*	(Allen Lane, 1983)
Noyes, Alfred	*The Accusing Ghost*	(Gollancz, 1957)
Pierrepoint, Albert	*Executioner: Pierrepoint*	(Harrap, 1974)
Potter, John Deane	*The Fatal Gallows Tree*	(Elek, 1965)
Radzinowicz, Leon	*A History of English Criminal Law and its Administration from 1750*	(Stevens, 1948-68)
Rowland, John	*Unfit to Plead?*	(John Long, 1965)
Rumbelow, Donald	*The Complete Jack the Ripper*	(W.H. Allen, 1975)
Scott, George Ryley	*The History of Capital Punishment*	(Torchstream Books, 1950)
Smith, Sir Sydney	*Mostly Murder*	(Harrap, 1959)
Stow, John	*The Survey of London*	(Everyman's Library edition, 1956)
Thompson, E. P.	*Whigs and Hunters*	(Allen Lane, 1975)
Watson, Eric R. (Ed.)	*Trial of Thurtell and Hunt*	(William Hodge, 1920)
	The Trial of George Joseph Smith	(William Hodge, 1922)
Wedgwood, C. V.	*The Trial of Charles I*	(Collins, 1964)
Wilson, Colin, and Pitman, Pat	*Encyclopaedia of Murder*	(Arthur Barker, 1961)
Young, Filson (Ed.)	*Trial of Frederick Bywaters and Edith Thompson*	(William Hodge, 1923)
Young, Sidney (Ed.)	*The Annals of the Barber-Surgeons of London*	(Blades, East & Blades, 1890)

2. Newspapers and journals

Bolton Journal
Bradford Telegraph & Argus
Catholic Herald
Daily Express
Daily Mail
Daily Universal Register
Empire News
Farnworth Journal
Gentleman's Magazine
Herts. Advertiser
Keighley News
Lancaster Gazette
London Evening News
London Evening Post
New Statesman

News of the World
Public Advertiser
Reynolds Newspaper
St Stephen's Review
Staffordshire Advertiser
The Lancet
The Observer
The Times
The Weekly Journal
Thomson's Weekly News
Warwick Advertiser
Yorkshire Evening Post
Yorkshire Gazette
Yorkshire Observer

3. Official documents, government papers, etc.

Hansard

Royal Commission on Capital Punishment, 1949-53.
    Report and Minutes of Evidence.   (HMSO, 1953)

Gibson, Evelyn, and Klein, S.
    Murder, 1957 to 1968 (A Home Office Research Study)   (HMSO, 1969)

Home Office papers in Public Record Office –
    HO 45/25843

Prison Commission papers in Public Record Office –
    PCOM 8/189
    PCOM 8/190
    PCOM 8/191
    PCOM 8/193

Index